Humour, subjectivity and world politics

Manchester University Press

Humour, subjectivity and world politics

Everyday articulations of identity at the limits of order

Alister Wedderburn

MANCHESTER UNIVERSITY PRESS

Copyright © Alister Wedderburn 2021

The right of Alister Wedderburn to be identified as the author of this work has been asserted by them in accordance with the Copyright, Designs and Patents Act 1988.

Published by Manchester University Press
Oxford Road, Manchester M13 9PL

www.manchesteruniversitypress.co.uk

British Library Cataloguing-in-Publication Data
A catalogue record for this book is available from the British Library

ISBN 978 1 5261 5069 1 hardback
ISBN 978 1 5261 9566 1 paperback

First published 2021
Paperback published 2026

The publisher has no responsibility for the persistence or accuracy of URLs for any external or third-party internet websites referred to in this book, and does not guarantee that any content on such websites is, or will remain, accurate or appropriate.

EU authorised representative for GPSR:
Easy Access System Europe – Mustamäe tee 50, 10621 Tallinn, Estonia
gpsr.requests@easproject.com

Typeset by
Deanta Global Publishing Services, Chennai, India

Contents

List of figures	*page* vi
Acknowledgements	vii
Introduction: taking humour seriously	1

Part I: Humour, subjectivity and world politics

1	'A way of operating': humour, subjectivity and the everyday	25
2	The parasite	51

Part II: Parasitic politics

3	Aesthetic parasitism: cartooning the camp	79
4	Physical parasitism: ACT UP and the HIV/AIDS pandemic	113
5	Parodic parasitism: clowning and mass protest	145

Conclusion: parasitic politics and world politics	169
Bibliography	179
Index	203

Figures

1 *Mickey au Camp de Gurs*, cover. (Reproduced with permission of the Mémorial de la Shoah, Paris.) page 92
2 *Mickey au Camp de Gurs*, fourth panel. (Reproduced with permission of the Mémorial de la Shoah, Paris.) 93
3 *Mickey au Camp de Gurs*, fifth panel. (Reproduced with permission of the Mémorial de la Shoah, Paris.) 95
4 Felix Nussbaum (1943): *Self-Portrait with Jewish Identity Card*. (Reproduced with permission of the Felix Nussbaum Haus, Osnabrück. Felix Nussbaum (1904–1944), *Self-Portrait with Jewish Identity Card*, around 1943. Oil on canvas, 56x49cm. Felix Nussbaum-Haus Osnabrück, loan from the Niedersächsische Sparkassenstiftung.) 96
5 *Mickey au Camp de Gurs*, final panel. (Reproduced with permission of the Mémorial de la Shoah, Paris.) 98
6 *Petit Guide à Travers Le Camp de Gurs*, cover. (Reproduced with permission of the Archiv für Zeitgesch.) 99
7 *Petit Guide à Travers Le Camp de Gurs*, first panel. (Reproduced with permission of the Archiv für Zeitgesch.) 101
8 *Petit Guide à Travers Le Camp de Gurs*, ninth panel. (Reproduced with permission of the Archiv für Zeitgesch.) 103
9 Karl Schwesig (1940–1941): Gurs 'stamps'. (Reproduced courtesy of Leo Baeck Institute, New York.) 105
10 Detail from the dining hall mural (1942–1943, artist(s) unknown), Camp des Milles. (Reproduced with permission of the Site Mémorial Camp des Milles.) 106
11 Detail from the dining hall mural (1942–1943, artist(s) unknown), Camp des Milles. (Reproduced with permission of the Site Mémorial Camp des Milles.) 106

Acknowledgements

It's taken seven years to get here, or slightly more than a fifth of my entire lifespan. That length of time is indicative of endless wrong turns and dead ends, many of which would have shattered my resolve without the help and support of many people who have variously picked me up, set me on the right track, guided me and offered me advice. I am grateful for the platform to thank them publicly here, and look forward to returning their kindness to the very best of my ability whenever the opportunity arises.

Three separate institutions have afforded me the time and space to research and write about humour and world politics. I spent three-and-a-half years as a doctoral student at King's College London, where I first started thinking about this topic and did much of the research that underpins this book. I never would have started my PhD without the help and support of Peter Busch, and I never would have finished without the diligence and generosity of my supervisor Claudia Aradau. In addition, my examiners James Brassett and Kimberly Hutchings made many suggestions that I have tried to implement in the process of transforming that project into this book, and I owe them a huge debt of gratitude for taking the time not just to read my thesis but to engage with it. I would also like to thank the Economic and Social Research Council for providing the funding that made my doctorate possible in the first place (grant number ES/S01117X/1).

I spent two exceedingly happy years as a postdoctoral fellow in the Coral Bell School at the Australian National University (ANU) in Canberra. My thanks are due to Mathew Davies, who took a punt on me when I was still doing my PhD, and whose mentorship was both exemplary and formative. Under his stewardship, ANU's International Relations (IR) department has generated a torrent of extraordinary research, all produced by warm, collegial and open-hearted scholars who represent the very best of what academia can be. I am very grateful indeed to have spent the initial period of my career in the Hedley Bull Building. Aside from Matt, my thanks are thus due to Ben Zala, Ben Day, Joe Mackay, Bina D'Costa, Luke Glanville, Bill Tow, Feng Zhang, Maria Tanyag, Eglantine Staunton, Sarah Logan, Mary-Lou Hickey, Jeremy Youde, David Envall, Cecilia Jacob, Nick Lemay-Hébert, Wes Widmaier and the department's superb cohorts of MA and PhD students.

My move to the University of Glasgow in January 2020 was swiftly followed by a strike and then a pandemic. Despite this, my new colleagues have made me feel at home very quickly, resisting the temptation to read my arrival as the portent or omen it must surely appear to be. In particular, I would like to thank Chris Carman, Andy Judge, Naomi Head, Ian Paterson, Allan Gillies, Ty Solomon, Rhys Machold, Sophia Dingli, Rhys Crilley, Mo Hume, Georgios Karyotis and Kelly Kollman. That I have been able to finish this book over the course of this year's lockdown is in no small part down to them.

I have been lucky enough to present various bits and pieces of this work at conferences and workshops around the world, including the 2014 AberLanc Graduate Colloquium in Warwick, UK; the 2015 meeting of the International Studies Association in New Orleans, USA; the 2015 International Political Sociology Doctoral Workshop and Winter School in Rio de Janeiro, Brazil; the 2015 Popular Culture and World Politics Conference in London, UK; the 2016 meeting of the International Studies Association in Atlanta, USA; the 2016 meeting of the British International Studies Association in Edinburgh, UK; the 2017 conference entitled 'The Interpretation of Global Politics: methods and epistemologies after the event' in Canberra, Australia; and the 2018 meeting of the International Political Science Association in Brisbane, Australia. These experiences have been invaluable, and I am grateful for all the sharp questions and challenging discussions they have generated. In addition, Jon de Peyer and Rob Byron at Manchester University Press have both been hugely encouraging and accommodating throughout the process of writing, refining and delivering this manuscript. I thank

Acknowledgements

them – and the reviewers they engaged on my behalf – for their professionalism, their understanding and their keen eyes.

Being an academic is always a privilege, but not necessarily always a pleasure. Navigating this profession has been made not just bearable but enjoyable by a huge crowd of superheroes. In addition to my colleagues and former colleagues, my appreciation and *solidarité* are thus also due to Henry Redwood, LucasDonna Hedlund, Hannah Partis-Jennings, Ciaran Gillespie, Andreas Papamichail, Clara Eroukhmanoff, Cian O'Driscoll, Tim Aistrope, Lindsay Clark, Dave Norman, Amy Doffegnies, Carol Futuro, Sol Gamsu, Mark Griffiths, Umut Ozguc, Roland Bleiker, Emma Hutchison and Federica Caso. Knowingly or unknowingly, you have all at various points inspired and challenged me, and you have been (and continue to be) dear friends.

The same is of course true of a large number of people outside academia, without whom the last seven years would have been impossible and overwhelming. My love and thanks are thus due to Ralph, Martha, Will, Martine, Dave, James, Thom, Hannah, Polly and the Canberra crew. Finally, my deepest thanks are reserved for my family: Mum, Dad, Susie and Elly. I love you all very dearly, and I owe you everything.

Introduction: taking humour seriously

Introduction

What is the relationship between humour and global politics? To some, the question might appear glib: surely the seriousness of the world's many problems demands a commensurately 'serious' scholarly focus? Yet humour is already woven into international affairs in ways that make it difficult to dismiss as flippant or facile. Consider the 2015 shootings at the offices of *Charlie Hebdo*, for example.[1] One cannot make much sense of the attack without understanding how humour served as a focal point for a variety of ethical and political anxieties. At stake for both *Charlie Hebdo*'s editorial team and their murderers were a number of complex questions: does 'free speech' have boundaries? How should any such boundaries be established, enforced, contested and/or resisted? What criteria ought to inform the construction and maintenance of political community in a context of social and cultural heterogeneity?

These questions have important global dimensions. Within hours, the *Charlie Hebdo* attack had been framed as an assault on 'Western' values, amid a transnational outpouring of solidarity with the magazine (cf. Eroukhmanoff, 2019). Outside Europe, meanwhile, protests against *Charlie Hebdo*'s continued publication took place in Niger, Algeria, Chechnya, Sudan, Mali, Pakistan, Mauritania and Jordan (Graham-Harrison, 2015). Taken together, these responses invite reflection on the contours and boundaries of European liberal democracy, and on the global matrices of inclusion and exclusion that define and sustain it. They demonstrate that questions about what is laughable are inextricable from questions about what is valuable, sacred, serious, rational and sensible – and about who gets to define these concepts' meanings. This in turn opens up further questions about order, hierarchy, privilege and status. All are of obvious significance to students of international politics.

This book's point of departure is the assertion that humour is a constitutive, active and potentially important ingredient of global-political discourse and practice. However, it is not just exceptional acts of explosive violence that demonstrate humour's relevance to international affairs. Humour also plays its part in a huge range of ordinary or everyday social practices, across communities and collectives of every imaginable stripe (Billig, 2005; Morreall, 1983; Palmer, 1994). Most people will have experienced the way a shared laugh can amplify and deepen the emotional ties that bind them to other individuals and to familial or friendship groups. Many will likewise recognise the sense of diminishment that comes with being the butt of a joke: the painful realisation that one's exclusion from a community of laughers is the precise thing around which that community has coalesced. These two functions are intimately connected. Anthropologists have long observed that, on one hand, conventions surrounding how, where, when and why people make one another laugh both reflect and help to codify social order (e.g. Radcliffe-Brown, 1940, 1949). When humour flouts or disregards these norms, on the other hand, it magnifies social tensions and contradictions in ways that can potentially provoke their reimagining (Douglas, 1968, 1975; Brassett and Sutton, 2017). Either way, humour plays a productive role in the organisation of its social field.

As a mode of everyday interaction and expression, humour also plays its part on the political and world-political stages. As feminist scholars have long argued, the local and the global are not discrete, independent domains, but are rather mutually constitutive of each other. On the one hand, international relations of domination and marginalisation are sustained and reproduced by everyday cultural practices: as Cynthia Enloe has argued, 'the bedroom's hierarchy is not unconnected to the hierarchies of the international coffee exchange or of the foreign ministry' (2004: 31). Yet on the other, it is precisely because of this 'not unconnected'-ness that these seemingly unremarkable fields of practice can also function as sites of questioning, disputation and resistance: sites where identity can be asserted, where agency can be claimed and where change can be both demanded and prefigured. In the words of Christine Sylvester, *pace* Alexander Wendt's claim that 'anarchy is what states make of it': 'anarchy is also what a variety of yet-to-be-heard people of international relations, and their "strange" politics and conversations and empathies, make of it' (2002: 261; cf. Rossdale, 2010: 494). For Sylvester, International Relations (IR) scholars must cultivate an attentiveness to what she calls 'the social relations of the international' – social relations that are themselves always already immanent within concerns of international reach and import – if they are adequately to address the layered complexities of global power relations (2002: 10).

In this book, I argue that a focus on humour not only provides one way to trace the production and reproduction of these 'social relations of the international', but also opens up hitherto under- or even unstudied sites where this production and reproduction takes place. In the body of artwork produced by detainees in concentration camps; in queer responses to the HIV/AIDS pandemic; and in carnivalesque tactics of contemporary mass protest, one can observe actors engaging through humour in the 'transversal' interrogation, negotiation and contestation of social, political and international relations.[2] These counterintuitive appeals to laughter, in contexts of little obvious levity, demand explanation. What is it about humour that makes it an attractive (and at times effective) mode of speech and action in circumstances defined by political and perhaps even existential urgency?

Underpinning my approach to this problem is the conviction that humour is not a tool, discrete and divisible from the subject who uses it, but rather a field of practice that makes a politically significant contribution to the processes by which actors come to position themselves as subjects in the first place. As post-structuralist IR scholars, among others, have suggested, linguistic, communicative and aesthetic practices are key to the formation of subjective identity (e.g. Der Derian and Shapiro, 1989; Campbell, 1992; Hansen, 2006). To engage in humour is therefore to participate in processes of social construction that blur the traditional distinction between doer and deed: humour, in short, is performative. To joke and laugh is not just to make a statement about who one is and how one relates to others: it is also a way of inhabiting the very form of life one is asserting (Butler, 2010: 155; Brassett, 2016: 171).

A handful of excellent articles within IR have begun to consider comedy, laughter and joking in these terms (e.g. Brassett, 2016; Salter, 2011; Dodds and Kirby, 2013; de Goede, 2005; Amoore and Hall, 2013; Brassett, Browning and Wedderburn, 2021). This body of work has done much to validate humour and comedy as objects of concern within the discipline, establishing them as sites where political identity and subjectivity are performatively brought into being in ways that raise challenging questions about hegemonic practices of security, leadership and market governance. One aspect of performativity theory towards which this literature has paid little attention, however, is its recognition that not everyone is permitted to participate in processes of subject formation. As Judith Butler argues, 'the exclusionary matrix by which subjects are formed … requires the simultaneous production of a domain of abject beings, those who are not yet "subjects", but who form the constitutive outside to the domain of the subject' (2011: xiii). What distinguishes my argument from existing studies is my focus on the ways in which humour often operates at and across this boundary between the 'abject' and the 'subject'. It is here, at the frontiers of what can and cannot be considered 'political', 'orderly', 'righteous' or 'civilised', that humour's transversal role in the production, reproduction and contestation of social relations of the international is most apparent.

One unique feature of my enquiry is that I ground this conceptualisation of humour in historical accounts of comic discourse and practice. Drawing on the Megarian theory of comedy that Aristotle outlines in the *Poetics*, I show how humour has historically been understood in relation to anxieties about subjectivity, estrangement and the circumscription and protection of the political sphere (Aristotle, 2006: 5–6). According to Aristotle, the Megarians conceived of comedy as a way of speaking from a position of 'disgrace', referring to a dishonour that debarred those burdened with it from participating in the political life of the *polis*. In ancient Greek comic poetry and drama, this function is embodied by the stock character of the parasite: an ambiguous figure who intrudes uninvited into social and political spaces from which they are by rights forbidden, sustaining their uneasy presence through the incitement or provocation of laughter (Corner, 2013a; 2013b). I interpret the parasite's appeals to humour as an 'interruptive' politicising act, performatively confronting an otherwise stable relational system with its excluded Other.[3] To act 'parasitically' is therefore to use humour in order to ask questions about the terms of belonging that govern who precisely is able to claim the status of 'subject', and who is instead condemned to the mute, undifferentiated realm of abjection that Butler identifies as its necessary corollary.

I use this theoretical 'parasitic' subject in order to illuminate my three concrete case studies. These interrogate humour's role in the political practice of three distinct groups: detainees in French concentration camps during the Second World War; people living with HIV/AIDS in the early years of the pandemic; and participants in the so-called 'global justice movement' around the turn of the millennium. All three are intimately concerned with issues of global reach and import, and all use humour 'parasitically', as a way of negotiating or contesting social and political relations from a position of 'disgrace'. Each demonstrates a different approach to parasitic performance, however, which I term 'aesthetic parasitism', 'physical parasitism' and 'parodic parasitism' respectively. Taken together, these three studies offer a layered and multi-dimensional understanding both of the ways in which humour functions politically and of the ways it can function 'parasitically' by conveying a performative claim to political subjectivity in the face of its violent, proscriptive denial.

Although my primary focus is on actors who have sought to challenge prevailing systems of governance and/or oppression, it is important to remember that humour has no political teleology. Humour can form part of reactionary, prejudicial and cruel political projects as well as radical, progressive and transformative ones. I thus have no normative commitment to humour *per se*. Rather, I am interested in humour as a practice: as a constitutive part of the multiple, various processes through which subjective identities and intersubjective relations are produced, reproduced and contested. This interest encompasses instances where change is demanded and/or enacted, as well as those where oppressive and violent dynamics are (re)produced. As will become clear, humour is as multiple and complex as the social and political fields in which it arises, and tends – even when mobilised as part of emancipatory political programmes – to pull in multiple directions simultaneously. As Judith Butler rightly notes, 'the mobilization of identity categories for the purposes of politicization always remain threatened by the prospect of identity becoming an instrument of the power one opposes' (2006: xxvi).

My study shows that IR has much to gain by taking humour seriously. In its exploration of humour's global-political purchase, this book makes a significant and original contribution to interdisciplinary debates about everyday practice, political aesthetics and the politics of subjectivity. In the process, it shows how international relations are engaged in a mutually constitutive relationship with everyday exchanges and interactions that cannot be unproblematically reduced to the broader intergovernmental context in which they take place. To speak of a 'parasitic politics' is therefore to foreground the role of humour in specific, local contests and negotiations, as well as the symbiotic, 'transversal' relationship between these struggles and global systems and networks of relations. Although the specificity of this focus means that this book cannot claim to be a comprehensive study of humour *per se*, it nevertheless opens a window onto yet-to-be-heard exchanges in a way that would be diluted by a more general enquiry. This promises in turn to deepen and enrich IR's understanding of how power and order are produced, maintained, understood and contested by virtue of engaging not just with the 'domain of the subject', but also with the abjection that functions as its 'constitutive outside' – as well as with the dynamic, shifting boundary between the two.

I proceed now to map this book's course in more detail. I begin by making the case for an analytic focus on humour within IR. Noting what Bonnie Honig (2013: 69) describes as the 'uncontested privileging' of tragedy within Western political thought, I argue that the discipline's failure to think more widely about the way it 'emplots' the international has caused it to overlook features of international affairs that sit uneasily within its prevailing archetype. These include (but are not limited to) humour, comedy and other patterns of everyday intersubjective communication. I then move on to establish why apparently unremarkable practices such as these might be significant for the study of world politics. IR has in many ways defined itself in opposition to the 'local' and 'cultural', relegating them to a sociological or anthropological realm outside its purview (Jahn, 2000; Lawson, 2006). In doing so, it has secured itself an analytic territory it can call its own – but at the cost of understanding the many forms of politics that spill untidily across the boundaries of 'the international'.

Humour, tragedy and international theory

The language surrounding humour is both varied and vague: in IR alone, articles have been written concerning not only 'humour' itself but also 'joking', 'laughter', 'satire' and 'comedy' (Dodds and Kirby, 2013; Adler-Nissen and Tsinovoi, 2019; Salter, 2011; Lisle, 2016; Brassett and Sutton, 2017; Hall, 2014; Brassett, 2016). In this book I make no attempt to classify or taxonomise these concepts, and instead take an inclusive view of my object of study: 'humour' is not a fixed analytical category but rather denotes a complex assemblage of practices, and its use throughout this book is thus more a matter of convenience than of principle. The practices that fall under its umbrella – practices that Umberto Eco describes (1984: 1) as 'a disturbing ensemble of diverse and not completely homogeneous phenomena' – defy easy categorisation, and are characterised loosely here by nothing more than the attempt socially to incite, provoke or express amusement.

Two aspects of this purposefully and determinedly open definition warrant further attention. First, an 'attempt' at humour does not have to be successful in order to be described as such. As Michael Billig has observed, 'unlaughter' – the lack of laughter when it is otherwise to be hoped for or expected; the deflated and deflating silence following a joke that has missed its target – is a crucial and often overlooked aspect of humour (2005: 175–199; Dodds and Kirby, 2013). In this respect, as Billig observes (2005: 7), 'we are the laughing animal only because we are also the unlaughing one': the charge that something isn't funny functions as a recognition of its status as humour rather than as a refusal. Second, 'humour' as defined here both encompasses and exceeds 'comedy', understood as a formal genre of performance that usually takes place in an overtly mediated setting (on stage, on a cinema or TV screen, through a radio speaker, within a text). In addition, humour also refers to the attempted incitement, provocation or expression of amusement in *any* social context (not just the theatre, cinema, radio or text *but also* the bedroom, café, office and street). Humour, in short, cannot be located solely in a particular, largely professionalised tradition of writing and performance, but rather in a diverse field of practice that includes (but is not limited to) the conventional 'comedic' channels.

Although a number of recent articles have asked what such practices might have to offer to the study of IR, the discipline nevertheless lacks any in-depth exploration of the topic. In relation to this relative lack of attention it is perhaps worth noting that IR, like other disciplines including philosophy, political theory, philosophy and psychoanalysis, has historically defined itself in relation to tragedy. What Bonnie Honig (2013: 69) calls the 'uncontested privileging' of the tragic in Western political thought is likewise manifest in a large and established body of IR theory, ranging across the discipline's various theoretical traditions (e.g. Appleman Williams, 2009; Butterfield, 1950; Dillon, 1996; Erskine and Lebow, 2012; Frost, 2003; 2008; Lebow, 2003; Mearsheimer, 2001; Morgenthau, 1947; 1962; 1969; Niebuhr, 1938; 1964; Thompson, 1972; cf. Wedderburn, 2018). According to this body of work, an engagement with tragic drama's themes and *motifs* enables an enriched understanding of some of IR's basic and foundational dilemmas. For Ned Lebow (2003: 20), for example, 'tragedy confronts us with our frailties and limits … and the disastrous consequences of trying to exceed them'. The 'tragic vision' he identifies as a key feature of classical realist theory is premised on the claim that there is a deep ontological correspondence between the tragic and the political: that we are all potential protagonists in a drama of our own making. As such, as Michael Dillon similarly argues (1996: 40), tragedy 'does not have to invent its characters or plots. It finds them already there in the human condition.' For these theorists, despite their many other differences, tragedy functions as a point of reference against which international politics can be measured and evaluated; it serves as a lens through which the world can be made legible to the analyst (Wedderburn, 2018).

One might reasonably ask whether and how a discipline oriented in this way might engage with aspects of political experience that fall outside its professed boundaries. After all, as Debbie Lisle rightly suggests (2016: 424), 'lurking within the experience of tragedy are a whole range of unruly, excessive, and in-between emotional states'. Foremost among these, for Lisle, are 'absurdity, comedy, satire, slapstick, mimicry, and laughter', 'states' that cannot easily be mapped onto IR's 'prefigured emotional pathways'. It is perhaps no surprise, then, that they have received little attention within the discipline. The handful of IR articles that *do* engage with humour bear witness to their own marginality through their diffusion: they refer to each other intermittently and inconsistently, and together comprise a piecemeal collage of ideas rather than a coherent body of literature.

As such, there is little theoretical or methodological consensus about humour among IR scholars. Some, like Riikka Kuusisto or Louiza Odysseos, can be situated within a broader turn to narrative in the social sciences. Both argue that international politics are given meaning by the interpretive and storytelling practices through which they are known: that one can only make sense of the world by constructing narratives that give shape to its otherwise overwhelming complexity. Comedy functions as one of these narrative scripts or frames – as one of many strategies for shaping and ordering the world. It is akin to what historian Hayden White (1975: 2) calls an 'emplotment':

> the historian confronts a veritable chaos of events already constituted, out of which he must choose the elements of the story he would tell. He makes his story by including some events and excluding others, by stressing some and subordinating others. This process of exclusion, stress, and subordination is carried out in the interest of constituting a story of a particular kind. That is to say, he 'emplots' his story.
> (White, 1975: 6n5)

White sees emplotment as the means by which the historian produces history, extracting a certain order from the 'veritable chaos of events' in front of her by selecting and organising them into a coherent narrative. For Kuusisto and Odysseos, IR scholars make sense of the stuff of international politics through an analogous process of composition and construction. As Kuusisto argues (2009: 601), 'truths ... depend on the story that constitutes their setting', while for Odysseos (2001: 709–710) a post-Enlightenment emphasis on reason has led to the predominance of what she calls 'rational narratives' in IR, of which the so-called 'democratic peace' hypothesis is emblematic.

Because they argue that 'the international' cannot be known except through the constellation of discursive practices that describe it, Kuusisto and Odysseos cannot claim that comedy offers an objective or universal 'vision' of world affairs. Instead, their argument is that comedy offers an instructive lens through which 'the international' might be perceived. Its value to the IR scholar can therefore be located in its capacity to illuminate otherwise disregarded features of the political landscape, or to suggest possibilities for action that would in other instances be overlooked. Comedy, in other words, carries the possibility of reframing or repoliticising IR's dominant narratives in a productive and/or beneficial way. To this end, Kuusisto argues that comedy can contribute towards processes of conflict resolution, because it accommodates more flexibility and understanding towards others than conventional scripts allow. Odysseos, meanwhile, uses a specific comedic narrative – Aristophanes' *Peace* – in order to disrupt the rational hegemony of the democratic peace hypothesis. Her aim in so doing is to 'reveal the importance of making use of the full spectrum of the human register in political and moral considerations' – a spectrum that includes the incongruous and irrational juxtapositions characteristic of Aristophanean comedy (2001: 731).

Kuusisto's and Odysseos' studies share important methodological similarities with the tragic visions of international politics that might be said to comprise the discipline's prevailing emplotment. Though they do not argue that comedy corresponds directly to political 'reality', both Kuusisto and Odysseos nevertheless seek to define certain, essential characteristics of the genre in a manner analogous to IR's tragic theorists. In so doing, they draw implicitly on archetypal literary criticism from the likes of Maud Bodkin and Northrop Frye, distilling complex traditions of narration and performance into formal models that they hope can shed light on various international political problems or dilemmas (Bodkin, 1965; Frye, 1973). 'Tragedy' and 'comedy' are therefore said to project particular, identifiable outlooks that can be applied to the political realm in a productive or enlightening way. They are 'pedagogical' resources for the IR theorist rather than sites of politics in their own right (Carpenter, 2016: 54–55; Williams, 2018).

Although this approach has made significant contributions towards the establishment of cultural and aesthetic media as legitimate sources of knowledge about international politics, it harbours significant methodological shortcomings. Foremost among these is the charge that has dogged archetypal criticism among literary critics since the 1970s: that it flattens the contours and folds of literary practice into a textureless sequence of formal characteristics, dislocated from the social contexts in which literature is written, read and performed. In so doing, archetypal criticism therefore 'rejects or perhaps simply excludes ... history from ... critical theory, and, what is more important, excludes along with it the whole chronological dimension – the "reality" of change, process, and time – in which history moves and has meaning' (Schroeter, 1972: 550; cf. Abrams, 1991: 217–233). A methodological outlook charged with depoliticising its object of study would seem a questionable tool for the analysis of world politics. If such ahistorical categories of textual form and meaning are unable adequately to account for the variability, diversity and historical contingency of literary practice, then they are also likely to be unsatisfactory reference points for the study of international affairs.

While in agreement with Kuusisto and Odysseos regarding the importance of narratives to the constitution of international-political 'reality', the separation of an archetypal ideal of 'comedy' from the textual and social practices that constitute it is reliant on an abstraction that is both methodologically and ontologically suspicious. Allowing a fixed and ahistorical emplotment to govern political analysis obscures the heterogeneous multiplicity of practices that comprise the political field, and ensures that aspects of everyday social and political life that do not fit neatly into one's prescribed archetype fall to the wayside. It also reduces literary, aesthetic and/ or cultural practices to a realm of representation, as opposed to acknowledging them as active political forces in and of themselves. As Jenny Edkins argues:

> It is not the novel or the fictional form *per se*, then, that challenges ... a certain distribution of the sensible in the name of politics – but a certain *type* of novel, a certain *type* of narrative, a certain *type* of story, even a certain type of academic account. What type might that be? Of course, it is always already impossible to answer this question in the manner in which it appears to be framed here, as a question of categories or of genres ... What is being asked here is a *practical* question – *a* question of *practice* – not a question of classification.
>
> *(2013: 286, emphasis in original)*

Recognising this, a number of scholars have recently made important steps towards establishing the practical global-political implications of humour. In so doing, they offer an alternative account of humour's relevance to IR that builds on insights first made by anthropologists in a series of studies focusing on the ritual 'joking relationships' typical of numerous peoples and societies around the world (Radcliffe-Brown, 1940; 1949; Douglas, 1975: 90–116; Brightman, 1999; Garde, 2008; Jackes, 1969; Arno, 1976: 71–86; Mead, 2012).

The 'joking relationship' is understood, in Alfred Radcliffe-Brown's words, as 'a relation between two persons in which one is by custom permitted, and in some instances required, to tease or make fun of the other, who in turn is required to take no offence' (1940: 195). The account that Radcliffe-Brown gives of the joking practices of the Dogon people in Mali suggests that humour can play a key role in the establishment and reinforcement of social order. For the Dogon, humour produces and sustains the hierarchical structures according to which their community is organised and governed, both internally and in terms of its outward relations with other peoples. In Radcliffe-Brown's words, it 'can be regarded as [a] means of establishing and maintaining social equilibrium' (1949: 135); it is a 'mode ... of organising a definite and stable system of social behaviour in which conjunctive and disjunctive components ... are maintained and combined' (1940: 200).

Radcliffe-Brown's analysis of joking as a socially situated practice allows for a dynamic account of the relationship between humour and its social and political field, in which respect it offers a more promising line of enquiry for IR than a turn towards narrative form. As Mary Douglas notes, however, Radcliffe-Brown's attempt to draw general laws from a specific case study makes for a limited, 'desiccated' (and, one might also add, implicitly colonial) account of joking relationships (1975: 91). Douglas argues that joking's social function is significantly more ambiguous than Radcliffe-Brown allows. She notes that people often choose *not* to follow whatever formal or informal social norms govern joking relationships: they might choose to joke at an inappropriate time, in an inappropriate way or to an inappropriate person, or they might fail to joke when it is expected of them (1975: 95–96). In so doing, they not only offer a formal challenge to the prevailing order, but also position themselves in a particular way in relation to it (1975: 98–99).

Humour can thus function either to maintain the continuity of social systems *or* as an engine of change: it is a mode of discourse and a field of practice through which the social and political fields can be delimited, organised, reproduced, negotiated and transformed in any number of contingent and provisional ways. Moreover, humour provides a way of tracing how people come to occupy, refuse or negotiate particular subject positions. How and to whom one jokes, in other words, helps to determine who one is. Humour thus plays an active part in the creation, maintenance and potential transformation of social and political relations. It follows that if one wishes to evaluate its contribution to these processes then one must study it as it occurs in practice. To speak, as Kuusisto and Odysseos do, of 'the comic narrative' as a lens through which global politics can be perceived, is to obscure the role played by comic practices in constituting the political field as an object of analysis in the first place.

Consider the 'locker room banter' that came to define the 2016 presidential election, for example.[4] By invoking the phrase, Donald Trump intended to designate and occupy a discursive space where his words would not correspond to his beliefs, to his prejudices or indeed to any sort of meaning at all. Instead, 'banter' denoted a space of insincerity, a space where language was simply sound signifying nothing: a space beyond politics. This attempt to cloak misogyny in a prophylactic layer of comic irony wilts under scrutiny. If humour is part of 'the processes of learning and imposing the disciplines of social life' – or the processes of resisting or refusing them – then to write it off as mere flippancy is a depoliticising move (Billig, 2005: 177). What happens in the 'locker room' does not necessarily stay there, as those who have studied the relationship between sports, masculinity and war have long argued (Shapiro, 1989b; Butterworth, 2017; Aistrope, 2020). Even if one accepts Trump's claim at face value, then, one can nevertheless assert that it is precisely because his remarks *were* 'banter' that they reveal something both about him and about the multiple, overlapping social *milieus* in which he moves and acts. The fact that so many accepted Trump's defence, meanwhile, suggests that the relevance of humour to the construction of identity and to the maintenance and contestation of order remains both under-theorised and poorly understood.

I turn now to suggest why this should be a matter for concern for the academic discipline of IR.

Everyday practice, subjectivity and global politics

As outlined by anthropologists like Mary Douglas, humour contributes to the establishment, negotiation and transformation of social and political relations. The ways in which individuals and groups make each other laugh not only reflect existing norms, but also help to shape and reshape them; to carve open subjective and intersubjective terrain where new possibilities for thought and action can be imagined and potentially brought into being. Humour is therefore of interest to scholars thinking about the production, reproduction and contestation of power relations, and about the ways in which subjects seek to position themselves within them. What distinguishes this book from the anthropological studies discussed in the preceding paragraphs, however, is its interest in the *global* implications of humour as a field of everyday practice. Why is humour of interest not just to anthropology and sociology, but also to IR? What does a focus on humour have to contribute to the study of *world* politics?

The analytic domain presided over by the academic discipline of IR is often understood to be coterminous with an anarchic interstate system. Among many IR scholars, there is a protective impulse towards 'the international' as an ontologically distinct sphere of political activity that relegates questions of social practice and of subjective identity to a sociological realm altogether beyond the purview of the discipline (cf. Lawson, 2006: 31). 'No sooner have we established that mainstream IR theory ... takes the cultural diversity of humanity as a defining feature of its problematic', Beate Jahn asserts, '[than] we find it leaving culture behind and grounding itself instead in a variety of versions of the concept of the state of nature' (2000: xii). Rob Walker likewise notes that 'within this ideological universe [of mainstream IR theory], categories of culture, class and gender have been repeatedly excised' (1993: 134).

Over the last thirty years, a wide variety of critical and dissenting voices have challenged the boundary-drawing practices required to define the international realm as a space distinct and discrete from the social and the everyday. Foremost among these have been feminist scholars, who have long maintained that the study of social practices opens up important perspectives on the maintenance and contestation of global relations of domination and marginalisation (Sylvester, 2002: 3). As Gillian Youngs argues, feminist IR has 'therefore been both deconstructive and reconstructive: focusing on revealing through critique the masculinist limitations of mainstream approaches, but also, crucially, going beyond those limitations and investigating political and economic processes in which women and men are engaged' (2004: 76–77). For feminists, the power relations that constitute 'the international' cannot be neatly cordoned off into a particular sphere of activity, but rather are (re)produced at any number of sites, from places of informal labour such as the home to places of leisure such as ambassadorial receptions or even bingo halls (Enloe, 2014: 37–82, 174–210; Elias and Roberts, 2016; Elias and Rai, 2019; Tickner, 1992).

Underpinning this scholarship is the conviction that power is not a concrete, quantifiable capacity, radiating outwards from sovereign centres, but rather something relational, produced through the practical and discursive normalisation of particular patterns of thought and behaviour. This is a claim that also lies beneath much critical and post-structuralist IR theory. Richard Ashley and Rob Walker, for example, assert that 'every historical figuration of sovereign presence … [is] a contingent political effect', and that 'to be practically effective any semblance of a sovereign centre … depends upon the *forgetting* of the ongoing labour of marginalising those ambiguities, uncertainties, and contesting interpretations that would … undo or disrupt the pretence of sovereign certitude' (1990: 368, 390, emphasis in original; see also Ashley, 1988; Der Derian and Shapiro, 1989; Campbell, 1992). The task of critical IR scholarship, then, is to draw attention to these 'ambiguities, uncertainties and contest[ations]', as well as to those subjects, occupying what Cynthia Enloe (2004) calls the 'margins, silences and bottom rungs', who not only embody but also expose and exploit these clefts in the prevailing system. Coming to terms with the untidy dynamics of global politics thus entails a focus on 'transversal' practices that spill messily across the putative boundaries between the 'international', the 'political' and the 'social', and ask questions of the processes and practices through which those boundaries are produced and policed. If humour makes a contribution to the drawing and redrawing of subjective identity and intersubjective relationality, as anthropologists have suggested, then it is reasonable also to ask whether it might function transversally to engage systems and apparatuses of global reach and significance.

This book argues that humour can and indeed often does play a transversal role in the maintenance and negotiation of global power relations. In making this argument, I build on a body of existing IR scholarship that has identified and explored instances of overlap between humour and global politics. James Brassett, for example, reads the work of professional comedians like Charlie Brooker, Stewart Lee and Russell Brand as a 'vernacular form of resistance' to established forms of 'market subjectivity' (2016: 170). While rightly stressing that humour is not *a priori* radical, Brassett nevertheless argues that it can project a 'subversive understanding' of contemporary capitalist subjectivity that enables its audience to reflect on the political limits and possibilities of a world forcefully driven by the disciplinary power of the market (2016: 170–171).

In contrast, Mark Salter focuses on the prohibition of humour in airports ('no joking!') as a way of reading the 'hypersecuritised' politics of 'surveillance and control' that govern mobility at the border (2011: 31–32). Salter posits the 'no joking' rule as one of many securitising measures intended to limit 'the possible [and] the sayable' within everyday life (2011: 33). A joke, he argues, carries the potential of disrupting the security mechanisms at work within airport spaces – mechanisms that discipline travellers to conform to certain patterns of behaviour. Joking does this by producing a subject who is opaque rather than transparent; whose identifying information is unreliable and inconstant instead of freely and soberly divulged (2011: 38–39). Theorising the airport checkpoint as a performative space, Salter implicitly constitutes joking in the same terms: the act of joking produces a subject whose illegibility short-circuits the presumptions of sincerity on which security practices depend. In Salter's words, 'ambiguity, on which jokes rely, fundamentally undermines the presentation of certainty that is crucial to security performances' (2011: 39).

Both Brassett and Salter, despite their different empirical foci, identify the subject as the point of intersection between humour and global politics. In the work of certain comedians, or in the securitised border space of the airport, dissonant and dissident subjectivities can

Introduction   17

be produced through the very act of telling a joke. Humour is constituted as a field of practice where alternative subjective possibilities can be experimented with, explored and enacted, in which sense it is performative: the comic subject does not precede her practice, but is constituted through it (cf. Butler, 2006: 195). This book builds on these brief studies insofar as it theorises humour as a field of everyday performative practice of interest to those concerned with the transversal politics of subjectivity. However, it also departs from them in one important regard. While both Brassett and Salter offer important insights regarding how humour might enable people to reposition themselves within the subjective field, they both take the category of 'subjectivity' as given. At stake in performativity theory, however, is not simply the problematisation of particular subjective identities, but also the destabilisation of the subjective realm itself:

> The 'abject' designates that which has been expelled from the body, discharged as excrement, literally rendered 'Other'. This appears as an expulsion of alien elements, but the alien is effectively established through this expulsion. The construction of the 'not-me' as the abject establishes the boundaries of the body which are also the first contours of the subject.
>
> *(Butler, 2011: xiii; cf. Kristeva, 1982)*

I argue that existing studies' failure to take account of the exclusionary dynamics at the heart of subjectivity is especially important when considering the politics of humour. This is because humour has historically been understood to operate at and across the boundary between the 'subject' and the 'abject': its politics do not just concern this or that mode of subjective being but also the terms of belonging that constitute and circumscribe the entire subjective field. Without taking these into account, IR lacks the theoretical and methodological tools necessary to engage fully with a world whose politics continue to condemn many of its inhabitants to silence and invisibility. This book addresses this gap.

Trajectory

This book is divided into two parts. Part I, comprising Chapters 1 and 2, explores the relationship between humour, subjectivity and global politics in more detail, and establishes the 'parasitic' understanding of comic-political subjectivity that informs my empirical analyses in Part II.

Chapter 1 develops a conceptual framework through which to understand the performative politics of humour. I theorise humour as a vehicle for the articulation and negotiation of political subjectivity: as one of many fields of practice 'through which "we" continually (re)produce ourselves and simultaneously mark ourselves off from that which is seen as different', in Ty Solomon's words (2015: 205). Humour plays an active and constitutive role (though also an ambiguous and indeterminate one) in the creation and maintenance of such distinctions, in which capacity it also helps to shape and reshape intersubjective relations both within and between political communities.

Drawing on the laugh that underpins Michel Foucault's investigations in *The Order of Things*, I argue that humour does not only participate in the performative production of different subjectivities, but also engages with the exclusionary terms by which a domain of the subject is initially made possible. Humour can therefore be understood, following Michel de Certeau, as a 'way of operating': as a field of everyday practice that is both irreducible to and inextricable from the broad network of relations that comprise its social and political terrain (1984: xiv, 30, 38–40). For de Certeau, 'ways of operating' are small resistances and deviations that disclose, occupy and exploit the liminal boundary-zones of social order. In the process, they facilitate a broader and deeper engagement with the 'mute processes' that constitute the boundaries of the thinkable, knowable, sayable and doable (1984: xiv). This understanding of humour provides the foundation for my enquiry.

Chapter 2 examines historical theories of humour. I focus on the ambiguous figure of the parasite, and show how an analytic focus on 'parasitic' appeals to humour can open up insights into the everyday politics of exclusion, struggle and resistance that underpin existing concerns in IR scholarship. I begin with the very earliest theory of comic practice that exists: a brief digression within Aristotle's discussion of tragedy in his *Poetics* (2006: 6). Aristotle's account is predicated on the belief that the Greek word for 'comedy' (*komoidia*) derives from the word for 'countryside' (*kômai*). Noting that Aristotle associates the countryside with 'disgrace' (*atimazoménous*), a word that denotes exclusion not just from the physical space of the city, but also from its political life, I argue that humour has historically been understood as a way of speaking when properly political speech is impossible.

I develop this understanding of comic-political subjectivity with reference to the parasite, a stock character of ancient Greek comic drama. Drawing on feminist theory, as well as the relational theory of Michel Serres, I argue that the parasite is an ambiguously 'interruptive' subject. The parasite 'operates' by enacting and sustaining an indeterminate encounter between a particular understanding of community, citizenship and identity on one hand, and all the things this understanding repudiates in order to achieve coherence and unity on the other. In the process, they induce an intersubjective relation where previously there was none, and open up space for the renegotiation of social and political relations. I argue that the parasite's interrogation of the terms of belonging that constitute the political sphere enables an examination of humour's transversal presence at and across the margins and limits of global political discourses and apparatuses.

Part II engages with three different sites where humour has contributed to a 'parasitic' claim to political subjectivity. I have chosen these particular sites for three reasons. First, all three touch upon existing concerns and literatures within IR. Second, the role of humour to the political dynamics in operation at each site remains under- or even unstudied. And third, each site manifests a different approach to the parasitic performance of comic-political subjectivity. Taken together, these three sites offer a thick, multifaceted interrogation and implementation of the framework established in Part I.

Chapter 3 outlines and evaluates an aesthetic approach to parasitism as demonstrated by three comic strips drawn by Horst Rosenthal, a German Jew detained at Gurs in Vichy France between 1940 and 1942 and later killed at Auschwitz-Birkenau. I read Rosenthal's three extant comic strips as examples of parasitic practice that seek to intervene into the extremities of the social context in which they were created on an aesthetic level. The three strips function by introducing dissonant aesthetic subjects into their representations of concentration: holidaymakers, and even in one case Mickey Mouse. In these ambiguous 'aesthetic interruptions',

Rosenthal sets up intersubjective encounters that enable him to engage with the desubjectifying and depoliticising effects of detainment with a latitude unavailable within the physical world of the camp. 'Aesthetic parasitism' thus refers to a performative claim to subjectivity made within an aesthetic sphere that stands as the cipher or avatar of a corresponding physical space.

Chapter 4 looks at 'physical parasitism' in the context of queer organisation against the AIDS crisis. Critical scholars have raised concerns that the post-2000 incorporation of the AIDS pandemic into United Nations and international security discourses might result in its governance according to a biopolitical logic of 'racism' (Elbe, 2005; cf. United Nations, 2000; United Nations Security Council, 2000). I argue, however, that these biopolitical responses to disease are merely extensions of an epidemiological discourse that in no small part has established and defined what HIV/AIDS signifies in the contemporary world. I focus on how people with AIDS engaged with and organised against the biomedical and biopolitical governance of their condition prior to the development of effective antiretroviral treatment in 1996, paying particular attention to the international AIDS activist group AIDS Coalition to Unleash Power (ACT UP). The importance of humour to the group's tactical approach has been largely overlooked by existing literature on the subject – a fact that several of its members have lamented (*ACT UP Oral History Project* [*AUOHP*] interview with Alan Klein, 2015). Building on these accounts, I argue that humour played an underappreciated role in ACT UP's attempts to resignify what it meant to live with (and die from) AIDS, a goal they pursued by physically occupying particular spaces associated with their marginalisation. 'Physical parasitism' thus refers to an intervention into an exclusionary discourse or system of power relations through the physical relocation and recontextualisation of bodies into spaces that produce or symbolise those bodies' abjection.

Chapter 5 interrogates the use of parody by global social movements in order to appropriate others' subjectivities. Drawing on Michel Foucault's concept of 'grotesque' or 'Ubu-esque' power (2003a: 11–15; cf. Jarry, 1968), in addition to Judith Butler's writing on parody (2006: 194–203; 2011: 84–95), I focus on the Clandestine Insurgent Rebel Clown Army (CIRCA), a group who played a prominent role in several large actions in the mid-2000s

Introduction

(cf. Amoore and Hall, 2013). I make the case that the carnivalesque parody characteristic of CIRCA and the so-called 'global justice movement' more widely intervenes into the prescriptive and established 'reality' of global capitalism by representing it in unfamiliar terms as something strange and 'grotesque' (cf. de Goede, 2005). In particular, I argue that the parodic militarism of the Clown Army served this function by highlighting the violent practices that enable global capitalism to operate on a day-to-day basis. CIRCA's 'parodic parasitism', I argue, draws on a long tradition of comic performance whose lineage can be traced back to ancient comic drama – and indeed, to the parasite. Questions arise, however, about the political meaning of parody – and indeed of humour more generally – in an age where various political figures, including the President of the United States, openly embrace the grotesque as a mode of governance.

The book's conclusion reviews the implications of its study of humour and the performance of subjectivity for the study of world politics. I emphasise three conclusions in particular. The first is the importance of everyday intersubjective interactions to the relational systems and networks that constitute international relations. A focus on humour, I argue, provides one way of tracing the symbiotic, transversal relationship between apparently mundane social practices and issues of global political concern. The second conclusion concerns the potential importance of humour to the making and unmaking of political subjectivities. Humour plays an active and sometimes important political role insofar as it is involved in the performance of political subjectivity and the (re)making of intersubjective social and political relations. Thirdly and finally, I emphasise the way in which a 'parasitic' understanding of comic-political subjectivity focuses analytic attention towards the political margins: towards the creation, reproduction, maintenance and contestation of political discourses, boundaries and orders.

Notes

1 On the morning of 7 January 2015, two men burst into an editorial meeting of the Parisian satirical magazine *Charlie Hebdo*. Opening fire, they killed ten people,* including the magazine's chief editor, Stéphane

'Charb' Charbonnier, who had commissioned and published work perceived to be making fun of the prophet Muhammad. The men fled, and after a forty-eight-hour search were themselves killed by police about twenty miles north-east of Paris.

* They also shot a contractor as they entered the building and a police officer as they made their escape, taking the total number of victims to twelve.

2 'Transversal' practices cut across the levels of analysis that commonly structure mainstream political enquiry. In Roland Bleiker's words (2000: 2), transversal action 'transgresses national boundaries, but also questions the spatial logic through which these boundaries have come to constitute and frame the conduct of international relations'. The term has been taken up by international political sociologists, whose critical outlook is often animated by a desire to 'fracture IR' by problematising the notion of a clearly bounded 'international' realm. Huysmans and Nogueira, 2016; Bigo and Walker, 2007a; 2007b. Cf. Basaran et al., 2017; Campbell, 1996; Ashley, 1989: 270, 296–299, 314; Foucault, 1982.

3 On interruption, see Butler, 2006: xxviii; Honig, 2013; Zalewski, 2007: 309; 2010: 50–51; Hall, 1992: 282.

4 On the morning of 16 September 2005, Donald Trump and Billy Bush shared a conversation aboard a bus in Burbank, California. Pulling up in the NBC Studios parking lot, they noticed the actor Arianne Zucker waiting to greet them. Trump commented that 'when you're a star, they [women] let you do it … [You can] grab 'em by the pussy. You can do anything.' On 7 October 2016, a recording of this conversation was published by the *Washington Post*, at the height of Trump's presidential campaign. In response to accusations that he was unfit to hold office, accompanied by calls to withdraw altogether from the race, Trump brushed the comments off as 'locker room banter'. He wins the election.

Part I

Humour, subjectivity and world politics

1

'A way of operating': humour, subjectivity and the everyday

Introduction

My aim in this opening chapter is to develop a framework through which to understand humour as a performative political practice. My starting point is a body of recent International Relations (IR) scholarship that has argued for the relevance of everyday life to global politics (e.g. Acuto, 2014; Björkdahl et al., 2019; Croft and Vaughan-Williams, 2017; Solomon and Steele, 2017). According to this literature, 'social relations, including international relations, are realised and produced by people': they are created and maintained, rooted in the contingencies of practice rather than pre-given structural or systemic realities (Davies and Niemann, 2002: 567; cf. Enloe, 2004: 19–20). Tracing and evaluating the production of these relations thus demands a methodological attentiveness towards the habitual and the routine: it entails '[a] move away from extant "grand" frameworks towards approaches … [that analyse] global systems and structures through the lenses of lived, embodied and experiential everyday processes' (Solomon and Steele, 2017: 275).

IR's turn towards the everyday is inextricable from a wider concern with the contours and limits of political subjectivity. For over thirty years, feminist, post-structuralist and other critical theorists have placed questions about subjectivity, intersubjectivity and their practical, everyday articulation at the heart of their analyses of world politics. As Ty Solomon (2014: 671) observes:

> The concept of the subject has been at the forefront of critically oriented IR studies for some time … In contrast to traditional rationalist, actor-centered approaches, and even conventional constructivism,

post-structuralism takes agents' social constitution as a problem to be interrogated rather than an analytical starting point.

Many of these 'critically oriented' IR scholars understand subjectivity in performative terms: as something generated through action without any ontological status prior to the practices that bring it into being (cf. Campbell, 1992: 8–9). This precludes the assumption of particular, pre-given centres of political authority, focusing attention instead on the practices through which authority is claimed and exercised (cf. Edkins, 1999). A concern with the social construction of subjective identity thus goes hand in hand with an interest in the everyday, insofar as it is understood to be through ordinary lived experience that 'human beings … take their place in the world' (Selimovic, 2019: 131).

To speak of humour as an everyday practice thus raises questions about its performative contribution to processes of social construction and subject-formation. Throughout this book, I will argue that humour is one of the 'lived, embodied and experiential everyday processes' through which subjective identities and intersubjective relations are performatively produced, reproduced and contested. Like obscenity (with which it is closely related), humour reveals much about power: about who speaks or acts with licence, and about what or whom is made the object of violation or vilification (Harris, 2018). How people joke and laugh thus says something about who they are (or want to be), about how they relate to one another and about the power relations infusing these relationships. As such, humour not only reflects the wider social orders in which it arises but also serves an active, productive role in their continuous and ongoing realisation.

An example: in December 2019, footage emerged of Canadian Prime Minister Justin Trudeau in conversation with French President Emmanuel Macron, Dutch Prime Minister Mark Rutte, British Prime Minister Boris Johnson and Britain's Princess Anne at that year's North Atlantic Treaty Organization (NATO) summit (Lyons and Wintour, 2019). In the video, Trudeau appeared to be mocking American President Donald Trump: 'He was late because he takes a 40-minute press conference off the top', Trudeau told the group. 'I've watched his team's jaws just *drop* to the floor.' Although much of the conversation is inaudible, the gist is clear: the group are smiling and laughing at what Trudeau and the others (in particular Macron and Rutte, whose backs are to the camera) are saying; they are trading anecdotes, stories and jokes behind one particular person's back and at his expense. When asked about the incident the following day, Trump described Trudeau as 'two-faced', before leaving the summit early, without holding a closing press conference. His departure was framed by both American and international media as a response to the leaked video: 'Trump leaves NATO summit early after video flap', the *Wall Street Journal* reported (Lucey and Meichtry, 2019), an angle repeated by the *Washington Post*, *Foreign Policy* and the *Guardian*, among other outlets (Birnbaum, 2019; Townsend and Kendall-Taylor, 2019; Wintour and Mason, 2019).

This incident reveals a great deal about humour as a social and political practice. The leaked video showed a group of people forging a common identity based on shared norms of foreign policy-making, public speaking and international diplomacy. This identity was reinforced by Trump's pointed exclusion: *we* are like each other, their joking affirmed, because *we* understand what being a statesperson means – unlike *him*. While Trump might have been excluded from the camaraderie privately cultivated by the group, however, his status as the leader of NATO's primary superpower made the leak not just socially embarrassing, but politically injurious. The video hinted at a set of interpersonal relations between various leaders that mapped awkwardly and unevenly onto the hierarchical relationships between the states they represented. Who people laugh with, and what (or whom) they laugh about, thus discloses important information both about their identities as subjects, as well as about the affinities, alliances and antagonisms through which these subjectivities find meaning.

In a sense, it is incidental that the exchange between Trudeau, Macron, Johnson, Rutte and Princess Anne took place within an elite political circle. My reason for focusing on humour throughout this book is not simply that it is an observable part of world leaders' informal (and sometimes formal) exchanges. That it is, of course, is noteworthy, and a number of scholars have consequently begun to evaluate humour's role in public diplomacy (e.g. Adler-Nissen and Tsinovoi, 2019; Brassett, Browning and Wedderburn, 2021). However, because humour can be found in almost all social situations and contexts (including those defined by political, ethical and even existential urgency), it opens up to enquiry a panoply of diverse lives, practices and struggles. It thus provides an opportunity to explore the construction, maintenance and contestation of social and political relations in places (and among people) usually considered marginal to world politics. How does humour contribute to people's attempts to 'take their place in the world'? How do these everyday articulations of subjective identity reproduce or alter global-political systems of power, knowledge and governance? And what do such practices disclose about the creation and maintenance of social, political and international orders? As a ubiquitous, perhaps even universal social practice, humour provides a revealing way to approach these questions.

Throughout this book, I theorise humour as a field of everyday practice that both reflects social, political and international relations and makes a performative, transversal contribution to their making and unmaking. Like other everyday practices, humour denotes a space where the day-to-day business of maintaining and reproducing existing orders takes place, as well as one where 'ideas and practices are formed and agential subjects emerge' (Selimovic, 2019: 133). It thus encompasses disputation and contestation as well as the reproduction and policing of existing relations. Humour is an arena where 'agential subjects' develop and test out various (and often multiple) articulations of themselves, and where they affirm, question and/or oppose the social, political and international contexts in relation to which these articulations take place.

I begin this chapter by discussing humour as a vehicle for the practical, everyday production of subjective and intersubjective identity. In particular, I focus on humour's performative qualities, by which I refer to its capacity for self-making: the idea that discursive practices 'do not provide a neutral reflection of an underlying reality, but rather create that very reality' (Wilcox, 2015: 8). Acknowledging international relations as an assemblage or convocation of such practices emphasises the ontological instability of its commonly assumed categories, concepts, hierarchies and centres of power. This in turn directs attention towards the dynamic, everyday interactions through which relational order is asserted, questioned and contested.

One aspect of performativity theory with which critical IR theorists have insufficiently engaged is its recognition that not everyone is able to participate in processes of subject-formation. Even when taking into account various and multiple performative articulations of subjectivity, IR scholars have tended to take the category of 'subject' for granted. As performativity theorists have emphasised, however, the circumscription of a political sphere – a space in which subjects can assert identities, jostle for position, form communities and develop patterns of interaction – is predicated on boundary-drawing processes that delimit precisely who can and cannot claim the status of 'subject' in the first place (cf. Butler, 2006). Drawing on the laugh that inspires Michel Foucault's enquiry into the discursive production of order in *The Order of Things*, I suggest that humour often engages with, probes at and/or reflects these boundary-drawing processes, as well as the vectors of in- and exclusion that they produce. It thereby offers a way into understanding the construction and contestation not just of this or that subjective identity, but also of the terms of belonging through which subjective being is initially made possible.

The chapter ends by considering humour as what Michel de Certeau calls a 'way of operating': a field of everyday practice both irreducible to and inextricable from its wider social and political fields. Ways of operating are 'the counterpart ... of the mute processes that organise the establishment of socioeconomic order' (de Certeau, 1984: xiv). As such, they facilitate an engagement with the anxieties and insecurities to be found at the limits of order: with the creation and production of new subjective articulations, new ways of living, new terms of belonging, and with order's often violent attempts to maintain control over its own boundaries. These themes will be expanded upon in Chapter 2 with reference to the parasite, a stock character of ancient comedy.

Humour, subjectivity and performativity

IR's turn towards the everyday can be understood as part of a wider project to 'reorient ... analysis [away] from [a] concern with the intentional acts of pregiven subjects to[wards] the problematic of subjectivity' itself (Campbell, 1992: 8). Underpinning this broad and diverse literature is an ontological conviction: that 'politics' is a dynamic set of practices through which various political identities and modes of being are continually brought into being, rather than a bounded field of interaction between a defined group of actors. Foregrounding the everyday negotiations and contestations that constitute the political sphere thus also foregrounds questions about subjectivity, and vice versa: the two are inextricable, part of the same ongoing processes of social construction, reproduction and transformation that define 'politics' as a whole.

This literature draws much from feminist scholarship. Feminists have long sought to politicise women's absence from political discourse and analysis by investigating the everyday practices that position some subjects at the centre of international affairs and others at the margins. As Cynthia Enloe argues (2004: 42):

> It is only by delving deeper into any political system, listening more attentively at its margins, that we can accurately estimate the powers it has taken to provide the state with the apparent stability that has permitted its elite to presume to speak on behalf of a coherent whole.

For Enloe, the critic's primary role is to investigate 'the yearly and daily business of maintaining the margin where it currently is and the centre where it now is' (Enloe, 2004: 20). This entails a focus on the lived experiences through which order (and the privilege of its mostly male elites) are imbued with qualities of naturalness or necessity. By showing how apparently enduring features of international affairs are in fact porous and pliable, feminist scholarship opens them to questioning. As Christine Sylvester emphasises (2002: 258), 'awareness of the identity borderlands we ... routinely transverse helps us to focus on [social] relations [of the] international as a phenomenon that has eluded IR theory'. Sylvester encourages reflection on these political margins and limits – 'the identity borderlands' – because they 'pos[e] different representations of the places, figures, and activities we think of as international relations ... [and] introduce[e] us to new locations of our field' (2002: 267). Rather than taking particular, privileged subjectivities for granted, then, a turn towards the everyday draws attention to the practices that produce privilege in the first place. In the process, it also brings into focus voices and subjectivities that are more usually dismissed as marginal or otherwise ignored.

IR scholars working on humour have built on these ideas in order to theorise their object of study as a field of practice involved in the making and unmaking of political subjectivities. James Brassett, for example, reads 'British comedy' – specifically, the work of Charlie Brooker, Stewart Lee and Russell Brand – as an everyday form of resistance against political-economic 'hierarchies, violences and exclusions' (2016: 170, 177; cf. Critchley, 1999: 119). Brassett argues that Brooker, Lee and Brand seek to problematise disciplinary 'norms of market subjectivity' by adopting and performing identities that gesture towards alternative forms and rhythms of social life (2016: 170–171; cf. Solomon, 2019). Though it is not *a priori* subversive or radical, 'British comedy' is nevertheless of political interest for Brassett insofar as it carves open space in which unconventional, dissonant or resistant subjects can be brought into being, and a life in excess of market norms imagined (2016: 174–175).

Klaus Dodds and Philip Kirby similarly read laughter as a practice that can contribute to the (de)construction of 'geopolitical subjectivities' (2013: 50). In particular, they argue that humour plays a 'role in the making of the citizen': it helps to define who can and who cannot be considered part of a particular geopolitical community. As such, it contributes to the drawing and redrawing of political identity: it is a field of practice through which forms of subjectivity are enacted, reinforced and/or resisted. Like Brassett, Dodds and Kirby stress humour's indeterminacy: it can entrench gendered, raced or violent political subjectivities as well as problematise them; it can close off possibilities for thought and action as well as open them up. As an example, they cite the 2005 cartoons of the Prophet Muhammad published in the Danish newspaper *Jyllands-Posten*, which they read as an attempt to strengthen a particular cultural and racial vision of 'Danish-ness' at the expense of a more open and inclusive sense of national identity (2013: 50, 55; cf. Hansen, 2011). The humour at work in these cartoons, Dodds and Kirby claim, posits and promotes an ideal (white, non-Muslim) Danish subject, constituting those excluded from this demographic as threatening, terroristic 'others' (2013: 49–56). For them as for Brassett, humour thus denotes 'a cultural space that can (*but does not necessarily*) reflect and resist political hierarchies, violences and exclusions' (Brassett, 2016: 177, emphasis added).

Finally, Mark Salter explores the 'no joking' rule common in the security spaces of contemporary airports (2011: 31–32). Joking subjects do not conform to the desired model of the security-conscious international traveller, freely and earnestly divulging information to the officials at the border (2011: 38–39). Instead, they short-circuit the presumptions of sincerity upon which airport security practices depend, thus undermining security officials' attempts to evaluate the danger or threat posed by particular subjects. Because joking subjects cannot be read or known in the same way as 'serious' ones, they embody an unruly and intransigent blockage in the airport's security machinery.

For Brassett, Dodds and Kirby, and Salter, humour is of political interest as a practice through which subjective identities can be created, experimented with and inhabited. Through humour, subjects reproduce, interrupt or otherwise participate in the economies of power and processes of ordering that comprise their social and political *milieus*. Crucially, however, these subjects are performatively produced: they do not pre-exist their practice, but are rather constituted by, in and through it. In Judith Butler's words (2006: 181):

> The foundationalist reasoning of identity politics tends to assume that an identity must first be in place in order for political interests to be elaborated and, subsequently, political action to be taken. My argument is that there need not be a 'doer behind the deed', but that the 'doer' is variably constructed in and through the deed.

Butler argues that performative identities are always provisional: rooted in performance, they are by definition unfinished, engaged in a never-ending process of becoming rather than occupying a state of being. In order for these identities to endure, the performance must therefore be continually repeated as part of what Butler calls performativity's 're-iterative temporality' (2010: 153). When identity, order and indeed politics are considered in these terms, it is clear that the assumptions of ontological stability that conventionally underpin political analysis can no longer hold. Relational order is instead established and fixed by assemblages of 'repetitive and iterative practices' that bring political 'reality' into being and imbue it with a sense of naturalness or necessity (Aradau et al., 2015: 70).

For Brassett, Dodds and Kirby, and Salter, humour can be understood as a performative practice through which provocative, unusual or dissident political subjectivities are iteratively brought into being. This book builds on these studies: if humour can 'politicise subjectivity' by 'inhabiting' relations of power 'as a form of life that is ongoing [and] political' (Brassett, 2016: 171; 184), then my goal here is to explore the terms by which such a 'form of life' might be understood. While IR's engagement with performativity theory provides an important point of reference for my study, however, there is one aspect of the performative as it is commonly conceived by feminists and other social theorists that remains under-explored within the IR scholarship on humour.

Theorists including Judith Butler, Julia Kristeva and Iris Marion Young have made clear that the performance of this or that subjective identity necessarily also makes claims about the texture and boundaries of the subjective field *per se*. According to this reading, the 'political sphere' – or in other words, the space in which subjects make claims regarding their identities and relative positions – is not simply a blank background on which human activity is projected, but is rather something circumscribed and delimited in such a way as to give precedence to some of these claims over others. Thinking performatively about the production and formation of subjects thus also entails thinking about whom is excluded from participating in these processes. As a performative practice, then, humour not only contributes to the articulation of subjective identities, but also makes particular claims about who can participate in such performances, and who is instead relegated to an obscure, illegible space altogether beyond the performatively constituted boundaries of order.

Performativity theorists have called this space 'abject', denoting a realm occupied by those determined to be incapable of full and proper selfhood, and consequently unable to participate in politics ('politics' being nothing more than a field of disputation and negotiation between those recognised as subjects). In Butler's terms (2011: xiii):

> The abject designates here precisely those 'unlivable' and 'uninhabitable' zones of social life which are nevertheless densely populated by those who do not enjoy the status of the subject … This zone of uninhabitability will constitute … that site of dreaded identification against which – and by virtue of which – the domain of the subject will circumscribe its own claim to autonomy and to life.

The abject thus denotes that which must be repudiated and rejected in order for the subject to be able to make performative claims to political selfhood and agency (cf. Kristeva, 1982). As such, the subject comes into being by defining (and distinguishing itself from) its abject other. As Lauren Wilcox explains, this distinction requires constant, vigilant maintenance if the boundaries of subjectivity (and thus of politics itself) are to be protected (2015: 9):

> in the subject's process of becoming, it must attempt to delineate its body from others, and to create clear boundaries between the self's inside and outside. To do this, it expels the abject or 'constitutive outside' that nonetheless shows up to haunt the self, as this founding repudiation is still included by its exclusion.

For Wilcox as for Butler, the subject's 'process of becoming' is always incomplete. As such, the abject can never truly be dispensed with: it 'shows up to haunt the self', a spectral presence constantly threatening to penetrate or even overwhelm the subject's meticulously constructed identity performances. It is for this reason that Iris Marion Young argues that 'abjection is the fear of losing the border between self and other we have constructed' (2005: 110): it denotes an ineradicable ontological insecurity that suffuses the experience of subjective being (cf. Steele, 2008). The abject and the subject are thus inextricable – not just at the moment of their foundation, but continuously. Neither is ontologically prior to the other (though this does not mean that the distribution of power that determines their relationship is ever equal). Instead, 'the abject, though expelled, is ... an essential part of the self, lingering or haunting the unconscious, rendering it permanently vulnerable to disruptions' (Wilcox, 2015: 84).

Although critical and post-structuralist IR scholars often acknowledge an exclusionary logic beneath political processes of ordering and identity-building, they are less forthcoming on the continuous 'haunt[ing of] the self' that these processes sets into motion. For David Campbell, for example, the United States of America performatively inscribes and re-inscribes itself into the world by producing an assemblage of threatening, dangerous others (1992; cf. Connolly, 1991). However, Campbell's concern with how 'the United States' constitutes itself through the production of foreign 'dangers' implicitly gives the former a certain analytical privilege over the latter. The others identified by Campbell, as

Claudia Aradau points out, thus remain obscure and interchangeable in their 'faceless' disavowal (2008: 60).

> Poststructuralists ... remain evasive on the subject that they consider. Many emphasize, in the wake of Connolly and Campbell, the constitution of identity/self through the exclusion of difference/other and the reproduction of identity. However, the 'other' they envisage is mostly a derivative of the constitution of 'us' ... In Campbell's analysis of how American identity is reproduced through rewritings of dangers, the others who are written out as dangerous, abnormal, risky are 'faceless faces', substitutable to one another. Different others succeed one another, subjected to the need of identity reproduction.

For Aradau, while Campbell's analysis seeks to develop an account of subjectivity alert to its ontological inextricability from processes of differentiation and objectification, its single-minded focus on 'identity reproduction' ends up reinforcing the privilege of the United States over its abject others by theorising the latter largely as the blank obverse of the former. As such, while Campbell problematises the specific political identity known as 'the United States', the subjective field in which that identity is articulated and finds meaning, as well as the abject 'dangers' against which it defines itself, feature in his analysis only as 'derivatives' of its primary subject.

IR's treatments of humour take a similar approach. For Brassett, Dodds and Kirby, and Salter, humour functions as a mode of play between multiple, performatively articulated subjectivities. The subjective field itself, however, is largely taken for granted. This limitation is significant because humour is commonly understood to operate at and across the boundaries separating the subject from the abject, the political from the non-political (a feature of its historical conceptualisation that I explore in detail both in this chapter's next section and throughout Chapter 2). While agreeing with Brassett, Dodds and Kirby, and Salter that humour makes important and understudied contributions to the performative production of (inter)subjectivity, then, my analysis here will focus more closely on the way humour engages not just with one or another subjective articulation, but also with the terms of belonging governing who precisely can claim the status of 'subject' in the first place. An example from the writing of Michel Foucault will serve to illustrate precisely what I mean.

Humour, order and otherness: Foucault's laugh

In his preface to *The Order of Things*, Foucault describes the incident that initially led him to embark upon his project. At first, he claims as his inspiration a particular passage of text, before correcting himself – it is not from the text itself that *The Order of Things* emerges, but rather from his response while reading it (2002: xvi):

> This book first arose out of a passage in [Jorge Luis] Borges, out of the laughter that shattered, as I read the passage, all the familiar landmarks of my thought – our thought, the thought that bears the stamp of our age and our geography – breaking up all the ordered surfaces and all the planes with which we are accustomed to tame the wild profusion of existing things, and continuing long afterwards to disturb and threaten with collapse our age-old distinction between the Same and the Other.

The passage in question is part of the essay 'John Wilkins' Analytical Language', in which Borges interrogates the seventeenth-century philosopher's attempt to construct a universal language by means of a comprehensive and meticulous scheme of classification (Borges, 1999). Wilkins divides everything in the universe (as he sees it) into one of forty categories, each of which is signified with a character. Subsequent letters are used to indicate subgroups within each category – and so '*Z*' denotes simply an animal, while '*Zα*', '*Za*', '*Ze*' and '*Zi*' add a level of specificity: 'exanguious' or 'bloodless' animals (i.e. insects and other invertebrates), fish, birds and 'beasts' respectively (Borges, 1999: 230; Wilkins, 1668). Further characters refine these classifications still more, until an individual species can be identified – '*Zana*', for example, means 'salmon' (1668: 415).

Wilkins imagines his language as 'a vast review of all knowledge establish[ing the] notions held in common by all rational beings', or in other words as a reflection of the ready-made categories which nature has already provided in order to enable distinction between its constituent parts (Eco, 1995: 238). Borges, however, compares Wilkins' taxonomy with that of a 'Chinese encyclopaedia' which catalogues animals not according to Wilkins' supposedly universal formula, but rather as follows (1999: 231):

> Animals are divided into: (a) belonging to the Emperor (b) embalmed (c) tame (d) sucking pigs (e) sirens (f) fabulous (g) stray dogs (h)

included in the present classification (i) frenzied (j) innumerable (k) drawn with a very fine camelhair brush (l) et cetera (m) having just broken the water pitcher (n) that from a long way off look like flies.

Foucault uses this extract – or rather, the laughter it inspires – as a provocation for thinking about the way in which order is created and imposed upon the world: 'I am concerned here with observing how a culture experiences the propinquity of things, how it establishes the *tabula* of their relationships and the order by which they must be considered' (2002: xxvi). Laughter, then, is the seed from which Foucault's intellectual endeavour in *The Order of Things* grows. Yet as Foucault sets out his project, he also sets aside the laughter that stimulates it, and it is this relation that I would like to reawaken and re-establish here. What mechanism is at work in Foucault's reading of Borges' text that prompts him to laugh? What function does that laugh serve in Foucault's broader intellectual undertaking – namely, his investigation into processes of ordering; into 'our age-old distinction between the Same and the Other'? And how does it reflect, contribute to or alter Foucault's sense of his own self as a thinking, knowing subject, woven into the system(s) of meaning he wishes to study?

I dwell on this particular laugh because it is indicative of the direction in which I will take my investigation into humour as a performative, everyday practice. Such practices are of political interest not simply because they contribute to the imagining of this or that subjective identity, but also because they probe at or oscillate across the limits and boundaries of the subjective field itself. This represents an expansion of the critical IR literature on performativity, but also of the cultural-theoretical and philosophical investigations into humour, laughter and comedy that commonly underpin political studies on the subjects.

Three theories of laughter

The philosophical literature on humour and laughter is often itself taxonomised: it is said that there are three broad categories to which theories of laughter can be assigned (e.g. Billig, 2005: 37–110; Critchley, 2002: 2–3; Morreall, 1987). The first is the 'superiority' theory (e.g. Aristotle, 2006: 9; Plato, 1997: 438–439; Hobbes,

2005: 43). According to this literature, laughter is an expression of eminence or supremacy: it signifies security and self-assurance.[1] The second category is the 'relief' theory (e.g. Freud, 2002; Spencer, 1878). For relief theorists, laughter can be explained as a release of nervous or unconscious energy: it opens up an emotional valve otherwise under unbearable pressure and strain. Finally, there is the 'incongruity' theory (e.g. Bergson, 1974; Hutcheson, 1758; Kant, 2007: 159–164; Schopenhauer, 1969, vol. 1: 59–61). In this instance, laughter indicates a recognition of contradiction or dissonance, either generally or of a particular type: for Bergson, for example, humour is predicated on an incongruity between the organic and the mechanical (1974: 79, cf. Lewis, 1928: 247).

Foucault's laugh does not obviously correspond to any of these models. As he frequently makes clear throughout the book's preface, *The Order of Things* is intended to undermine any residual sense of cultural privilege or supremacy harboured either by him or his readers: 'in attempting to uncover the deepest strata of Western culture, I am restoring to our silent and apparently immobile soil its rifts, its instability, [and] its flaws' (2002: xxii). For this reason, his cannot be a laugh of superiority. Yet neither is it a laugh of relief: on the contrary, the overriding emotion provoked in Foucault by Borges' text is anxiety. As he admits, 'that passage from Borges kept me laughing a long time, though not without a certain uneasiness that I found hard to shake off' (2002: xix).

At first glance, the incongruity theory appears to provide a more suitable interpretive scaffold than its two counterparts. Borges' fictional encyclopaedia is recognisably presented in the form of a taxonomical classification, but its organising logic and grammar are nevertheless wildly at odds with Wilkins' hyper-rational system. Anyone even vaguely versed in Western scientific classification will struggle to group a list of animals into the categories given in the 'Chinese encyclopaedia', which include dead animals ('embalmed', 'sucking pigs'), mythical or fictional animals ('sirens', 'fabulous') and animals defined by quantity rather than quality ('innumerable').

For an incongruity theorist like Schopenhauer, this sort of encounter provokes laughter because it presents a 'suddenly perceived incongruity between a concept and the real objects that had been thought through it' (1969, vol. 1: 59). According to this reading, if one laughs at the encyclopaedia it is because one recognises that categories like 'having just broken the water pitcher' are unable *truly* to characterise the relations between different types of animal. However, a laugh of this sort would also be a laugh of superiority: an Orientalist laugh directed at the Chinese encyclopaedia and its 'concepts'; its ostensible inability to acceptably or rationally organise the 'real objects' of zoological enquiry.[2] Such a laugh would reinforce rather than 'shatter' the 'familiar landmarks of … thought' (Foucault, 2002: xvi). In contrast, it is not the fictional encyclopaedia's 'absurdity' that Foucault laughs at, but rather the awareness it provokes of his own thought's limits and boundaries, and the artifice of its assumed privilege. For this reason,

> there arose in [the laugh's] wake the suspicion that there is a worse kind of disorder than that of the *incongruous*, the linking together of things that are inappropriate; I mean the disorder in which fragments of a large number of possible orders glitter separately in the dimension, without law or geometry, of the *heteroclite*.
> (2002: xix, emphasis in original)

To identify incongruity in the Schopenhauerian sense, one must first have a sense of *con*gruity: a conception of what is 'correct', 'orderly' or 'true'. In contrast, Foucault's 'suspicion' is provoked not simply by the foreignness of the encyclopaedia's classification, but by the reflexive recognition that his own logic is equally arbitrary and strange: that there is no agreed scale, no 'law or geometry', against which the (in)congruity of either system can be measured. 'When we say that a cat and a dog resemble each other less than two greyhounds do, even if both are tame or embalmed, even if both are frenzied, even if both have just broken the water pitcher, what is the ground on which we are able to establish the validity of this classification with complete certainty?', Foucault asks (2002: xxi).

Upsetting the epistemological assumptions and presumptions through which Foucault had previously made sense of the world around him, the encyclopaedia thus also destabilises his identity as a thinking, knowing subject: 'the fundamental codes of a culture … establish for every man, from the very first, the empirical orders with which he will be dealing and within which he will be at home' (2002: xxi).[3] In this context, the laugh that inspires *The Order of Things* functions as an indication that the 'fundamental codes' through which Foucault had previously used to make sense of the world (and his place in it) can no longer be considered 'fundamental' at all. It denotes the dissolution of the line between 'subject' and 'abject' upon which his identity depends, and in so doing it cuts him adrift from his subjective moorings.[4]

Instead of simply observing and marking incongruity, *The Order of Things* thus seeks to interrogate the terms by which incongruity is made possible. It examines the codes, the lenses, the grids, the *epistemes* which allow subjects to link things together, to arrange things as part of the same classification, to identify things as similar or establish the terms by which their difference or otherness can be thought. Foucault's laugh thus indicates a realisation that the terrain on which his identity as a subject finds meaning has shifted beneath his feet:

> The monstrous quality that runs through Borges's enumeration consists ... in the fact that the common ground on which such meetings [between different things] are possible has itself been destroyed. What is impossible is not the propinquity of the things listed, but the very site on which their propinquity would be possible.
>
> *(2002: xvii)*

For Foucault, the relational logic by which he makes sense of both himself and his world is not fixed *a priori* by nature or reason; is not universal, is not all-encompassing. Instead, it has been constructed, it has conditions of possibility, it is symbiotically entwined with the historical and political contexts from which it has emerged, it is limited and indeterminate, and it can be contested. The laugh that begins *The Order of Things* thus denotes Foucault's questioning of his subjective field, and of the terms of belonging that designate alternative ways of organising the world as 'absurd', 'irrational' or 'nonsensical'. It marks the opening of space in which Foucault can reconsider and reimagine his subjective terrain; it signifies a shift in his relationship to what he had previously considered the immovable and unchanging 'landmarks of our thought'. Crucially, it does so in a way which refuses to give priority or precedence to any particular vision of subjective order, and which in so doing also refuses to abject *a priori* any particular standpoint or perspective.

In speaking of humour as a performative practice, I build on the small but significant body of IR work that suggests that humour 'perform[s] subjects in creative, vital terms' (Brassett, 2016: 171). Like the examples discussed in these pieces, Foucault's laugh produces and makes legible a new subjective orientation. Yet it also reveals something about the instability and indeterminacy of his broader epistemological and relational terrain – terrain whose terms of belonging help to determine what kind of being is able to claim the status of 'subject' in the first place. Laughter is for Foucault a way into the problem of order, a way to acknowledge the boundary line separating the subjective realm from its abject other and a way to keep both sides of that line simultaneously in view. It is the ambiguous and volatile limit-zone thus occupied that this study seeks to inhabit: what does humour reveal about the exclusionary terms by which a 'domain of the subject' is initially made possible? In what ways does humour enable subjects to inhabit or engage with this domain, or the terms of belonging by which it is defined? And how does humour accommodate the instances of failure and undoing that accompany such efforts?

To end this chapter, I turn to Michel de Certeau in order to suggest that humour might profitably be understood as what he calls a 'way of operating': a field of practice that is inescapably woven into a broader network of relations to which it is nevertheless irreducible (1984: 29–42). Humour can be brought to bear on politics insofar as its performatively constituted subjects can not only 'inhabit' but also 'operate', productively and creatively, at and across the exclusionary boundaries of the political field. Theorised in these terms, humour is constituted as an everyday practice that can illuminate not only processes of subject-formation but also the distinctions and differentiations, the 'tabula of relationships' that constitute and delimit the subjective field itself (Foucault, 2002: xxvi).

Humour as a 'way of operating'

The laugh that opens *The Order of Things* exemplifies those aspects of humour's everyday performativity that I will foreground throughout this book. It marks a space in which particular subjective formations can be asserted and negotiated, and from which the limits of the subjective field can be acknowledged, traced and reimagined. While Foucault's laugh lays the groundwork for his enquiry, however, there is little beyond his preface to suggest how humour might illuminate or help to produce the 'modalities of order' with which he is concerned (2002: xxiii). Laughter provides a way into Foucault's problem in *The Order of Things*, but it does not sustain his analysis. How, then, can one understand humour as something that circulates between subjects, that mediates and modulates their interactions and their engagements with the world? Foucault's laugh raises these questions, but it does not answer them. My project in this book is thus to give an account of humour that acknowledges its embedded-ness in the everyday, iterative production and reproduction of subjective and relational order.

In addressing this problem, it is crucial to stress humour's indeterminacy and ambiguity. Philosophical, theological and political-theoretical literatures have often succumbed to the temptation to fix *a priori* humour's relationship to the political sphere. They do this in two ways. For some, humour is conceived as a force that threatens political and/or spiritual order from the outside: it is a rebellious or revolutionary practice, incommensurable with any and all systems of social organisation. For others, humour upholds these systems from within by enabling subjects cynically to avoid engaging with their more coercive or discriminatory characteristics. In this section I will outline both of these positions with reference to Umberto Eco's novel *The Name of the Rose*, before drawing on Michel de Certeau in order to theorise humour as a 'way of operating'. Ways of operating comprise a collage of creative, productive practices; a 'network of … antidiscipline' both inextricable from and irreducible to the systems and networks into which they intervene (de Certeau, 1984: xiv–xv). As a 'way of operating', humour thus occupies an ambiguous ethical and political position (cf. de Certeau, 1984: 37–38). Its political effects cannot be decided in advance, but rather emerge and are generated performatively, in the mutually constitutive interaction between subjects and their fields.

The Name of the Rose follows William of Baskerville, a fourteenth-century Franciscan monk on theological business at a Benedictine abbey, as he investigates a series of deaths that appear to be connected in some way to the monastery's mysterious library. It transpires that the deaths are the work of an old, blind monk named Jorge, who is determined to prevent the library from giving up what he sees as its most powerful and destructive secret: the lost second book of Aristotle's *Poetics*, on comedy (cf. Watson, 2012). Jorge believes the book to be a 'subtle weapon' that will 'sweep away' Christian truth and order by justifying laughter – hitherto a symbol of 'weakness, corruption, the foolishness of our flesh' – as an agent of wisdom and learning (Eco, 2004: 507–509). Despite William's protestations, Jorge refuses to give up the manuscript. In the struggle that follows, he snatches and casts away William's torch, igniting a blaze that engulfs the entire monastery, including the library and its contents.

In *The Sublime Object of Ideology*, Slavoj Žižek briefly sets out what he sees as the 'basic underlying thesis' of the novel:

> the source of totalitarianism is a dogmatic attachment to the official word: the lack of laughter, of ironic detachment ... [there is an] underlying belief in the liberating, anti-totalitarian force of laughter, of ironic distance.
>
> *(2008: 23–24)*

For Žižek, Eco's central claim is that humour poses an insistent and uncompromising threat to tyranny, dogmatism and indeed political and social order more generally. The necessary gravity and solemnity of 'the official word' depends for its onto-political stability on the suppression of any and all instances of 'ironic detachment'. Humour thus occupies a space external to the systems, orders, practices, knowledges and institutions through which power is exercised: it carves open autonomous spaces from which the prevailing order of things has no choice but to recede.

This oppositional logic can be found elsewhere in the philosophical and political-theoretical literatures on humour and comedy. One can identify it in Plato's injunctions against laughter in *The Republic* (1987: 84–85, 322–323), for example, or in the widespread monastic prohibitions common both in Eastern and Western orders (Halliwell, 2008: 8; Constantinides Hero and Thomas, 2000, vol. 1: 24, 141; 2000, vol. 2: 472–474, 489, 594, 806; 2000, vol. 3: 895–897, 1026, 1082, 1133; 2000, vol. 4: 1501, 1602). In these instances, humour is constituted as an agent of corruption and instability, serving as a conduit for antisocial or sinful thoughts and behaviours. For Plato and St Benedict alike, humour undermines their prescribed systems of social organisation: it expresses something fundamentally insubordinate or ungovernable that picks irrepressibly at the threads of order.

While ancient thinkers tended to argue that this unruliness made humour socially or spiritually undesirable, modern liberal defenders of free speech have instead valorised it as a way of moderating the threat posed to personal freedoms by prescriptive political systems. For Salman Rushdie, for example, 'satire ... has always been a force for liberty and against tyranny, dishonesty and stupidity': it opens up space from which authority can be questioned, and must therefore be defended and protected (2015; cf. Stanley, 2015). Humour here functions as a corrective: a necessary check/balance on political overreach, and a sign of healthy liberal-democratic exchange. Although he celebrates rather than condemns its recalcitrance, Rushdie aligns himself with Eco, Plato and St Benedict insofar as he also presumes that humour undermines the codes by which social, political and/or spiritual life are commonly ordered. Notwithstanding their differences, then, these accounts all theorise a relationship of mutual incompatibility between humour and political order. The 'ironic distance' humour produces disrupts or destabilises political claims to universality, totality or necessity: it produces rebellious, ungovernable subjects, and in so doing prefigures or foreshadows social change.

Žižek rejects these accounts, and in their place offers his own. Suspicious of the dualism between laughter and politics that he identifies in *The Name of the Rose*, Žižek claims that laughter is in fact internal to the prevailing political machinery: 'cynical distance, laughter, irony, are, so to speak, part of the game. The ruling ideology is not meant to be taken seriously or literally' (2008: 24; cf. Zupančič, 2008: 4). According to this reading, the mocking or trivialisation of coercive institutions cultivates a cynical distance that enables them to exercise their power smoothly and without friction. Preoccupied with the superficial manifestations of power, the comic subject unwittingly lubricates the channels through which it is really exercised. By way of illustration, Žižek points to the soldiers in Korean War comedy *M*A*S*H*: 'the military doctors are involved in all sorts of sexual escapades, make jokes all the time ... We should always bear in mind[, however,] that the soldiers, with all their practical jokes, making fun of their superiors and so on, operate perfectly as soldiers. They d[o] their duty' (Žižek in Fiennes, 2012; cf. Zupančič, 2008: 30–31).

The connection Žižek draws between humour, cynicism and indifference is often associated with the contemporary 'mediatisation' of politics. Peter Buse, for example, argues that 'clowning [has become] somehow coterminous with power, as the inevitable consequence of a political-entertainment complex that compromises all conventional authority and ends with the investiture of the buffoon' (2015; cf. Foucault, 2003a: 11–16). According to Buse, the clownish personae of Silvio Berlusconi and Boris Johnson do not undermine or subvert their authority but rather allow them to act freely in an environment in which the line between politics and entertainment has become inextricably blurred. For Buse as for Žižek, humour is thus conceived as a constitutive part of a political hyperreality that demands as part of its strategy *not* to be taken seriously. The extravagant absurdities of political power do not have to be hidden at all cost lest they be illuminated by the harsh and hostile light of satire, as Rushdie argues. Rather, they can be openly displayed, made light of in order to inspire a cynical, ironic distance that short-circuits the possibility of meaningful critical engagement. Humour is thus constituted as an internal component of political order: it produces subjects whose attempts to perform autonomy end up reproducing or enabling the very systems against which these performances are directed.

Both these ways of understanding humour as a political practice require assessment and critique. On the one hand, Eco's oppositional logic constitutes humour as a force of almost limitless transformative political potential, deriving from (or even producing) a subjective space outside politics from which the comic subject is able to resist or transform a dominant political or epistemic regime. On the other, Žižek presents an almost total incapacity on the part of humour to perform any such function, locating it within an all-encompassing political-ideological apparatus. In short, while for Eco humour appears to be incommensurable with the demands made by the prevailing order on its subjects, for Žižek it is an important vehicle for ensuring those demands are met.

Both these readings, however, presume a fixed, pre-determined relationship between humour and politics: humour is either a vehicle of change and transformation, *or* it is a way of ensuring the maintenance and reinforcement of the status quo. This sits uneasily with the performative approach advanced in the previous paragraphs, which conceives of humour as a field of practice whose political effects cannot be decided in advance. The performatively produced comic subject does not pre-exist her practice, but is rather constituted *through* a contingent, unpredictable and mutually constitutive assemblage of interactions with her political surroundings. With reference to Michel de Certeau, I thus offer a third approach towards humour that is able to accommodate its indeterminacy as a temporally and geographically situated field of everyday practice. Humour performs a range of ambiguous social functions that are not predetermined, but which instead emerge through its reiterative and symbiotic interaction with the broader field in which it operates.

Building on the performative understanding of humour already advanced, I would thus like to theorise humour as what de Certeau calls a 'way of operating'. For de Certeau, everyday practices can neither be detached from the productive systems or networks within which they take place, as implied by Eco, nor entirely reduced to them, as Žižek claims (de Certeau, 1984: xi, xix, 30; cf. Bleiker, 2000: 201–202). Rather, they intervene creatively in the social field, in such a way that they are able potentially to transform relations of which they are nevertheless still very much a part. Importantly, however, their capacity in this regard has no necessary political trajectory: ways of operating cannot 'tabulate and impose ... spaces', but instead 'use, manipulate and divert [them]'. To 'operate' is therefore to enter into a negotiation with a particular system, rather than conclusively and unilaterally to decide upon its shape or strategy (de Certeau, 1984: 30). As de Certeau says (1984: 37):

> [A way of operating] must vigilantly make use of the cracks that particular conjunctions open in the surveillance of the proprietary power. It poaches in them. It creates surprises in them ... It is a guileful ruse.

To consider humour as a 'way of operating', then, facilitates an engagement with the anxieties to be found at the limits (or in the 'cracks') of the political sphere. It is for this reason that Roland Bleiker cites early-modern carnival as an example of the sorts of 'everyday forms of resistance' that de Certeau takes as his objects of analysis (Bleiker, 2000: 203). Bleiker's analysis demonstrates how carnival's 'popular culture of laughter' was, on the one hand, productive and socially transformative, and yet on the other also reproduced particular (gendered and/or racialised) vectors of hierarchy and exclusion (2000: 203–204). While it might provide a way for subjects creatively to (re)imagine, (re)configure or otherwise find their place within their social and political fields, then, humour cannot be considered an independent force of pure rebellion. Instead, it opens a window onto positional struggles: onto the everyday performances through which subjects both take their place in the world and seek to reshape or redefine it to their advantage. This conclusion is also implicit in de Certeau's association between 'ways of operating' and 'wit' (1984: 37–38):

> a tactic boldly juxtaposes diverse elements in order suddenly to produce a flash shedding a different light on the language of a place and to strike the hearer. Cross-cuts, fragments, cracks and lucky hits in the framework of a system, ... ways of operating are the practical equivalents of wit.

This approach departs from Eco's and Žižek's for two reasons: firstly, because of the contingency that de Certeau emphasises is key to the ways in which 'wit' operates ('lucky hits in the framework of a system'). And secondly, because the relation of these 'ways of operating' to their broader political context cannot be determined in advance, but rather emerges performatively, through everyday practice itself. Humour is one of the 'microbe-like operations' that proliferate within all systems, ensuring that society cannot be wholly reduced to the mechanisms and institutions by which it is governed (de Certeau, 1984: xiv). As a 'way of operating', humour thus 'intervenes in a field which regulates it at a first level ... but [it also] introduces into [that field] a way of turning it to [its] advantage that obeys other rules and constitutes something like a second level interwoven into the first' (de Certeau, 1984: 30). It is something like this process that one can identify in Foucault's reading of Borges' fictional 'Chinese encyclopaedia': though it is ostensibly framed as a counterpoint to Wilkins' 'rational' taxonomy, Foucault's laugh reflexively folds the encyclopaedia into his understanding of rationality itself.

The question of whether humour is radical or conservative is therefore the wrong one. Rather, one needs to ask how humour interacts with its social, political and international fields. Theorising humour as a 'way of operating', then, constitutes it as an assemblage of disparate and diverse phenomena which engage creatively with the networks of relations within which they are constituted, but without ever escaping them. It sets up a dynamic and interdependent relation between social, political and international relations and the everyday, performative practices that bring them into being. As one such practice, humour not only discloses information about how subjects 'take their place in the world', but also offers an unusual perspective on the 'mute processes' that constitute the boundaries of the thinkable, knowable, sayable and doable, and that enable subjects to differentiate themselves from their abject others.

Conclusion

Drawing on IR literature on the everyday has enabled me to theorise humour as an everyday practice that makes a contribution to performative processes of subject-formation. I also noted, however, that performativity theory does not just describe a play between subjectivities, but also seeks to understand the processes by which the subjective field itself is defined and circumscribed. I used Foucault's laugh at the beginning of *The Order of Things* in order to illustrate and illuminate humour's intimate association with questions about the limits of subjective order, about what (or who) lies beyond these boundaries, and about the subject's ontological complicity with the abject others that constitute their 'constitutive outside'. Drawing on Michel de Certeau, I suggested that humour might be understood as a 'way of operating': a creative and productive practice both inextricable from and irreducible to its broader social field. As a 'way of operating', humour sheds light both on the practices through which subjects seek to define their own identities, and on the logics and rationalities through which social, political and international orders are organised, regulated and marked off from that which they define as abject or other.

Foucault's appeal to laughter at the beginning of *The Order of Things*, and de Certeau's turn to 'wit' as an exemplary 'way of operating', are both telling. In both instances, there is an intuitive sense that humour provides an access point into questions about subjectivity, intersubjectivity and their social and political organisation. These are questions with which theorists of humour and comedy have also been preoccupied. In my next chapter, I will ask in more detail how the comic's performative production of subjectivity might 'operate' in the manner outlined here – and why this might be of interest to IR more specifically. I identify and establish a particular 'way of operating' focused on the ambiguous figure of the parasite, a stock character of ancient Greek comedy. I will show how an analytic focus on 'parasitic' appeals to humour opens up insights into the everyday politics of ordering, exclusion and struggle underpinning existing concerns within IR.

Notes

1 In fact, as Quentin Skinner notes, Hobbes' theory is a little more nuanced than this: for Hobbes, laughter is an expression not simply of 'superiority' but more specifically of a sense of superiority deriving from the desire to erase or overcome a more fundamental inadequacy. It is a coping mechanism tinged with vainglory. Nevertheless, Hobbes' understanding of laughter is usually presented as the paradigmatic example of the superiority theory (Skinner, 2004: 163–164).
2 It is notable in this respect that some of Schopenhauer's own examples of incongruity are racist (1969: vol. 2, 95).
3 It is surely no coincidence that Borges makes his fictional encyclopaedia 'Chinese', for this designation is likely immediately to conjure up for many of Borges' (European and American) readers an imagined space of otherness and of difference; it denotes 'a vast reservoir of utopias' against which 'Western rationality' is often measured, but by which it remains haunted (2002: xx).
4 A similar understanding of laughter's relationship with disorder can be found in George Orwell's essay 'Shooting an elephant', in which he describes being called to attend to an escaped elephant while working as a colonial policeman in what is now Myanmar. Upon arriving at the scene he notes that the elephant is calm, and unlikely to cause any more damage to life or property. Nevertheless, 'to come all that way, rifle in hand, with two thousand people marching at my heels, and then to trail feebly away, having done nothing – no, that was impossible. The crowd would laugh at me. And my whole life, every white man's life in the East, was one long struggle not to be laughed at' (2002: 47). Laughter is here constituted as an acknowledgment of imperial fragility: there is a sense that the colonial order Orwell is charged with upholding and reproducing is held together by nothing more than empty displays of strength. In this light, the laugh that he imagines accompanying any failure to perform such displays is akin to Foucault's in *The Order of Things*: both indicate the dissolution of the 'fundamental codes'

structuring their respective lives as thinking, knowing, ordering and/or governing subjects. Something like this, one presumes, underpins Judith Butler's assertion that 'laughter in the face of serious categories is indispensable for feminism' (2006: xxviii; cf. Irigaray, 1985: 162–163; Enloe, 2016).

2

The parasite

Introduction

In my first chapter, I outlined a theory of humour focused on its performative contribution to the production of political subjectivity. Humour is a field of everyday practice through which people come to negotiate and occupy particular subject-positions – in which capacity it also plays an active and constitutive role in the making and unmaking of intersubjective relations. With reference to the laugh that opens Michel Foucault's *The Order of Things*, however, I also noted that humour often operates across the boundary separating the 'domain of the subject' from the realm of abjection that functions as its 'constitutive outside' (Butler, 2011: xiii). Humour does not just participate in everyday performances of subjective identity, but also intervenes into the logics and processes determining who or what can be made legible as a subject in the first place. As such, it can be theorised as what Michel de Certeau calls a 'way of operating': as a field of everyday practice through which the limits and boundaries of social order can be uncovered, interrogated and/or made strange.

In this chapter, I consolidate these ideas by demonstrating their origins in some of the earliest surviving accounts of humour as a field of social and political practice. I draw on the mythical-theoretical discourses through which comedy was first established as an object of critical and philosophical concern in order to develop an account of its complex entanglement with questions and anxieties about political modes of being. Revisiting the earliest surviving account of comedy's origins that we have – the Megarian theory recounted (and dismissed) by Aristotle in the *Poetics* (2006)

– I read it in tandem with Jacques Derrida's account of the ritual of the *pharmakos* (1981). I suggest that the association between comedian and scapegoat produced by this reading opens up terrain from which to theorise a foundational complicity between comedy on the one hand and political forms of subjectivity on the other. As the Megarian myth reveals, comedy's origins are woven into those of the Greek *polis*: each institution implies the other, insofar as both derive from the same originary moment of sacrificial violence.

Comedy might therefore be said to occupy a supplementary position with respect to politics, simultaneously threatening the ontological self-identity of the political sphere and providing the means for its potential augmentation and renewal (cf. Derrida, 1997: 144–145). On the one hand, comedy can be understood as a way of speaking when properly political speech is impossible; as a way of making a claim to political subjectivity from a position of political 'disgrace'. On the other, however, it is precisely because of comedy's apparent exteriority to the political sphere that its incorporation into political practice can also serve as a means for the *polis* to strengthen its claims to universality.

These parallel significations are personified in the ancient literature by the stock character of the parasite (Athenaeus, 1854: 372–373; Corner, 2013a; 2013b; cf. Serres, 2007). An ambiguous and indeterminate figure, the parasite intrudes uninvited into social or political spaces, sustaining her uneasy presence by provoking laughter among the other – invited – guests. While her interruptive entry unsettles the exclusionary terms of belonging by which a properly 'political' space is defined and maintained, however, it also provides a focal point for their potential renegotiation and regeneration. Embodying the constitutively intertwining ontologies of comedy and politics established by the Megarian origin-myth, the parasite thus sheds light on humour's contribution to questions about the limits and boundaries of the political sphere.

My argument in this chapter will proceed in three stages. The first offers a radical re-reading of the Megarian theory of comedy that Aristotle recounts in the *Poetics*. Contemporary writing on the origins of comedy by classicists, literary theorists, political philosophers and theorists of humour and comedy has almost entirely neglected this Megarian narrative, which is predicated on the belief that the Greek word for 'comedy' (*komoidia*) derives from the word for 'countryside' (*kômai*). Observing Aristotle's equation of politics with the city-space of the *polis*, I expand upon this account in order to argue that humour has historically been conceived as a discourse spoken from a position of political abjection: it is a way of speaking when properly political speech is impossible; a way of acting when meaningful agency is otherwise denied.

In ancient poetry and drama, this function is embodied by the parasite. The parasite stages an encounter across the boundary between subject and abject, troubling the processes through which both categories are defined, circumscribed and secured. She thus offers a lens through which to think about how humour might 'operate' productively, creatively and transversally, opening up insights into the everyday politics of exclusion and struggle that underpin a number of overlapping concerns in International Relations (IR) scholarship. These include the construction and transformation of political identities and communities, the possibilities and limits of agency and the processes and practices by which certain subjects or subject-groups are produced as different or 'other'.

In the chapter's second section, I will examine how this theoretical parasitic subject might be brought to bear on the contemporary study of IR. I draw on feminist theory, in tandem with Michel Serres' *The Parasite*, in order to suggest that the parasite is an 'interruptive' subject whose invasive presence forces a particular network, order or system of relations to reckon with that which it has excluded as a condition of its own being. An analytic emphasis on 'parasitic' appeals to humour therefore focuses attention not only towards exclusionary global-political processes, but also towards the everyday negotiations and contestations that occur at their limits. To think 'parasitically' about humour thus entails engaging with a number of complex questions concerning the ways in which political discourses, communities, identities and orders are brought into being, maintained and contested. In particular, the parasite opens up terrain from which to consider how those constituted as abject might engage with the terms of their abjection. I conclude the chapter by outlining my intentions for the remaining chapters.

The *polis*, the *pharmakos*, the comedian and the parasite

In the *Poetics*, Aristotle cites the Megarian belief that comedy had originated there rather than in Attica:

> The Megarians lay claim to comedy – both those on the mainland (who allege that it arose in the period of their democracy), and those in Sicily ... They use the names as evidence. They say that they call outlying villages *kômai*, while Athenians call them *dêmoi*, the assumption being that comedians were so-called not from the revel or *kômos*, but because they toured the villages when expelled from the town in disgrace.
>
> *(2006: 6)*

According to the Megarians, who inhabited a Greek city-state with a colonial outpost north of Syracuse in Sicily, the first comedians were neither revellers in the festive procession of the *kômos*, as the Athenians claimed,[1] nor theatrical performers. Rather, they were *pharmakoi*: people in exile, disgraced and scorned, who nomadically roamed around rural settlements, unable to re-enter the city.

Jacques Derrida notes that the word *pharmakos* is completely absent from Plato's dialogues, despite the frequent occurrence of related words like *pharmakeia*, *pharmakon* and *pharmakeus* (1981: 130). He speculates that this is because the term had been 'overlaid by Greek culture with another function' which made it impossible to be incorporated within Athenian political and philosophical discourse:

> The character of the *pharmakos* has been compared to a scapegoat. The evil and the outside, the expulsion of the evil, its exclusion out of the body (and out) of the city – these are the two major senses of the character and of the ritual.
>
> *(Derrida, 1981: 130)*

The *pharmakoi* were outcasts, banished in disgrace both from the city and from its political-philosophical vocabulary. Yet their exclusion was not simply a question of judicial retribution or punishment: the ejection of these bodies, incurably and irreconcilably other to the *polis*, was what enabled the city to renew or restore itself whenever it deemed it necessary or desirable to do so:

> The city's body proper thus reconstitutes its unity, closes around the security of its inner courts ... by violently excluding from its territory the representative of an external threat or aggression.
>
> *(Derrida, 1981: 133)*

The *pharmakoi* thus played two roles. First, they signified a poisonous, pathogenic presence within the political space of the *polis*; they were the incarnation of a cancerous evil by which the city had been corrupted or infected, and from which it needed to be inoculated. Second, however, they also embodied a cure insofar as their removal or excision was able to resuscitate or reconstitute the city at moments of crisis (Derrida, 1981: 133; cf. Frazer, 1954: 540–541).

The *pharmakos* was thus both irretrievably other to the *polis* and yet also essential to its metaphysical coherence and unity: as Derrida says, 'the ceremony of the *pharmakos* ... [is] played out on the boundary line between inside and outside, which it has as its function ceaselessly to trace and retrace' (1981: 133). For Derrida, then, the pharmacotic ritual enacted the very limits of the political: it clarified who precisely was part of the *polis*, who could be considered a political subject – and who was not, and could not ever be. Both unincorporable into the political realm and yet simultaneously the principle of its being, the *pharmakos*' embodied pathogenicity determined both her own abjection and the subjective space of the *polis* from which she had been excised.

While Derrida focuses exclusively on the political connotations of the *pharmakos*' expulsion, however, the Megarian account of comedy offers an alternative perspective on the ritual. According to the Megarians, even if the exclusion of the *pharmakos* functioned to clarify the boundaries of the *polis*, it did not do so without also producing a supplement or remainder, namely a gaggle of itinerant exile-comedians left to wander outside the city walls. If Derrida's analysis illuminates the first of these functions, however, the process behind the second – not to mention the relation between the two – remains obscure. A path between Derrida's account and that of Aristotle's Megarians must therefore be traced: how does the *pharmakos* become the comedian?

From the pharmakos to the comedian

Derrida's enquiry breaks down at the moment the *pharmakos* crosses the city's threshold: as she passes into exile, she dissolves off the page. This is perhaps no surprise: as the passive object of the city's violence, Derrida's *pharmakos* cannot argue or plead, cannot speak, cannot participate in discourse. She is instead wholly determined by the space from which she has been evicted: denied any positive content of her own, she is nothing more than a pollutant, and as such she is no subject at all.

The abjection that marks and defines Derrida's *pharmakos* can also be ascribed to the *pharmakoi*-comedians described in the *Poetics*. The word used by Aristotle to signify the 'disgrace' of the Megarian exiles (ἀτιμαζομένους [*atimazoménous*]) is most often used elsewhere in Greek literature precisely to signify a specifically political type of dishonour: a dishonour that waives the right to speak and be heard; a dishonour that debars those to whom it refers from participation in political discourse, and thereby from political subjectivity altogether. During the Mytilenean debate in Thucydides' *History of the Peloponnesian War*, Diodotus argues that political discussion must take place without fear of reprisal from opposing parties (1900: 213). 'The wise city ought not to give increased honour to her best counsellor, any more than she will deprive him of that which he has; while he whose proposal is rejected not only ought to receive no punishment, but should be free from all disgrace [ἀτιμάζειν [*atimázein*]]'.[2] Here, to participate discursively in the city's political processes debars one from a 'disgrace' that is presumably reserved for those who cannot do so: those who speak should not be burdened with *atimázein*, even if their speech is dismissed. The capacity to speak and be heard thus functions as a basic marker of political subjectivity (an equivalence reinforced by Aristotle's own dictum that it is speech that distinguishes [hu]man[ity] as a specifically *political* animal from other social creatures such as bees or other insects (1992: 60). *Atimázein/atimazoménous*, then, are qualities ascribed to those – like the *pharmakoi* – who cannot speak at all.

Derrida conceives of the *pharmakos* only within the terms of the *atimazoménous*, or 'disgrace', that marks her dislocation from the political sphere. As such, the *pharmakos* is no longer of relevance to his argument once she has been cast from the city, and can be disregarded. Yet this overlooks what is a key, transfigurative moment in the ritual, for even if the *pharmakos* cannot speak in the city, or to the city, or within the political-philosophical register of the city (as Derrida makes clear she absolutely cannot), it is nevertheless also apparent that something changes as she shuffles through the gates and into the wilderness.

In exile, according to Derrida, the *pharmakos* is at total remove from the *polis*, for in order to avoid being re-infected, the community must cast her entirely to one side, into a symbolic void standing at an absolute distance from the political realm. As far as the *polis* is concerned, the *pharmakos* traipsing between villages thus no longer exists at all: she is simply waste, flushed out to a place from which she can no longer contaminate the reconstituted unity of the body politic (1981: 133). While it is for this reason that the expelled *pharmakos* disappears from Derrida's text, this elimination can only be sustained if one takes the city-state itself – or the processes by which it (re)constitutes its unity – as the analytic focus of one's enquiry. Such a step is by no means necessary: despite her physical expulsion and political annihilation, the *pharmakos* is still alive, after all. As Michael Dillon has noted, while 'the constitution of a people, a nation, a state, or a democracy necessarily specifies who is estranged from that identity, place of regime ... [the] act of delimitation ... does not dispense ... with the stranger' (1999: 119).

What might it mean, then, to reconfigure the ritual of the *pharmakos* around the figure of the scapegoat, rather than the *polis* from which she is evicted? Derrida's failure to do so is significant because it leads him to overlook a transformative moment that is vital to understanding how the pharmacotic ceremony might produce a subject like the wandering Megarian exile-comedian. This metamorphosis is made possible by the fact that the 'disgrace' of the *pharmakos* is only intelligible within the relational framework of the *polis* from which she has been wholly and absolutely evacuated. As she passes into exile, the *pharmakos* thus sheds her 'disgrace' like an old skin – a transformation that empowers her as she wanders around the countryside to reclaim an attenuated capacity for speech. This speech cannot belong to any sort of political register, of course, emerging as it does from a position of banishment, but is instead compelled to take on a different character. In speaking, then, the Megarian exiles instigate a new idiom, a new dialect – and it is *this* that became known as 'comic', from *kômai*, ultimately meaning a discourse that emerged from the countryside rather than from the properly political space of the city.

Comedy, in this instance at least, thus appears to be predicated on a certain, attenuated reclamation of subjectivity in the face of a political prohibition or silencing: it is a way of speaking when properly political speech is impossible. But what form might this new, 'comic' mode of discourse have taken, and how might it have engaged – if indeed it could – with the subjective space from which it had been disqualified? How, in other words, might one bring the *pharmakos*-comedian to bear on the political terrain from which she has been outlawed?

From the comedian to the parasite

The speech of the Megarian wanderer-comedians is lost. It is impossible to know how this early comic discourse might have interacted with the ostracism of those who spoke it, or with the political realm from which they had been expelled. Nevertheless, similar preoccupations with otherness, with difference and with the limits of political subjectivity are frequently at play in ancient Greek comic drama. As James McGlew (2002: v) has argued, the central questions posed by these plays concern precisely those same anxieties that the rite of the *pharmakos* was intended to resolve: who is or is not a citizen? How and where should boundaries be drawn and maintained? And how ought a political community to manage its encounters with those it deems different or other to itself?

It is perhaps with a sense of this that Derrida offhandedly describes the *pharmakoi* as 'parasites', for the parasite is a stock figure in ancient comic drama (1981: 133; cf. Corner, 2013a, 2013b; Damon, 1997; Davidson, 1997: 270–277; Wilkins, 2000: 71–86). Presenting herself uninvited at a home, dinner or symposium, the parasite secures her entry, her presence and her feeding by provoking laughter among the invited guests (Corner, 2013a: 53–54, 72–74; Tylawsky, 2002: 2–3).[3] Epicharmus, the earliest Greek comic poet whose work survives – and himself a Megarian, according to Diogenes Laertius (1853: 368–369) – summarises the parasite's social role in one of the few pre-Aristophanean comic fragments that we have:

> I'll dine with a willing host – he has only to invite me.
> I'll dine with an unwilling host – he need not even invite me!
> I am charming at the event, I turn up the
> Laughter ...
> And then, when I have eaten a lot and drunk a lot,

> I go away. No boy carries a lamp for me.
> I creep, slipping in the darkness,
> Deserted. And if I happen on the patrols
> I say, by the gods, it is a good thing
> Because they only want to beat me up.
> And then, roughed up, I go home,
> And I sleep, without bedding.⁴

Although Epicharmus' parasite lives physically within the city walls, she is clearly not *of* the *polis* (cf. Thalmann, 1984: 100–102, 146). Instead, she occupies an abstract and fugitive realm in which she sleeps without bedding and is subject to indiscriminate and capricious beatings. She is apparently nothing, then: a non-social, non-relational, pathogenic being; the passive object of others' will, much like Derrida's *pharmakos*. Yet unlike the *pharmakos*, the parasite also participates in the social spaces from which her otherness would appear to prohibit her. She sustains this awkward and ambiguous juxtaposition through the comedic incitement and provocation – the 'turn[ing] up' – of laughter (cf. Corner, 2013a: 44).

On one level, then, the parasite mirrors the Megarian exile-comedians in her adoption of a comic register from an abject position of exile. Yet the parasite nevertheless differs from these originary comedic figures in one crucial respect: unlike them, she is able to return to the spaces from which she has been forbidden, not just once but again and again. If the Megarian exiles can speak, can provoke laughter, they can only do so in the countryside through which they tramp. Wandering from village to village and back again, they remain haunted by the exclusion from the city that provides the background to their restlessness, for they cannot return to the *polis* without re-assuming their *atimazoménous*, or 'disgrace'. This prohibition appears to be absent for the parasite, however, who speaks *despite* her *atimazoménous*; who operates in the same social and political spaces from which she has been banished, and who uses humour as a way of initiating and sustaining an uneasy encounter with the host and guests of the 'event' she gatecrashes. Though her entry into the festivities is always subject to negotiation, it seems she is never finally barred, just as she is never finally included or integrated. Instead, she is able to defy her host's order even after an initial refusal ('I'll dine with an unwilling host – he need not even invite me!'), and when she is eventually kicked out, she simply finds some nook to sleep in before starting the whole game up again the following day.

If the *pharmakos* is the abject non-subject who cannot speak, and the Megarian exile-comedian is the figure who can speak only by virtue of having undergone a final and absolute expulsion – the figure whose speech depends on having left the *polis* entirely and forever, never to return – then the parasite is the figure whose expulsion is never final; the figure who, despite having been cast out, still returns, and still speaks. In so doing, she embodies comedy's intimate association with political subjectivity, political order and the exclusionary violence through which both are delimited, circumscribed and brought into being. Traversing the frontiers defined by her eviction, the parasite undermines the assumed metaphysical integrity of the *polis* and the supposed fixity of its terms of belonging. In the process, she revives and resuscitates a number of tensions lurking beneath the political domain (tensions, moreover, that the ritual of the *pharmakos* promised to resolve): how should communities be organised? Where should their boundaries be drawn? How ought they to be secured, and from whom?

If on one level the parasite poses an interruptive challenge to political order, however, then on another she provides the means for its reconstitution and renewal. Her hosts tolerate her presence, they permit themselves to be entertained and amused by her – but they also reserve the right to kick her out onto the streets whenever they have had enough, relying on the patrols to ensure that any future encounter remains (so far as possible) on their terms. The parasite thus occupies a supplementary position with respect to the political sphere: she simultaneously confronts it with its ontological incompleteness and provides the means for it to reaffirm its unity, either by abiding her or by ejecting her in a restaging of the pharmacotic rite.[5]

The parasite as a performative 'way of operating'

The *pharmakos*, the comedian and the parasite represent three stations on the same circular trajectory between expulsion and return. The first of these – the ritual expulsion of the *pharmakos* – produces both political subjects (those who remain within the city walls, their civic identity reconstituted and made whole again by the removal of the pharmacotic pathogen), and *pharmakoi* (those banned from the *polis*, cast into abjection and compelled to find a new discursive idiom in exile). Yet while the pharmacotic rite seeks to enact a clear, distinct boundary between inside and outside – between those who can be considered part of the *polis* and those who cannot ever be – the return of the parasite troubles and blurs this distinction by making the ontological interdependence of its two poles ambiguously manifest in a single body. The parasite, then, both is and is more than the *pharmakos*: 'is' insofar as she represents the return of the banished, pharmacotic 'other', and 'more than' insofar as this return, made possible by her appeal to humour, enables her to occupy an entirely new subject position, 'neither fully integrated nor entirely rejected, [a] stranger whose status is not properly resolved but who remains an outsider within' (Corner, 2013a: 44).

As Corner goes on to argue, the parasite's ambiguous subjective status enables her – like Borges' Chinese encyclopaedia – to probe at the terms of belonging governing who can claim the status of 'subject' in the first place. She is 'a figure belonging … to an image of the world by which a society represents itself to itself, an image constituted by and embodying the complex of norms and beliefs by which people understand themselves as social and ethical subjects and evaluate and make sense of their world' (Corner, 2013a: 43). In the Greek context, this 'complex of norms and beliefs' was of course deeply exclusionary: to be a citizen (and thus a 'social and ethical subject') one had to be a free (i.e. non-slave), property-owning (i.e. non-poor), male (i.e. non-female) (Corner, 2013a: 67–68; 2013b: 231). As Corner notes, the parasite pushed across all these boundaries. Simultaneously slavish, destitute and of indeterminate gender, she forced an ambiguous and indeterminate encounter between Greek social order on the one hand and all that it rendered unintelligible in order to establish and secure its own intelligibility on the other (2013b: 228).

The parasite's appeals to humour are what enable her to fulfil this function, because it is only by provoking laughter that she is able to sustain her dissonant and ambivalent presence among her host and his invited guests. By returning to and inhabiting this space – a space whose onto-political coherence is predicated upon her absence – the parasite undermines the boundaries secured by her initial expulsion, dragging them onto a plane of contestation where they can be questioned, stretched and reshaped (or upheld, asserted and reaffirmed). While Epicharmus' parasite clearly never transcends the 'otherness' imposed upon her – it is reinscribed each night with her withdrawal into darkness, after all – she nevertheless avoids being reduced to it by virtue of her habitual return to the subjective domain from which she has been abjected. The appeal to humour that sustains her presence in these spaces, then, is typical of 'ways of operating' insofar as it

> must play on and with a terrain imposed on it and organised by the law of a foreign power ... It does not, therefore, have the options of planning general strategy and viewing the adversary as a whole within a district, visible and objectifiable space. It operates in isolated actions, blow by blow. It takes advantage of 'opportunities' and depends on them, being without any base where it could stockpile its winnings, build up its own position, and plan raids ... It must vigilantly make use of the cracks that particular conjunctions open in ... the proprietary powers.
>
> (de Certeau, 1984: 37)

The parasite intrudes onto 'a terrain ... organised by the law of a foreign power', improvising opportunities and opening 'cracks' by making appeals to humour in such a way as to both prolong her presence at the table, and redirect its flows (of food, drink, attention, conversation) to suit her purpose and caprice (de Certeau, 1984: 39). Crucially, this struggle can never be finally won or lost: the parasite's eventual (re-)ejection into the night might reprise the pharmacotic ritual, but this merely resets the game until the following day. Thus set into motion is an endless cycle of expulsion and return, without hope of closure; a continually repeated encounter between the subjective domain of politics and the obscure realm of abjection that it both produces and rejects as a condition of its own being. Brought into focus by these encounters are a number of important questions: how are political identities, communities, and orders constructed? Whom do they exclude? How are their boundaries maintained, secured, negotiated and contested? And what political possibilities are available to those they abject? It is in these capacities that this theoretical parasitic subject can be brought to bear on the study of world politics.

Parasitic politics and world politics

The parasite and The Parasite

For Michel Serres, there is an originary act of violent exclusion – a ritual of sacrificial purgation or scapegoating akin to that of the *pharmakos* – that haunts all human relations (2000: 117, 131–134; Assad, 1999: 11; Brown, 2004: 391–392; cf. Girard, 1986; 2005):

> Our collective is the expulsion of the stranger, of the enemy ... The laws of hospitality become laws of hostility. Whatever the size of the group, from two on up to all human kind, the transcendental condition of its constitution is the existence of the Demon.
> *(2007: 56)*

Serres seeks to construct a theory of intersubjectivity capable of accommodating the relational interdependence between collective and stranger, and it is in pursuit of this aim that he invokes the parasite:

> The order in the sense of the order of things and the order in the sense of structures of order cannot emerge without this element of relation of order. The parasite is an element of relation; it is the atom of relation, the directional atom ... The theory of being, ontology, brings us to atoms. The theory of relations brings us to the parasite.
> *(2007: 184–185)*

For Serres, the parasite provides a framework through which to understand *all* communicative, social and political relations: '[parasites] constitute our environment' (2007: 10). The parasite operates as interference in a system, as 'noise'[6] contaminating a channel intended for the smooth passage of a particular 'signal' or meaning. It is for this reason that parasitism is a constant in human affairs, because no system (political or otherwise) ever functions perfectly, 'without losses, flights, wear and tear, errors, accidents, opacity' (2007: 12–13). For perfection to be achieved, a system would need to operate without resistance or friction, without anything obscuring, obstructing or diverting its productive capability. Such perfection is not only unattainable, but also – counterintuitively – precludes the possibility of any sort of relational understanding at all. This is best understood with reference to theories of communication:

> Given, two stations and a channel. They exchange messages. If the relation succeeds, if it is perfect, optimum, and immediate; it disappears as a relation.
>
> *(2007: 79)*

If two stations were to communicate perfectly, without any interference or noise, then the difference between them would be eradicated, and their relation would consequently disappear (Brown, 2002: 7–8; 2004: 383–384; 2013: 86–88; Serres, 1982: 66–67; Serres with Hallward, 2003). Yet if communication were entirely impossible – if there were nothing *but* noise – then the difference between the stations would be infinite, and their relation would similarly evaporate (Brown, 2004: 385). Noise's interference with meaningful signals is thus not to be understood as that which shackles or smothers the relation, but rather that which makes it possible: 'as soon as we are two, we are already three or four ... In order to succeed, the dialogue needs an excluded third' (Serres, 2007: 57).[7] And later: 'Relation is nonrelation. And that is what the parasite is ... The parasite is the essence of relation. It is necessary for the relation' (2007: 79). Crucially, however, for Serres this parasitic interruption is not to be thought negatively: as he makes clear in *Genesis*, the book directly following *The Parasite*, '"noise" [is] the sole positive word for describing a state we otherwise can only designate in negative terms, such as disorder' (1995: 20). The parasite is thus the principle of relational order in all its ceaseless instability, for which reason she is creative as well as disruptive:

> The parasite invents something new ... [S]he crosses the exchange, makes it into a diagonal ... People laugh, the parasite is expelled, [s]he is made fun of, [s]he is beaten, [s]he cheats us; but [s]he invents anew ... [S]he speaks in a logic considered irrational up to now, a new epistemology and a new theory of equilibrium. [S]he makes the order of things as well as the states of things – solid and gas – into diagonals.
>
> *(2007: 35–36)*

For Derrida, the ritual of the *pharmakos* exemplifies the way in which identities, orders and systems are constituted through processes of sacrifice, expulsion or extirpation – processes that aim to flush the system clean of noise, in other words. Serres accepts this: everywhere in *The Parasite*, one finds examples of this kind of emetic or purgative cleansing in operation. Communicative systems aim to 'eliminate the [noise] from the channel so the message can go through as best it can' (2007: 56), while social and political systems constitute their collectives through an analogously pharmacotic procedure:

> What is the collective? Politics is the set of theatrical discourses of magicians who want us to believe that they know what it is. However, there is at least one clear answer to the question. And professional politicians usually know it. For unanimity to appear within a group, sometimes all that is necessary is to bring about general animosity toward the one who will be labelled public enemy. All that is necessary is to find an object of hatred and of execration ... Union is produced through expulsion.
>
> *(2007: 118–119)*

In the contemporary political sphere, this 'union' commonly manifests in the form of the state's claim to a monopoly on the legitimate use of violence – what Serres describes as 'the lie told everywhere' (Serres, 2015: 79). This monopoly functions precisely as an attempt to silence any and all parasitic interruptions of the state's authority; it expresses an intolerance towards any 'relations between elements except for the very ones imposed by it' (2015: 79). Yet this is merely a modern iteration of a mechanism that for Serres permeates all human history, from the prehistoric development of agriculture ...

> Men chase out life from a given location. The inundation was not wished for, the labour was not executed in order to irrigate or to sow; everything was done for cleaning. Hence this tear, this catastrophe, through which the multiplication of wheat, rice or corn could pass, depending on the location, chance and circumstances ... The first one who, having enclosed a field or bit of land, decided to exclude everything there, was the true founder of the following historical era ... Agriculture and culture have the same origin or the same foundation, a white spot ..., a clean spot constituted through expulsion.
>
> *(2007: 176–179)*

... to the constitution of the Cartesian subject:

> The Cartesian meditation eliminates, expels, banishes everything, hyperbolically. Once again, a clean slate and a clear spot in the religious major mode, and this slate and this spot are the extent of which I am

the master and possessor of my thought. The thinking ego chases the parasites out, ... [and] thus chases everything out, speaking absolutely.

(2007: 180)

Humankind is *always* attempting to clean up the social, political, communicative, subjective or symbolic spaces in which it lives; attempting to create a 'clean slate and a clear spot' where one can be heard, listened to, understood and obeyed. 'The message of order must pass through silence. There must be silence. The parasites must be chased' (2007: 95). The repetition of the pharmacotic ritual through the constitution and expulsion of an 'other' is thus woven into the fabric of social and political intersubjectivity.

While Derrida's account ends with the exclusion of the *pharmakos* from the *polis*, however, Serres focuses on the enduring instability that inevitably accompanies these acts of boundary-drawing – indeed, he sees these points of disputation as the primary location of history and politics.[8] The 'white spot' – the space entirely cleansed of pharmacotic 'noise' – is also a space cleansed of plurality, change, agency and time. It is only when this 'clean slate' is 'contaminated' by the return of its excluded others that it comes alive. 'History begins with the parasitism of this space, the tiny deviation which makes the blank space diversify. The parasite is then the motor of history, or rather this occurs through the parasite's seizing of the white space' (Brown, 2004: 391–392). Dissonance and interference thus ground intersubjective relationality even as they disrupt and divert its flows: the expulsion of the *pharmakos*, in other words, is always accompanied by the parasitic return.

As such, while Serres acknowledges a pharmacotic logic at the root of practices of social ordering, he also emphasises that there is no way to make this expulsion final, to achieve the ultimate equilibrium of identity in all its transcendent unity. We are all, whether in the singular or in the plural, relationally constituted. And this means that there will always be parasites:

> The parasite is indeed this repressed one, the chased entity that always returns ... I have undoubtedly found a good definition of the parasitic function. It is ineluctable and almost a necessity. The force that excludes it is immediately overturned to bring it back. What is repressed is always there.
>
> *(2007: 78)*

A theory of (inter)subjectivity that acknowledges the processes through which otherness and difference are inscribed and re-inscribed must therefore also take account of the inevitable parasitic incursions into the systems and orders that seek to chase them away. The parasite is to be found wherever the pharmacotic system breaks down or disintegrates – and to think parasitically about political processes of ordering and identity construction thereby does more than simply acknowledge the exclusions and differentiations through which identity, community and order are constructed. In addition, it also focuses attention on the ways in which these mechanisms fall short of their intended aim. Noise is immanent within the meaning-making channels of political discourse, and it is in those liminal spaces where noise and signal meet and interfere – not in order's 'white spot' – that politics takes place.

The parasite thus illuminates the negotiations and contestations that oscillate ceaselessly across the boundaries distinguishing signal from noise, order from disorder, subject from abject (cf. Ozguc, 2020). For Serres, these boundaries can never be wholly secure: the unity they seek to produce will always fray and disintegrate (while any purity they do manage momentarily to realise turns out in any case to be desiccated and lifeless). As such, there can be no politics without parasites: the pharmacotic exclusions on which subjective and intersubjective order are founded are always haunted by the prospect or possibility of feedback.[9] And as the Megarian origin-myth reveals, this is the place not only of politics, but of comedy.

Interruption

The parasite of ancient Greek comedy emerges from the wilderness and disrupts the equilibrium of a particular socio-political system by producing 'noise' both figuratively through her dissonant presence and literally through the production and incitement of laughter. In so doing, she embodies Serres' description of the parasite as 'an interrupter': interposing herself into apparently stable intersubjective channels, the parasite politicises them by opening up their terms of belonging to dynamic processes of contestation and questioning (2007: 111). However, to speak of parasitic politics as a politics of 'interruption' is also (even if only implicitly) to draw on a large and diffuse tradition of queer and feminist thought and activism that has used the latter term in order to describe or explain its own practice (cf. Honig, 2013; Zalewski, 2010: 50–51; Zalewski, 2007: 309). In *Gender Trouble*, for example, Judith Butler outlines the role of identity categories in political struggle:

> There is no political position purified of power, and ... that impurity is what produces agency as the potential interruption and reversal of regulatory regimes ... Those who are deemed 'unreal' nevertheless lay hold of the real ... and a vital instability is produced by that performative surprise.
>
> *(2006: xxvi)*

For Butler, to 'interrupt' is to introduce into a particular epistemic, relational or political system an element deemed to be extraneous to it, in so doing destabilising its hold over meaning and order by compelling it to recognise or engage with a body or idea that it has silenced or rendered invisible. *Gender Trouble*, she says, is therefore a book designed to 'interrupt' established discourses on sex and gender by contributing to a more general 'collective struggle' by and on behalf of 'those who live, or try to live, on the sexual margins' (2006: xxviii). It is, in short, an attempt to introduce recalcitrant 'others' into otherwise accepted, presumed-universal discourses: the very others, indeed, that those discourses more commonly marginalise or obscure in order to secure their own hegemonic privilege.

Stuart Hall's account of the challenge made by feminism to cultural studies describes how such an interruption might be experienced by those on its receiving end:

> For cultural studies (in addition to many other theoretical projects), the intervention of feminism was specific and decisive. It was ruptural ... As a thief in the night, it broke in, interrupted, made an unseemly noise.
>
> *(1992: 282)*

Hall conceives of the 'interruptive' qualities of feminist thought in a similar way to Butler. For him, too, 'interruption' can be understood in terms of the intrusion of the 'unreal' into the 'real': feminism introduced 'unseemly noise' into cultural studies' settled, comfortable debates and in so doing offered a radical challenge to the relational order by which that very 'noise' was constituted as such. Interruption, then, can be said to induce an intersubjective relation where previously there was none, confronting existing systems with what lies behind their boundaries, and in so doing providing them with three possible responses. First, to ignore the interruptive noise and hope it goes away of its own accord; second, to forcibly exclude the noise in the hope of achieving or maintaining a nominally spotless purity; or third, to transform in such a way as to incorporate the noise within itself.[10] It is for this reason that Jacques Rancière argues that 'politics comes about *solely* through interruption', and that 'the political community is [therefore] a community of interruptions, fractures, irregular and local' (1999: 13, 137, emphasis added). The 'inter-' of 'interruption', in short, parasitically opens up a relational 'between' that performatively establishes the intersubjective multiplicity choked and denied by the attempt to establish and fix order.

Within IR, Cynthia Weber has expanded upon this to think about interruption in relation to critical practice: to interrupt, she argues, is 'to break the uniformity or continuity of *x*', in so doing 'methodically pluralising' a discourse or apparatus presumed to be final, settled or complete (2010: 977–979). To 'interrupt', then – to introduce an 'unseemly noise' into the discursive channels through which knowledge and truth about international politics are produced and transmitted, and in so doing to 'forc[e] a conversation' – is a critically and politically vital act that may be exemplified by queer and feminist critique, but is not necessarily limited to it (Weber, 2010: 979). To consider humour's contribution to the everyday politics of subjectivity in 'parasitic' terms it is therefore necessary to look for instances where it enables subjects to position themselves in relation to an apparatus that seeks to deny them any sort of positionality at all; instances where those deemed 'unreal' nevertheless 'lay hold of the real', in Butler's terms. It is here that one might bring parasitic humour to bear on world politics.

Prominent among the processes and practices that constitute international relations are mechanisms of differentiation and othering that seek to shore up or secure a particular identity, order or relational framework by producing a 'foreign' body to be expunged into a dark and silent realm of abjection. This is of course true of international politics itself, which is defined by widespread and pervasive patterns of exploitation and dispossession, and the consequent creation of 'a diverse population shuffled to the margins of freedom, dignity, social participation, and affluence' (Connolly, 1991: 203–204). Yet it is also true of IR as an academic discipline. Feminist scholars have asked why IR has marginalised the experiences and agency of women in its analyses of world affairs. Decolonial scholars have sought to excavate IR's roots in colonial thought and practice, suggesting with Naeem Inayatullah and David Blaney that 'IR fails to confront seriously the role of colonialism, neocolonialism, and various postcolonial responses to colonialism and its legacies ... [because] the current shape of IR is itself partly a legacy of colonialism' (2004: 2). Scholars working on race and racism have built on these insights to argue first that the birth of IR as an academic discipline was inspired by concerns regarding the maintenance and continuation of global white supremacy, and second that racist hierarchies 'continue to subliminally structure contemporary world politics, in both material and ideological ways' (Anievas, Manchanda and Shilliam, 2015: 3; cf. Mbembe, 2001; Abrahamsen, 2003; Vitalis, 2015).

In these respects and others, IR has reproduced the differentiations and abjections that structure the world it both purports to describe and aims to transform. Certain subjects (white, male, 'Western'), certain actors (states, transnational corporations, international organisations, non-governmental organisations) and certain spaces (battlefields, international summits, parliaments and foreign offices) are understood to be central to the business of international politics. Their centrality inevitably comes at others' expense (cf. Enloe, 2004). Such mechanisms are analogous to the ritual of the *pharmakos* insofar as they not only produce particular subjects as unintelligibly different or other but also, in so doing, trace and fortify the limits of a subjective realm in relation to which that difference or otherness can be articulated and given meaning. When these hierarchies become reified, their conditions of possibility, the processes that bring them into being and the parasitic noise that buzzes at and across their edges all fade from view.

In this light, it is hardly surprising that a growing body of critical work has sought to bring neglected voices and perspectives to bear on debates within the discipline. IR's 'turn' towards the everyday can be read as part of this broad undertaking. For Sophie Harman, for example, 'how to make the invisible visible and use the everyday as a basis for thinking about international power relations underpins feminist method in International Relations' (2018: 791). Such approaches have also inspired researchers to reflect on their own positionality with respect to the research they do and the research subjects they (ab)use in the process of doing it (cf. Dauphinee, 2010, 2013; Harman, 2018). Such reflections have brought into focus the ethical issues at play when researchers seek to redress the silences, marginalisations and hierarchies that structure global politics (cf. Dingli, 2015). Notwithstanding the validity of these concerns, however, it nevertheless remains true that 'debates over how to bring the "silent subject" into analytical and political view ... [are] central to critical IR scholarship' (Hansen, 2017: 602).

The parasitic subject I have outlined in this chapter provides one way to navigate these choppy waters. In the juxtaposition of a particular order with its 'constitutive outside', the parasite enacts an indeterminate encounter between a particular understanding of political subjectivity and all the things it repudiates as a condition of its own coherence. In so doing, however, it interruptively destabilises the boundaries on which such distinctions rely: subject and abject, order and disorder, inside and outside, signal and noise, speech and silence. Thinking parasitically does not entail bringing an otherwise passive subject from a realm of silence into a world of speech (a colonial or neo-colonial enterprise that always *a priori* frames the boundaries of speech for and on behalf of the silent subject). Rather, it involves acknowledging the noise that is always already there: oscillating across the purported boundaries of order, making use of its cracks, operating on its terrain. Focusing on humour provides one way to access these dynamic sites of interference and disputation.

My aim throughout the second part of this book is therefore to examine and evaluate humour's presence at and across the margins and limits of global political discourses and apparatuses. Doing so will allow me to trace not only the pharmacotic processes that underpin the establishment of the intersubjective realm, but also the parasitic encounters and skirmishes inevitably to be found at its margins. When considered parasitically, humour opens up insights into the everyday political struggles that seethe and hiss at the limits of subjective, political and international order. In so doing, humour functions transversally: it is one of the everyday practices through which individuals and groups engage with and seek to change the international relations in which they live (Bleiker, 2000: 7). To allow that world politics is pervasively productive and powerful – that the way in which power is organised internationally shapes and determines the everyday lives of all sorts of people around the world – mandates an engagement with the methods and tactics through which people, in turn, interact with the global forces that shape and delimit their possibilities for action. As Part II will demonstrate, humour is often important to these negotiations.

Conclusion

In this chapter I looked to the ancient figure of the parasite in order first to establish one way in which humour contributes to the performance of political subjectivity, and secondly to assess why this might be of relevance or importance to IR. The parasite emerges from a realm of exile and invisibility into a space in which her uneasy presence, sustained through humour, compromises the norms, assumptions and terms of belonging by which that space is delimited and secured. In so doing, she carries the possibility – though only a possibility – of problematising or even transforming the relational framework[s] whose unity her original banishment sought to secure. Moving from the parasite to Michel Serres' *The Parasite*, I built upon this analysis in order to show how the parasite might contribute to debates about difference and otherness within IR. The parasite can be understood as an 'interruptive' subject who confronts a particular vision of order with that it abjects as a condition of its own coherence.

The remaining chapters of this book will interrogate three separate sites at which humour has been used to make parasitic claims to political subjectivity. To what extent and how does a focus on humour enrich an understanding of these sites? How might humour contribute to the reclaiming of subjectivity or to the voicing of grievances in situations when subjectivity or voice is denied? In what ways might it 'operate' on and with systems of power, governance, marginalisation or domination? And where are its political limits to be found? The three sites to be evaluated here have not been chosen in order to provide any sort of systematic or general perspective on humour, politics or the parasite. Instead, they have been chosen for three connected reasons: firstly, because of their heterogeneity, which can be understood in terms of the subjects under consideration, the practices in which they participate and the systems they seek to engage. Secondly, because these sites each demonstrate a different approach to the everyday performance of comic-political subjectivity. Chapter 3 looks at 'aesthetic parasitism' with a study of previously unpublished cartoons drawn in concentration camps. Chapter 4 considers 'physical parasitism' with reference to the bodily occupation of particular politically charged spaces by AIDS activists. Chapter 5 is concerned with 'parodic parasitism', focusing on the appropriation of particular subjective identities as part of carnivalesque mass protest tactics. Finally, these three sites all touch upon existing concerns or literatures in IR, to do with the role of the camp in contemporary sovereign practice, the biopolitical management of disease and neoliberal global governance respectively. Yet despite this, the relevance of humour to the political and subjective processes and dynamics at play has hitherto been neglected.

First, I will look at a collection of comic strips drawn in French concentration camps during the Second World War. IR often theorises the camp as a space 'beyond politics', a space where the hubristic ambition of sovereign power to determine the outcome of all political decisions and disputes would appear in fact to have been realised. An analysis of this sort would appear to constitute the camp as an entirely non-relational, anti-political realm of abjection in which no political activity is conceivable. This has led scholars to overlook testimony produced *within* the wire by detainees themselves. With reference to a series of comic strips drawn by Horst Rosenthal, a German Jew detained in Gurs and later killed at Auschwitz-Birkenau, I argue that this small but significant body of work offers a valuable perspective on the possibility of politics in a context of unimaginable extremity. I argue that these strips demonstrate a mode of 'aesthetic parasitism' defined by the parasitic introduction of 'noise' into an aesthetic realm that stands as the avatar of the actual, material camp space. The subjects who populate these strips interrupt the intersubjective terrain upon which they move and act precisely in order to problematise the logics and rationalities supporting the practices of concentration, detention, deportation and killing underpinning the camps in their material actuality.

Secondly, I will evaluate humour's role in the attempts of the AIDS Coalition to Unleash Power (ACT UP) to engage the biopolitical-epidemiological rationality governing the HIV/AIDS crisis in the United States during the 1980s/1990s. While IR has tended to examine the biopolitical implications of health governance in relation to transnational attempts to manage the virus, examination of the initial epidemiological response to the AIDS crisis in the early 1980s shows how such dynamics were in fact in operation from the very moment the syndrome became an object of medical concern. Although ACT UP possessed a wide and varied emotional palette, the group nevertheless made frequent appeals to humour that can be understood in terms of the interruptive introduction of disruptive and transformative 'noise' into the discourses governing AIDS. By physically recontextualising the bodies of people living with HIV and AIDS into the very spaces working to produce their pharmacotic invisibility and silence, ACT UP sought to resignify what it meant to live – and die – with the virus. In so doing, they sought to produce the person with HIV/AIDS as an active political subject, rather than simply the passive recipient of scientific and (bio)political 'expertise'.

Finally, I will interrogate the carnivalesque protest tactics of the 'global justice movement' in the early 2000s, and in particular the use of parody by the Clandestine Insurgent Rebel Clown Army (CIRCA) in order to appropriate and undermine established, powerful subject-positions. Drawing on Michel Foucault's concept of 'grotesque' or 'Ubu-esque' power, I argue that parody appropriates, denaturalises and makes strange the signifiers and symbols that constitute global capitalism as necessary and natural. In particular, CIRCA's parodic militarism aimed to short-circuit the grids of intelligibility underpinning neoliberal globalisation by highlighting the violent practices that sustain it.

Notes

1 This is of course the claim to which Aristotle (as an Athenian himself) subscribes. The *kômos* was a procession that roamed the city streets, spreading merriment and at least occasionally doing so by entering private social spaces without invitation (most famously, in Plato's *Symposium* [2005]). There is no clear historical reason why one should accept either account over the other, though the Athenian theory is

certainly more commonly cited in literature about the origins of comedy (e.g. Cornford, 2011; Rusten, 2006). However, the Megarian version of events is not so much dismissed in this literature as it is ignored: I can find nothing that engages with it at much greater length than Aristotle himself (about sixty words – e.g. Cornford, 2011: 192). While it is clear why Aristotle might prefer an Atheno-centric narrative, it is less obvious why later scholars should follow his lead. I have chosen to take this Megarian narrative seriously for three reasons. First, because no-one else appears to have done so. Second, because of the happy coincidence (or telling detail) that Epicharmus – the earliest comic poet whose work survives – was a Megarian. Third, because the comparative plausibility of these claims does not seem to me to be particularly relevant. What seems more important than whether the Megarian account is 'true' or not (which, after all, can and will never be known) is the rather less speculative assertion, inferred from Aristotle himself, that people believed it to be true, or perhaps more accurately that this was a story which was told as if it were true. In other words, either or both of these stories (and who knows how many more besides) formed the mythical-historical background in relation to which ancient comic discourse was given meaning.

2   Benjamin Jowett, whose translation I have used here, uses 'reproach' for *atimázein*. It should be noted, however, that the word is more commonly rendered as 'disgrace', as in the translations of Thomas Hobbes, Richard Crawley and Martin Hammond. I have followed their lead, rather than Jowett's. Thucydides, 1843: 308; 2004: 132; 2009: 150.

3   As Sean Corner argues, the gender of the parasite is frequently ambiguous or even indeterminate (2013a: 72–75). Their function was to intersect and problematise any boundaries or logics which could be used to generate a sense of unity and community, of which – in a society made up solely of free men and their households – gender was obviously one (Corner, 2013b: 228). I use a feminine pronoun here partly to emphasise this indeterminacy – especially important because the parasite is usually thought of as unproblematically male (see, for example, almost all of the parables cited in Serres, 2007) – and partly to emphasise the continuity between the parasite and the *pharmakos*, who I have also here referred to using a feminine pronoun. Nevertheless, it should also be noted that in a dramatic or theatrical sense the parasite was always male: women were not allowed to act or perform on the Athenian stage.

4   Quoted in Konstan, 1997: 86. This fragment has been preserved in Athenaeus, 1854: 372–373.

5   'Whether it adds or substitutes itself, the supplement is exterior, outside of the positivity to which it is super-added, alien to that which, in order

to be replaced by it, must be other than it' (Derrida, 1997: 145). The parasite, in short, is always an outsider – for which reason her relation to the *polis* is different from that of the *parrhesiastes*. As Michel Foucault outlines (2001: 21), *parrhesia* is something that 'takes place between citizens ... the agora is the place where parrhesia appears'. Though the *parrhesiastes* speaks from below, he must nevertheless possess the capacity to speak in the first place, for which reason 'one must first be a male citizen to speak the truth as a parrhesiastes' (2001: 18). The parasite, who speaks despite not being a citizen, cannot claim this status.

6 In French, 'parasite[s]' signifies 'noise' or 'static' in addition to the biological and social meanings familiar to English speakers. Serres, 2007: 5–6; cf. Brown, 2004: 388.
7 For a more detailed exploration of 'noise', see Serres, 1983; 1995.
8 It should be noted that Derrida's late work emphasises that the sovereign claim to wholesome monophony undoes itself in its very articulation: at best, the sovereign 'can only tend, for a limited time, to reign without sharing' (Derrida, 2005: 102; cf. Derrida in Borradori, 2003: 124; Mansfield, 2008).
9 The only permanent solution to the problem of the parasite, Serres argues, is Leibniz's: to construct a monadology, and in so doing to eliminate social relationality altogether (Serres, 2015: 78–79). Such projects are of course profoundly anti-political.
10 'We have all been programmed to respond to the human differences between us with fear and loathing and to handle that difference in one of three ways: ignore it, and if that is not possible, copy it if we think it is dominant, or destroy it if we think it is subordinate' (Lorde, 1995: 285).

Part II

Parasitic politics

3

Aesthetic parasitism: cartooning the camp

Introduction

In Part I, I established a conceptual framework through which to understand humour as a political practice. Building on International Relations (IR) literature on the everyday, I suggested that social, political and international relations are 'transversally' produced and reproduced by all manner of seemingly banal, ordinary or routine social practices. From this perspective, international relations are dynamic and changeable, rooted in the messiness of (inter)action rather than in structural necessity or an inalienable human nature. This 'turn' towards the everyday is inextricable from a wider concern among critical IR scholars with the contours and limits of political (inter)subjectivity, and their practical, everyday articulation. Theorising humour as a vehicle for the performative production, reproduction and contestation of (inter)subjectivity, I suggested that a focus on the ways in which humour circulates can illuminate a great deal about the power relations at play both within and between groups: it reveals who is able to speak with license and freedom, who is not able to speak at all (or whose speech is not listened to) and who is commonly violated or vilified.

Humour is thus part of a wider field of everyday practice through which subjects act and interact, and through which they performatively claim, construct and contest particular identities and positions. One aspect of performativity theory to which IR has paid insufficient attention, however, is its assertion that not everyone is able to participate in these processes of subject-formation. The circumscription of a subjective realm inescapably marks others off as 'abject': incapable of full and proper selfhood, objectified and condemned to silence. Drawing on the laugh that begins Michel Foucault's *The Order of Things*, I noted that humour is often understood to oscillate across this boundary between subject and abject, and to probe at the terms of belonging by which a 'domain of the subject' is initially made possible. In this respect, humour can be understood with Michel de Certeau as a 'way of operating': as an everyday practice that illuminates (and exploits) anxieties, insecurities and leftover spaces at the liminal boundary-zones of social, political and international order.

In ancient comic drama, this role and function is embodied by the stock character of the parasite. In Chapter 2, I suggested that the parasite's 'interruptive' appeals to humour function as a way of making a claim to political subjectivity from a position of 'disgrace', or political abjection. In so doing, the parasite enables and sustains an encounter between subject and abject that illuminates the exclusionary and violent boundary-drawing processes through which order is created and maintained. Humour's presence at and across the boundaries of subjective order thus makes it a suitable place at which to investigate the performatively constituted (inter)subjectivities that constitute social, political and international relations.

In the chapters to come, I will interrogate three sites where one can identify 'parasitic' appeals to humour. Though historically and geographically distinct, all three illustrate how humour might facilitate performative claims to subjectivity from a position of political abjection. These sites have been chosen for three reasons. First, because they all touch upon existing concerns, debates and literatures within IR. Second, because the role or function of humour in relation to each site is under- (or even un-) studied in the existing critical and analytical literature. And third, because each demonstrates a different approach to what I have termed 'parasitic politics', namely 'aesthetic parasitism', 'physical parasitism' and 'parodic parasitism' respectively.

This chapter will look at a series of cartoons and comics drawn in concentration camps in the south of France during the Second World War, focusing in particular on two strips drawn by German Jewish artist Horst Rosenthal.[1] The network of work, prison, death and transit camps set up in order to facilitate the concentration, enslaving and mass murder of Jews, Roma, communists, homosexuals and others have been considered by IR scholars as spaces of such desperate abjection as to be altogether beyond politics (e.g. Edkins and Pin-Fat, 2004; Kalyvas, 2005). In this sense, they appear to denote the fulfilment of the sovereign claim to rule absolutely and univocally, without limit or remainder – a claim that critical IR scholars have long argued represents an anti-political attempt to suffocate difference, deliberation and dissent. What shape or form can politics possibly take in a place of such political, ethical and existential extremity?

Without denying or mystifying the appalling and murderous cruelty inherent to the camps' existence and day-to-day functioning, in this chapter I look at artwork produced within the wire in order to identify ways in which detainees sought to engage 'parasitically' with the terms of their abjection.[2] This body of work exemplifies what I call 'aesthetic parasitism', referring to claims to political subjectivity made within the confines of a representational universe that stands as an avatar to the actual, physical terrain of the camp. In contexts where the possibilities for political action are desperately impoverished, this work creates and circumscribes a parallel space in which aesthetically constituted subjects can explore, interrogate and operate with a latitude unavailable to the detainee-artists themselves. 'Aesthetic parasitism' thus refers to the use of humour to make a performative claim to subjectivity within an aesthetic realm standing as the cipher of a corresponding physical space.

Whether considered individually or together, these cartoons demonstrate how a certain form-of-life (even if diminished, even if partial, even if in despair, even if in a mere few out of a countless many) might have been able to manifest itself (even if only for the duration of a few small scribbles) *within* the wire (cf. Edkins and Pin-Fat, 2004: 8). Although the material limitations of such a mode of practice remain many and obvious, the chapter will conclude by arguing that these muffled, often obscured, almost inaudible 'noises' nevertheless constitute fragmentary interventions into the overwhelming sovereign 'signal' of the camp's coercive apparatus.

The chapter will proceed in three stages. The first will engage with critical IR literature on sovereignty in order to demonstrate the singular and perplexing place of the camps of wartime Europe in relation to debates about political (im)possibility and sovereign violence. The second will establish the terms of the 'aesthetic parasitism' mentioned already. The third will look at two of Horst Rosenthal's comic strips in order to evaluate the role of humour in creating and sustaining parasitic encounters within aesthetically constituted spaces. In these works, and in others like them, one can identify detainees operating on and with their wider relational terrain in ways that have been largely overlooked by IR scholars. In so doing, these comics demonstrate one way in which (to however painfully limited a degree) the political might be 'brought back in' to discussions about sovereign power, even in its most extreme manifestations (cf. Edkins, 1999).

Sovereignty, multiplicity and political possibility

For more than thirty years now, sovereignty has been a prominent object of critique among post-structuralist, feminist and other IR theorists (e.g. Ashley, 1984, 1988; Ashley and Walker, 1990; Bartelson, 1995; Edkins et al., 1999; Peterson, 1992; Vaughan-Williams, 2009; Walker, 1993; Weber, 2016). At stake in this body of work is not so much an empirical question about the extent to which the state's importance to international political affairs has been eroded,[3] but rather an analytical question about the ways in which the boundaries of political possibility are circumscribed and policed (Walker, 2004: 241; Bigo and Walker, 2007b: 731; Edkins and Pin-Fat, 2004: 1–3). This literature is therefore concerned with how sovereignty functions and operates: with how it gains and maintains substance, significance or self-evidence, and with how it comes to delimit and determine the political realm (Ashley, 1988: 248). In the process, sovereignty is recast as something that does, rather than something that is: in Rob Walker's words, it is 'an act that works by producing a ... state of being, exactly where there is and can be no such thing' (2004: 242; cf. Weber, 1998).

This 'state of being' can be understood as an articulation of what Michael Dillon describes as a 'metaphysics of presence' (1999: 117), a logic that looks to resolve difference and division by uniting individuals and communities under a pure and uncorrupted sovereign identity. For Richard Ashley and Rob Walker, sovereignty can thus be described as

> a problem posed amidst a crisis of representation: an unmappable region of ambiguity, uncertainty, indeterminacy, and multiplying cultural possibilities where time knows no certain measure, space knows no certain bounds, and human conduct reliably obeys no law

> ... It is a problem of enclosing this boundless region, defining what is alien to it, making a territory in space and time, giving it a temporal metric, and imposing thereupon a centre of judgement beyond doubt that can effectively police the boundaries, fend off the alien, preside over all questions of difference and change within, and decide for one and all what every disputed happening must mean.
>
> *(1990: 381)*

In order to establish itself, sovereign power must inscribe boundaries: it must mark off a physical territory, locate this territory within a temporal matrix and define a symbolic commonwealth of people over whom it has complete authority. The sovereign himself, as the central and sole referent of this space, is consequently positioned as a necessary condition of order: in his absence, there can be no society at all, but rather only a seething whorl of indeterminate brutality that renders undecidable any and every disagreement. Sovereignty is thus constituted as the principle by which this chaotic volatility – this 'unmappable region of ambiguity', as Ashley and Walker describe it – can be made orderly: the derogation of each person's will to a central authority produces a community of people whose unity and coherence are functions of their individual and collective genuflection to the sovereign singularity.

Conventionally, then, sovereignty is understood as that absolute, universal and univocal authority – 'the One, the homogenous' (Bigo and Walker, 2007b: 735) – whose ideal terrain is the 'white spot' from which all parasitic 'noise' has been chased (cf. Serres, 2007: 179). If the 'unmappable region of ambiguity' in which sovereign discourse claims politics to be impossible can be understood an impenetrable hiss of 'noise', then the sovereign enclosure of this space aims towards the opposite extreme: a 'clean slate' whose channels pulse with an unadulterated sovereign 'signal', broadcast unceasingly and without interruption. This means that the sovereign must not only chase out all parasites, but also take measures against their return: the edges of the sovereign space must be vigilantly policed, in order to preserve, maintain and perpetuate its blank and monophonic clarity, free from parasitic noise. It is for this reason that sovereignty is understood to be a- or even anti-political: in its endeavour to demarcate and occupy a closed and homogenous space, it seeks to establish and secure a dominion in which the intersubjective relations that constitute 'politics' – contestation, dissent, resistance, deliberation, counter-conduct, play and so on – would be either unviable or unnecessary. It thus projects a voice that can 'decide for one and all what every disputed happening must mean'; a 'voice ... beyond politics and beyond doubt' (Ashley and Walker, 1990: 368).

Yet as Walker notes, even if sovereignty 'is', insofar as it exists as an identifiable set of discursive assertions and claims, it also 'can[not] be', because it is necessarily incapable of fulfilling the conditions it sets for itself: it is, in other words, a discourse defined by *hubris* (2004: 242). To this end, critical IR theorists have drawn attention to the dissenting voices, the marginal texts, the practices of resistance, the moments of interruption, the friction, the fog – the 'noise', in other words – that also contribute(s) to the constitution of the political field. In so doing, they have stressed the decentralised and relational ways in which power operates, the fragmentary and negotiated character of all identity claims, and the consequent impossibility of overcoming, finalising or perfecting the political field (Ashley, 1989; Ashley and Walker, 1990: 413; Edkins, 1999).

Even if sovereignty attempts to eliminate these disturbances and in so doing reorient politics around its own, singular centre, then, its homogeneity cannot be assumed or even allowed. There is always something blocking and obstructing the channels of sovereign power, something impeding its smooth functioning, disclosing its limitations and insufficiencies and betraying its inability truly to homogenise a space. These critical theorists thus reconfigure sovereignty as a particular 'grammar of power' (Edkins and Pin-Fat, 2004: 3) operating on a broad plane of political contestation defined by a multiplicity of voices and struggles that in their very multiplicity offer a challenge to its onto-politics of closure (cf. Campbell, 2005; Connolly, 2009). If sovereign power seeks to produce a space 'beyond politics', then to bring these other voices under consideration – to draw attention to the multiplicity sovereign power seeks to suffocate – is to contest these depoliticising effects, and to preserve a sense of political possibility.

This literature can potentially be brought into dialogue with a number of other theoretical discourses within IR. These might include the emphasis within Critical Security Studies on the ontological complicity between security and insecurity, or the broadly Foucauldian affirmation of the immanence of resistance within practices of governance – both of which similarly seek to problematise claims to an anti-political wholeness or monophony (cf. Dillon, 1996; Bigo and McCluskey, 2018; Foucault, 2005; Brassett, 2016). In this chapter, however, I will pursue this literature's decentralised, fragmented, contested, incomplete and relational understanding of politics within a specific historical context of such dire privation that meaningful political activity has, to some, appeared genuinely unviable: the concentration camp. Jenny Edkins and Véronique Pin-Fat, for example, identify the concentration camp as an environment in which 'sovereign' violence and coercion operate so overwhelmingly that politics is entirely and absolutely impossible:

> what examples might [there] be, in practice, of a mode of being where resistance is impossible, and hence where there is no power relation[?] It can be argued, following Agamben, that the concentration camp is such an example ... [The camp] is an example of where power relations vanish. What we have in the camps is not a power relation ... What we have is ... *an impossibility of politics.*
> (2005: 10–12, emphasis added)

Although Edkins and Pin-Fat allow for the possibility of resistance in contemporary refugee or asylum camps, they posit the Nazi camps – which they consider together, in the abstract – as limit zones of violence to which the 'opposite pole can only be passivity' (Foucault quoted in Edkins and Pin-Fat, 2005: 13). For Edkins and Pin-Fat, then, the camps of wartime Europe are spaces in which an overwhelming, arbitrary violence holds complete and uncompromising sway, without interruption or disturbance. They are spaces, in other words, in which the broad critical project previously outlined breaks down: truly non-relational, non-political spaces in which the supposedly hubristic ambition to govern without excess or remainder appears in fact to have been realised.

How, then, might one identify the possibility or even the practice of politics in such a devastating, extreme environment – if indeed one can? What can 'politics' even signify in a context like this, and how can any discernable political engagement with such overwhelming material circumstances be theorised or understood? In this chapter, I will address these questions with reference to two comic strips drawn by Horst Rosenthal, a German Jew detained at Gurs[4] in Vichy France and later killed at Auschwitz-Birkenau. Although there is a sizeable literature on camps within IR, as well on the global-political significance of comics and other visual and popular-cultural media, these fields of study have not previously been brought to bear on each other.[5] Political theorists, meanwhile, have more commonly concerned themselves with how to bear witness after the event: with the profound practical, ethical and epistemological challenges associated with the retrospective visualisation or narrativisation of concentrationary atrocity. This focus either on the exhausting and exhaustive totality of the power relations at play, or on testimony produced by survivors in retrospect, has inadvertently served to obscure the small but significant body of work produced in the camps themselves, most of which remains little- or unknown.[6]

To read Rosenthal's comic strips as expressive of a political will and agency is the task of this chapter. What is at stake here, I would like immediately to make clear, is by no means the profound physical, mental, emotional, political and ethical extremity of camp spaces, the everlasting silence of the vast majority of detainees, or the dreadful figures cut by the *Muselmänner* (the 'drowned', the 'non-men', the ones whose deaths Primo Levi 'hesitates to call … death' (1959: 103)). While Rosenthal's comics can be seen to represent the pursuit and practice of politics in an environment of unthinkable privation, to understand them in 'parasitic' terms is also to recognise the manifold ways in which they were woven into the material context from which they emerged, in relation to which they operated and by which they and their author were disciplined (and in the latter case, destroyed). Nevertheless, these strips, and others like them, offer one way of potentially 'bringing the political back in' – in however fragmented or diminished a form – to a constellation of events that is often discussed as though it were beyond the limits of political possibility (cf. Edkins, 1999).

'Desolation' and aesthetic parasitism

For critical IR theorists like Richard Ashley and Rob Walker, the complete suffocation of difference by which the sovereign 'state of being' is defined is a hubristic impossibility (1990). For Jenny Edkins and Véronique Pin-Fat, on the other hand, the Nazi concentration and death camps actualise the non-relational, aporetic zones of violence that constitute Ashley and Walker's vision. For Edkins and Pin-Fat, the camps construct a space in which deliberation, disputation and dissent are genuinely impossible, and in which questions about subjectivity, performativity and politics have no purchase at all. This depiction of the camps echoes a number of survivors' accounts. In the words of Primo Levi, for example:

> The evil and insane SS men, the Kapos, the politicals, the criminals, the prominents, great and small, down to the indifferent slave *Häftlinge*, all the grades of the mad hierarchy created by the Germans paradoxically fraternized in a uniform internal desolation.
> *(1959: 142)*

For Levi, Auschwitz's 'uniform internal desolation' designates an unintelligible swirl in which all distinctions have collapsed into squalor and ruin. The hierarchies nominally underpinning the camp's functioning dissolve, it seems, in the face of a universal human degradation that produces a catastrophic relational void within which all can be considered 'uniform'. If such a space represents an 'impossibility of politics', as Edkins and Pin-Fat suggest, it is precisely because it so comprehensively shatters the intersubjective conduits upon which politics depends, in favour of a monophonic violence whose amplification diminishes victim and perpetrator alike.

What is perhaps more contentious about Edkins and Pin-Fat's account is their equation of this non-relational, non-political concentrationary limit zone with Giorgio Agamben's account of the camp as the paradigmatic space of contemporary sovereign power in the first instalment of *Homo Sacer* (1998). Agamben's work has been much discussed by IR scholars, and a summary of his ideas and arguments in their totality is not necessary here (see Vaughan-Williams, 2009 for an outline of Agamben's influence on IR). Nevertheless, it should be stressed that while Edkins and Pin-Fat are not alone in interpreting his account of the camp in terms of politics' potential eclipse (cf. Connolly, 2007; Kalyvas, 2005; Laclau, 2007), subsequent literature has challenged these readings. William Watkin, for example, argues that for Agamben the camp is the place where 'the political is at its most dangerous but also its most exposed', and argues that this sense of crisis is exactly what makes a new politics not only necessary but possible (2010: 200). Agamben himself, meanwhile, has turned in subsequent instalments of the *Homo Sacer* series to the question of whether and how politics can proceed from the very state of degradation that his earlier work sought to diagnose, advancing what might be described, with Sergei Prozorov, as a 'politics of inoperativity' (Agamben, 2011; 2015; Prozorov, 2014: 30–59).

It is thus Levi's idea of the camp as a non-relational, non-political space, rather than Agamben's account, that I would like to engage with here. It should be emphasised that I have neither the capacity nor the intention to question or criticise Levi's description of his own concentrationary experience. Nor do I want automatically to equate Levi's experiences in Auschwitz with Rosenthal's in Gurs, or with any other detainee's in any other camp. The homogenisation of the transit, concentration, labour, death, prisoner-of-war and multi-purpose camps into a single, undifferentiated mass is an unfortunate feature of contemporary Holocaust discourse that is reinforced by the tendency to see Auschwitz as a synecdoche for the camp system as a whole. Notwithstanding this important qualification, however, the 'uniform internal desolation' Levi describes is nevertheless of use here insofar as it illuminates the aesthetic terrain that Rosenthal's comics both construct and 'interrupt'. This twin movement constitutes the aesthetic mode of parasitism that informs my reading of these comics in this chapter's next section.

Aesthetic parasitism

There is a growing body of work within IR that engages with cartoons and comic books as popular media that can (and do) play an important and active role in international politics (e.g. Dittmer, 2013; Dodds, 2007; Hansen, 2011; 2017; Shim, 2017). The idea that one might potentially speak of a comic book as in some sense 'parasitic', then, is one which builds upon this literature insofar as it acknowledges that aesthetic, visual and/or popular media are productive both of international politics and of the epistemic frameworks through which it is studied and known (cf. D. Campbell, 2003; Grayson, Davies and Philpott, 2009). Importantly, however, the productive potential of comics and cartoons does not mandate any particular political function or trajectory: they can be disruptive or constitutive, critical or conservative. In the words of Lene Hansen:

> When analysing comics ... one should study how text and images are mobilized such that coherent identities are produced, for example, through representations of human subjects. However, one should also ask where and how such 'cohesion' is destabilized through specific characters – visually and textually – that challenge representations of homogeneous collective identity.
>
> *(2017: 589)*

Although comics and cartoons do not have to act in an interruptive manner, then, they nevertheless can do so, insofar as they possess the capacity to introduce 'noise' – dissonant, resistant or transformative ideas, images, narratives or symbols – into the meaning-making channels of political discourse. In the case of Rosenthal's comics, however, so little is known about the circumstances surrounding their creation that it is impossible to draw any conclusions regarding how and why they were made, who saw them or to what effect. It is not even known if anyone else within the camp was aware of their existence beyond Rosenthal himself, while the comics' journeys out of the camp and into the collection of the Hansbacher family – who donated them in 1978 to the archival wing of the Mémorial de la Shoah in Paris, where they remain – is similarly obscure (Kotek and Pasamonik, 2014: 52–3; Rosenberg, 2002: 275). Rosenthal's comics cannot therefore be read with any confidence as immediate interruptive intrusions into the environment in which they were drawn: such a reading would demand answers to simply unanswerable questions about the comics' reception. Instead, I would like to argue that these strips exemplify an alternative, aesthetic mode of parasitic practice.

If the 'interruptive' qualities of the parasite are predicated on a performative claim to political subjectivity from a position of abjection – bringing the 'unreal' to bear on the 'real' through the introduction of 'unseemly noise', in Stuart Hall's words (1992: 282) – then 'aesthetic parasitism' can be understood as the introduction of 'noise' into an aesthetic realm that stands as the avatar of the 'real'. The representation of a concentration camp within an artistic medium like the comic strip opens up an alternative, parallel camp space where an engagement with the camp's day-to-day practices (or with the epistemic frameworks that underpin and sustain them) can be pursued with a latitude that would be impossible within the material camp itself. Rosenthal's comics thus stage or enact an interruptive encounter within their own aesthetic space. They do this by introducing into their representation of Gurs what Michael Shapiro has termed 'aesthetic subjects': aesthetically constituted beings whose 'movements and actions' can function to 'map and often alter experiential, politically relevant terrains' (2013: xiv; 2010; cf. Grayson, 2016: 130–169).

In the first of Rosenthal's comics, *Mickey au Camp de Gurs*, this subject is Mickey Mouse, whose indecipherable, 'noisy' presence radically destabilises the logics sustaining the imagined Gurs through which he wanders. Rosenthal's second comic – *Petit Guide à Travers le Camp de Gurs* – functions slightly differently, by ironically reconfiguring the camp as a holiday camp, and its detainees as tourists: blithe, happy and carefree. The implicit suggestion made by this latter strip is that if Gurs is an exceptional space, it is only so on a temporary and transitory basis: a return to 'normal' life for the 'holidaymakers' is imminent.

One reason for Rosenthal's pursuit of an aesthetic mode of interruption, one imagines, is at least potentially to establish a degree of separation from the camp itself and from the retributive violence likely to befall any open act of dissent. Yet even if aesthetic parasitism is a clandestine means of resistant practice that can (hypothetically, and only ever relatively) insulate its author from reprisal, it nevertheless remains important to recognise that it also potentially opens up an expansive sweep of narrative and imaginative opportunities that enable a depth of interruptive engagement not necessarily available by other means. In short, by operating in relation to an aesthetic facsimile of the 'real' as opposed to the 'real' itself, the political possibilities open to Rosenthal – or rather, to the aesthetic subjects that serve as his proxies – multiply dramatically. This is of particular relevance in a context like a concentration camp where the material possibilities for disruptive, resistant or transformational action are curtailed to an all-but-absolute extent.

When considered together, these comics thus suggest that some sort of political engagement with the logic and machinery of the camps (even if vicarious, even if displaced, even if 'only' aesthetic) *did* remain possible, even in the face of an otherwise overwhelming coercive apparatus. The pieces to be considered in this chapter

Aesthetic parasitism 91

thus not only offer an important, critical perspective on the world[s] they depict and explore, but also enable an acknowledgement of the agency and subjectivity of those who created them: they draw attention to (a few of) the detainees' voices, *as well as* to the productive forces sustaining their detention. These comics thus carve open aesthetic spaces in which Gurs itself can be explored, opposed and operated upon. In so doing, they represent the introduction of an almost imperceptible but nevertheless vital 'noise' into the channels of sovereign power.

These strips have been selected for three reasons. First, that they are directly accessible to the twenty-first-century researcher in a way that interruptive events like the Treblinka Uprising – events that can only be studied today through the mediations of secondhand historiography – are not (cf. Arad, 1987: 282–294). Secondly, that although there is a sizeable body of artwork that derives from Gurs and indeed the Nazi camp system more widely,[7] these pieces in particular allow for an especially rich parasitic engagement with their author's concentrationary context, adopting as they do the extended, narrative form of the comic strip (McCloud, 1994; Groensteen, 2013). And finally, that their exemplification of an aesthetic mode of parasitism provides an unusual and valuable perspective on questions of agency and identity in contexts of political and existential extremity. It is in these terms that I now turn to read the comics themselves.

Cartooning the camp

Mickey au Camp de Gurs

The basic plot of *Mickey au Camp de Gurs* (Figure 1) is simple – as indeed it has to be, given its length of just fifteen panels. Mickey Mouse, striding happily about France, is arrested. Without papers, he is sent to Gurs, where he is detained. Roaming around the camp, he engages with its various characters, practices and rituals, before in the final panel deciding to depart for greener pastures: 'And so, because I'm nothing more than a drawing, I rubbed myself out with a stroke of the eraser … and … ta-da …!!! The police can always come and look for me in the land of lib…ty, eq…ity and frat…ity (I'm talking about America!)'.[8]

Figure 1 *Mickey au Camp de Gurs*, cover. '*Mickey au Camp de Gurs*: published without the permission of Walt Disney'.

The strip, then, presents an impossible encounter between an actually existing place and an imagined, fabulous subject with no material referent at all. The comic strip, it might be argued, is a medium that suits this purpose, given that it not only openly eschews representational realism, but also formally exemplifies a series of dissonant juxtapositions in its combination of image and text, animal and human, spatial frame and temporally indeterminate 'gutter' (McCloud, 1994).[9] Rosenthal plays upon some of these joint articulations in the comic's fourth panel, where Mickey, having been arrested, encounters Gurs for the first time (Figure 2). Here two different worlds collide: the cartoon on the one hand, and the camp in its actuality on the other, a drawing and a photograph presented in tandem yet still warily distinct. Mickey's obvious expression of alarm appears to denote an understandable unwillingness to insert himself into the concentrationary sphere. Yet despite his reluctance, the rest of the strip articulates mouse and camp in concert, slurred together despite their apparent incompatibility and obvious incongruity.

The comic thus constructs an aesthetic space in which an encounter between Gurs and Mickey can be sustained – an encounter whose impossibility is reinforced by the multiple media across

Aesthetic parasitism 93

Figure 2 *Mickey au Camp de Gurs*, fourth panel. '… GURS!!! My first impression was pretty bad. As far as it was possible to see, hundreds of little dog kennels in lines, between which a swarm of people busied themselves with mysterious tasks. But I had no time to look any closer, because I was taken into an office, in the middle of which I could see a large pile of … [papers, see Figure 3]'.

which they are introduced. Crucially, however, the tension signified by the formal incoherence of this initial meeting is preserved even after Mickey enters Gurs, insofar as the camp is unable fully to accommodate him within its epistemic and juridico-political coordinates. Like the parasite among a party's invited guests, then, Mickey might be in Gurs, but he is never of it, occupying a wholly different subjective position to the human detainees he encounters. Moreover, in the same way that the parasite maintains her presence at the feast by provoking laughter, it is the humorous absurdity of Rosenthal's juxtaposition of camp and cartoon mouse that enables their joint articulation to be sustained throughout the strip's narrative.

A dissonant and otherworldly aesthetic subject, physically within Gurs but nevertheless illegible according to its governing logic, Mickey is able to 'operate' on and with the camp's relational terrain in a manner altogether unavailable to its human inhabitants. As such, he functions as a proxy through which the abjection imposed upon Rosenthal and his fellow detainees can be both illuminated and interrogated. Mickey's alien presence must be unscrambled, understood or disciplined into some kind of intelligible sense if the camp is to bring him under effective control. Yet despite its evident efforts in this regard, the camp turns out to be incapable of deciphering or decoding him: its attempts to identify him, to incorporate him into the camp's governing logic, meet nothing but thin air.

It is in these terms that *Mickey au Camp de Gurs* might be read as an example of 'aesthetic parasitism', insofar as its introduction of an ungovernable aesthetic subject performatively cultivates a vital instability within an exclusionary and violent system and order. Although Mickey occupies the same huts as his human contemporaries, takes the same rations as them and answers to the same rules, he is nevertheless not a 'regular' detainee. For this reason, the camp cannot locate him within its epistemic and juridico-political co-ordinates, and its officials cannot objectify him in the same way as the other detainees. Mickey thus short-circuits the rationality according to which the camp space is circumscribed and on the basis of which it functions. This is evident from Mickey's first interchange within the wire, in which he speaks to a clerk who attempts to identify him and in so doing determine the terms of his detainment (Figure 3). The dialogue reads:

—*You're a Jew?*
—*What?*
—*I asked if you were a Jew!!*
Shamefully, I professed my complete ignorance on the subject.

In the accompanying picture, Mickey gazes up at the clerk, wide-eyed and with a question mark in a speech bubble above his head, understanding neither the content nor the context of the question. When Mickey eventually declares that although he was born in America, he is really international, the clerk assumes 'with a horrible grimace' that he is identifying as a communist. Mickey, of course, is doing nothing of the sort: he cannot be ascribed any national, cultural or political identity, and appears almost entirely unaware of what such titles might signify: he is of no race, of no nation, of no political affiliation, of no family.[10] As such, the attempts of the clerk

Aesthetic parasitism 95

Figure 3 *Mickey Au Camp de Gurs*, fifth panel. '[I was taken into an office, in the middle of which I could see a large pile of ...] ... papers!! After a few minutes' waiting, a head popped out of the pile. "Your name?" the head asked. "Mickey". "Father's name?" "Walt Disney". "Mother's name?" "My mother? I don't have a mother". "What?! You don't have a mother? You're fucking with me!!" "No, really – I don't have a mother!!" "No kidding! I've heard of people who don't have a father, but no mother ... Anyway, we'll move on. You're a Jew?" "What?" "I asked if you were a Jew!!" Shamefully, I professed my complete [ignorance on the subject]'.

to ascribe Mickey to one of the categories underpinning the camp's terms of detainment meet nothing but thin air.

The childlike naïveté evident in this particular panel is key to Mickey's aesthetic subjectivity throughout the strip. Understanding nothing of the logic underpinning the camp's existence and practice, he is baffled by his experiences rather than angered or horrified by them; he is a *tabula rasa*, unable to participate in the camp's identity games as a result of his ignorance of the terms by which they are played. In this respect, he might be contrasted with Felix Nussbaum's 1943 *Self-Portrait with Jewish Identity Card* (Figure 4), in which the artist displays his yellow star and identity card prominently to the viewer. These signifiers, of course, worked to govern how Nussbaum was to be recognised, classified and distinguished – as a Jew, as a person whose identity was determined by the papers he carried, and whose movement was consequently constantly checked

Figure 4 Felix Nussbaum (1943): *Self-Portrait with Jewish Identity Card*. In 1944, Nussbaum painted *Self-Portrait in the Camp*, a companion piece to the former that is now in the collection of the Neue Galerie in New York.

and curtailed. Yet the picture – as a *self*-portrait – also appears to suggest that this vision had become normalised and internalised. This, it seems, is how Nussbaum now conceives of himself.

Nussbaum's self-portrait depicts an environment in which a restrictive, arbitrary violence has worked productively to alter the terms by which he sees himself, and in so doing to circumscribe a desolate space in which the relations and interactions that constitute 'normal' social life become impossible to sustain.[11] In *Mickey au Camp de Gurs*, the same processes and practices are in evidence – the obsession with papers, with identity defined in racial or political terms, with constraint and curtailment, checkpoints and barriers. The human detainees Mickey meets consequently exist in a state of desperate degradation, and variously spend their time pimping, fencing or spivving, fussing over a 'garden' consisting of a single weed or cooking up some vile concoction with whatever material is available, edible or otherwise. They do not interact either with each other or with the camp's various officials, who are themselves likewise diminished; lost within mountains of paper (cf. Figure 3) or, in one case, literally faceless. Yet Mickey – uniquely – is able to resist the camp's attempts to drag him onto its plane.

If, as Primo Levi argued, 'the [camp] was a great machine to reduce us to beasts', then Mickey is the ghost in this machine, unable to be bestialised because he already *is* non-human (1959: 39). While his physical body can seemingly be confined (although the camp's ability even in this regard is limited, as his ultimate self-erasure from the strip attests), the camp's attempts to rationalise his detention through the imposition, designation or production of a particular subjective identity make no headway whatsoever. Mickey instead plays the part of a blithe *flâneur*; a renegade ethnographer whose mere presence interruptively alters the terms of belonging determining the group in which he has embedded himself.

It is here that one might note how Mickey's interruptive presence within Gurs serves not only to map the desolation of the camp, but also to probe at the practices that sustain it. Manoeuvring about the camp on his own terms, diverting and deflecting its attempts to govern him, Mickey unconsciously traverses the categories and boundaries by which the camp's day-to-day practices are organised. His wanderings around the camp are 'parasitic' by virtue of their performance of a particular subjective identity that cannot be incorporated into the camp's ordering logic even as he strides across its terrain.

In this sense, Mickey might be described as 'Chaplinesque', in Henri Lefebvre's terms: 'he comes as a stranger into the familiar world' (2014: 33). According to Lefebvre, the 'point of departure' for Chaplin's understanding of humour is 'the simplicity of a child, a primitive and a wonderfully gifted barbarian, suddenly plunged (as we all are at every moment) into an everyday life that is inflexible and bristling with ever-new difficulties' (2014: 33). This description applies to Mickey insofar as Rosenthal transports him into a universe that he does not understand but must nevertheless navigate, in the process of which he 'confront[s] the established ... world and its vain attempts to complete itself and close itself off' (Lefebvre, 2014: 33). In his Chaplinesque naïveté, as well as his irreducibility to the abjection of the other detainees, Mickey's meanderings around the camp introduce an indeterminacy into Gurs that the camp apparatus, bent as it is on securing the uncontaminated purity of its own 'signal', cannot tolerate.

It thus comes as no surprise that by the end of the comic strip, Mickey has come to realise that whatever the camp is, it is not for him: 'decidedly, the Pyrenean air did not suit me at all' (Figure 5). Describing the camp as a corruption of the French revolutionary ideals of liberty, equality and fraternity, he chooses to rub himself out of the comic strip altogether and relocate to the United States, where such values are still to be found (Figure 5). With this move, Rosenthal reverses the polarities of Mickey's initial encounter with Gurs, in which the former shrinks away from the latter (Figure 2). While *Mickey au Camp de Gurs* at first appears to depict Mickey's entry into the material world of the camp, this final panel suggests that the comic strip might equally be read the other way: perhaps it in fact describes the submission of Gurs to the comic absurdity of Mickey's own cartoon world. 'Laying hold' of the terrain upon which he has

Figure 5 *Mickey au Camp de Gurs*, final panel. 'But decidedly, the Pyrenean air did not suit me at all. And so, because I'm nothing more than a drawing, I rubbed myself out with a stroke of the eraser … and … ta-da …!!! The police can always come and look for me in the land of lib…ty, eq…ity and frat…ity (I'm talking about America!) Signed, Mickey (copy certified by Horst Rosenthal, Gurs, 1942)'.

Figure 6 *Petit Guide à Travers Le Camp de Gurs*, cover.

unwillingly been thrust, Mickey therefore demonstrates once and for all its inability to contain him by heading across the Atlantic.

If Mickey's self-erasure is in some sense an interruptive triumph, however, it is important to remember that it also carries with it an obvious overtone that also looms over *Mickey au Camp de Gurs* more generally. This is of course Rosenthal's own continued legibility within the very space that Mickey interruptively frustrates: his (and his peers') abject detainment within the same wires that Mickey simply ghosts through. There is a pathos in Mickey's self-erasure that arises from the understanding knowledge that such measures are unavailable to any of Gurs' human inhabitants: that the flip side of his illegibility is Rosenthal's abject legibility as a German Jew. *Petit Guide à Travers le Camp de Gurs*, another of Rosenthal's strips, takes a different approach to camp life that seeks to reconfigure what detainment means even for Gurs' human inhabitants.

Petit Guide à Travers le Camp de Gurs

In the 1997 comedy *La Vita è Bella* (*Life is Beautiful*), an Italian-Jewish waiter called Guido Orefice (Roberto Benigni) is sent with his wife Dora (Nicoletta Braschi) and their young son Giosuè (Giorgio Cantarini) to a nameless concentration and death camp (Benigni, 1997). In an attempt to shelter Giosuè from the gravity and severity of their situation, Guido tells him that the camp is actually an enormous, immersive game in which the 'contestants' – i.e. the detainees – must perform certain tasks, in exchange for points. The first player to reach a thousand points, Guido says, will win a tank. Giosuè believes his father's story, and dutifully performs the tasks he is set. Although Guido is killed as the Germans flee the camp in the face of the Allies' impending arrival, the film ends with Giosuè's and Dora's joyful reunion, Dora having been detained in the women's block throughout the latter part of the narrative, separated from her husband and son.

La Vita è Bella has rightly been criticised for its sentimentality, as well as for its ultimate message of redemption (Giosuè's passage from the exceptional space of the camp back into the normality of his mother's loving embrace might be contrasted with the inexpressible pathos of Primo Levi's 'child of Auschwitz', Hurbinek).[12] However, the relevance of the film here lies not in its narrative trajectory but in the strategy that Guido adopts in order to navigate the concentrationary space in which he and his family have been detained, and in so doing to enable them to elude the abjection it imposes upon them. Guido does not actively or materially oppose the camp apparatus: he does not refuse to work, or fight back against the guards, or try to escape. Instead, he attempts to alter what the camp signifies: the guards may be 'mean', but that's because they're always looking to dock points from slack or slothful competitors; Guido might have to spend all day hauling anvils around a big steel mill, but that's because he's helping to build the tank that the winner will receive as a prize; he and Giosuè might not get fed properly, but that's a challenge, all part of the 'game' – because points are deducted if you complain about being hungry. Rather than opposing it directly, Guido instead seeks to impose an entirely different epistemic framework upon the camp, and in so doing to reimagine it as a playful space as opposed to a coercive, murderous one.

It is in this respect that *La Vita è Bella* is of relevance to Rosenthal's *Petit Guide à Travers le Camp de Gurs*. The *Petit Guide* is written like a tourist brochure, and as such attempts to persuade its reader of all the reasons why s/he might wish to visit Gurs.[13] The first page (Figure 7) reads:

> For a while now, we have seen a charming poster in every train station and travel agency that invites travellers to spend their holidays at Gurs. What is this famous camp? We have created this brochure in order to satisfy your healthy curiosity.[14]

In the same way that Guido seeks to shape Giosuè's concentrationary experience by reconfiguring it according to an alternative rationality, so Rosenthal's *Petit Guide* seeks to incorporate Gurs into an alternative regime of sense: to constitute it as a holiday

Figure 7 *Petit Guide à Travers Le Camp de Gurs*, first panel. The poster reads: 'If you want to lose weight – come to GURS! Its cuisine is renowned! For more information, head to your local police station!'

rather than a concentration camp, as a space of leisure rather than of sovereign power.[15]

By reimagining the camp space in this way, the *Petit Guide* short-circuits the logic according to which it functions. If the camp denotes a non-relational 'desolation' in which all division and distinction has dissolved, then the *Petit Guide* re-establishes some of these differentiations. A holiday, for example, is by definition temporally bounded (one cannot *always* be on holiday), with a clearly defined beginning and end (one is always aware of an impending return to 'reality'; one must always depart for home). Gurs, as a 'holiday camp', is thus ironically constituted as a brief and anomalous excursion from 'normality'; a sabbatical from which those who visit will no doubt soon return, refreshed and ready to re-assume their regular routines.

While *Mickey au Camp de Gurs* presents an aesthetic subject, unincorporable into the camp space, *Petit Guide à Travers le Camp de Gurs* reconfigures and reimagines the space itself, recalibrating the terms by which it is understood such that it signifies something else entirely. Yet this also transforms the detainees themselves: holidaymakers rather than the desperate abjects that Mickey encounters in *Mickey au Camp de Gurs*, the 'tourists' can enjoy the 'renowned cuisine' of the camp, and perhaps even take in a show from its 'permanent theatre troupe', before returning home.[16] By reimagining the camp, in other words, Rosenthal also produces a different type of camp subject: just as Guido transforms Giosuè from detainee to game-player, and just as it is in this capacity that Giosuè experiences the camp, so Rosenthal produces the residents of Gurs as sightseers and day-trippers rather than the objects of arbitrary and overwhelming violence. Although the camp is materially the same, it has nevertheless been radically reshaped – bent out of all recognition, forced to submit to a different, alien logic: beasts organised according to the terms of Borges' 'Chinese encyclopaedia' rather than Wilkins' hyper-rational taxonomy.[17]

Throughout the *Petit Guide*, however, there is a sense that all is not what it seems: the strip cannot consistently maintain its artifice. As such, it occasionally gestures towards the inevitable shortcomings of its own irony. One page of the 'brochure', for example, displays a censor's stamp crashing through the panel, with the text beneath overtly and heavily redacted (Figure 8):

Aesthetic parasitism

And now, I would like to talk to you about ... and about ... and about the ...

Finally, I would like to tell you something extremely interesting. These are the sensational revelations about ...

In this panel, the camp shatters the illusion established over the course of the preceding pages (quite literally shattering, indeed, in the form of the censor's stamp bursting through the frame).[18] The stamp suggests that the strip's vision of Gurs as an idyllic holidaymaker's paradise is concealing something – that there is some abstract force lurking beneath the brochure's cheery façade that will intervene if necessary in order to ensure that its trickery or pretence does not go too far. Rosenthal's aesthetic and ironic reimagining of the camp space thus begins to crumble, placed in tension with the very force it is trying to veil.

Figure 8 *Petit Guide à Travers Le Camp de Gurs*, ninth panel.

This violent juxtaposition between the strip's ironic reimagining of Gurs on one hand and the violence governing the camp in its material actuality on the other serves to ensure that the strip cannot be read simply as a flight of fancy or as an imaginative exercise. The *Petit Guide* is not a fairy tale. Instead, it carves open an aesthetic space (however provisional, contingent or absurd) in which the productive mechanisms of the camp can be contested (though never transcended, as the stamp's intervention makes only too clear). Within this space are produced subjects – in this case, 'holidaymakers' happily enjoying their break in the Pyrenees – who can 'operate' within the camp in a way that is impossible if it is understood as a space of unthinkable privation.

The *Petit Guide*'s ironic sense of humour thus functions 'as a vital and creative resource for thinking through ... "limits"' (Brassett, 2009: 237). Rosenthal's ironic reimagining of the camp space can be read as an attempt to 'interrupt ... dominant narratives ... provoking us to rethink their central assumptions and perhaps, resist them' (2009: 240). More specifically, by depicting the violent intrusion of the censor's stamp into the pages of the 'brochure', the *Petit Guide* portrays the camp asserting itself through naked violence in order to re-establish its hold over the aesthetic vocabulary by which Rosenthal is presenting it. In so doing, the comic draws attention to the violence inherent in the camp machinery by forcing its governing powers openly to declare their hand. This undermines the brochure's vision of the camp as a leisure space, but it also carves open a space of confrontation and contestation where previously there was none (Brassett, 2009: 242).

Other work from the camps

There are a number of other works, both from Gurs and from other camps, that use humour and irony in order to operate on and with the material camp spaces in which they were produced. Karl Schwesig's Gurs 'stamps' (Figure 9), for example, might be compared to Rosenthal's *Petit Guide* insofar as they also ironically constitute Gurs as a tourist destination: as the sort of place from which one might wish to send a postcard home. Schwesig constitutes Gurs as a sovereign state, giving it the capability to issue stamps in the first place,[19] underlining this implication by associating Gurs with

Aesthetic parasitism 105

Figure 9 Karl Schwesig (1940–1941): Gurs 'stamps'.

the ideals of liberty, equality and fraternity that supposedly underpin the French Republic (the same ideals, of course, that Mickey cites in order to justify his departure from Gurs). The pictures accompanying these invocations, however, illustrate the bankruptcy rather than the fulfilment of these values: if the stamps imply that Gurs is in some sense a sovereign state, then it is in the disjuncture between ideal and actuality that it should be assessed. For Schwesig as for Rosenthal, then, irony provides a way of throwing the camps' violence into sharp, stark relief.

On the walls of the dining hall at Camp des Milles in Aix-en-Provence, meanwhile, an unknown artist (or artists) painted a mural or frieze. As a testimony, one presumes, to their hunger, they drew a series of men staggering or falling under the weight of food they were attempting to carry; flush with the excess of their consumption (Figure 10). Depicting an overflowing abundance of food and drink, this mural would have contrasted starkly with the scarcity and dearth experienced by detainees in the very same room. This disparity is made explicit on the (unfinished) opposite wall (Figure 11), which presents a scene of alimentary excess captioned with the words 'if your plates are not full enough ...'.

The frieze's depiction of plenty both occupies the very space at which its dissonance with the actuality of the concentrationary

Figure 10 Detail from the dining hall mural (1942–1943, artist(s) unknown), Camp des Milles.

Figure 11 Detail from the dining hall mural (1942–1943, artist(s) unknown), Camp des Milles.

experience would have been most acutely felt, and plays upon this dissonance. The mural does not reconfigure the camp in the manner of the *Petit Guide*, but instead throws its material paucity into relief by juxtaposing it with a distant, aesthetically constituted realm of abundance. In so doing, it suggests that for some detainees at least, an ironic sense of humour was an important resource with which to negotiate or engage with the situation in which they found themselves.

These pieces use humour either to reimagine the camps by incorporating them into an unexpected logical framework (the holiday camp, the liberal ideals of revolutionary France), or to contrast them with a diametrically opposed realm of freedom and plenty. Like Rosenthal's strips, however, they function by creating an interruptive dissonance between the actuality of the camp space and an aesthetically constituted, ironic space. In so doing, these pieces can also be read as instances of aesthetic parasitism, insofar as they create and sustain an encounter between the camp's self-contained epistemic and coercive terrain and (aspects of) social, political, international or everyday life beyond the wire.

> Without breaking down the distance between the two of them, the fact of the word forces the sovereign to become an interlocutor and enter a space of discourse with the stranger. It is a space of discourse that these two parties have not rendered transparent; indeed, it never will be transparent, but it manifestly exists between them in the facticity of their encounter by virtue of the existence of language itself. Of course, this is not a space that they occupy with equal force and advantage, but it is there.
>
> *(Dillon, 1999: 125)*

Conclusion

In August 1942, Horst Rosenthal was sent from Gurs to Drancy, near Paris, and then on to Auschwitz, where he was killed upon arrival (Kotek and Pasamonik, 2014: 167–169). In this light, it would be grotesque to suggest that his comics represent any sort of means by which its author might have overcome the situation in which he lived and ultimately died, and consequently I do not make this claim: there are obvious and potentially profound limits to the aesthetic mode of parasitism that I have advanced in this chapter. This is not to say that aesthetic parasitism is necessarily politically powerless or incapable, however: a large literature exists both within IR and without concerning the ways in which visual and/or popular-cultural media like comic books might contribute to the (re)definition of the limits of political possibility (cf. Rancière, 2004). Yet it is important to acknowledge that any interruptive effects identifiable beyond the aesthetic sphere of the strip are provisional and indeterminate, dependent on the circumstances of production, dissemination and reception that are incumbent on artistic activity as much as any other field of practice. These circumstances are unknowable in relation to the work discussed here: in these instances, questions of reception must reluctantly be left open.

Nevertheless, in recent years, it seems that sovereignty has become increasingly entrenched within a number of Western states, feeding (and feeding off) a growing border anxiety that has on occasion (but not always) found material form in camps of one sort or another: in Calais, on Nauru, on Manus, at Yarl's Wood and, more recently still, in Immigration and Customs Enforcement (ICE) detention centres in the United States (cf. Aradau, 2016). Underpinning all these sites is a desire for control, a desire whose fulfilment relies on the reduction of the political field to a singularity and the consequent production of what Nick Vaughan-Williams describes as 'the subjects of sovereign power: mute; undifferentiated; and depoliticised' (2009: 135; cf. Wilcox, 2015: 87).

In such times, it is more important than ever to keep an ear cocked for the interruptive buzz that belies the hubris of this desire, and to remain open to the possibility that such interventions might find aesthetic expression. The works discussed here thus gesture towards other sites of potential interest to IR scholars: the work of, among others, Abbas al Aboudi, an Iraqi artist detained by the Australian Department of Home Affairs on Nauru; Eaten Fish, an Iranian cartoonist formerly detained on Manus Island, Papua New Guinea; and Behrouz Boochani, a Kurdish novelist and journalist who lived in New Zealand at the time of writing.[20] Like *Mickey au Camp de Gurs* and *Petit Guide à Travers le Camp de Gurs*, their work manifests a diminished yet existent political possibility; it both describes and (to a painfully limited degree) defies the desubjectifying and depoliticising effects of sovereign power. It is important not because it offers a way to escape or transcend coercive violence, nor because it represents some residual, ethically vital 'humanity' left in an otherwise inhuman space. Rather, this work's refusal to accept 'desolation', its refusal to be 'mute, undifferentiated, and depoliticised', is important because it testifies to the possibility and indeed the necessity of politics, even in the most chastening of contexts. It is important because it *is*.

Notes

1 Little is known of Rosenthal: he was born in Breslau (now Wrocław, Poland) and held at Gurs between 1940 and August 1942. While detained there, he drew (at least) three short comic strips – *Mickey au*

Camp de Gurs (*Mickey in the Gurs Camp*), *La Journée d'un Hébergé* (*A Day in the Life of a Hébergé* [Resident]) and *Petit Guide à Travers Le Camp de Gurs* (*Little Guide Through the Gurs Camp*). The first two of these were donated to the Centre de Documentation Juive Contemporaine in Paris in 1978, although nothing is known of their whereabouts up to that point. The third was given or sold to a Swiss nurse in Gurs, who smuggled it out of the camp before donating it in 1986 to the Skovgaard Museum in Viborg (Denmark). Rosenthal himself was transferred to Drancy in August 1942 and then to Auschwitz-Birkenau a month later, where he was killed upon arrival. None of Rosenthal's three extant comics have ever been published outside France. Biographical information taken from Kotek and Pasamonik (2014: 167–169); see also Rosenberg (2002).
2 The use of the word 'parasite' in relation to subjects who were frequently constituted as subhuman raises obvious ethical and political questions, and may well inspire a certain amount of unease. This is not without good cause: Andreas Musolff has recently traced the metaphorical use of the term 'parasite' within Nazi discourses on Jewishness, and this is an association from which I obviously wish to distance myself entirely (2014: 1–10; cf. Bein, 1964). Two points should be raised at this juncture. First, that I use the term 'parasite' in this chapter to refer not to the detainees themselves but rather to the aesthetic subjects produced by and through their artworks. And second, that the way in which I have theorised parasitism in this book's first part should make clear that my use of the word has a meaning and derivation at some remove from its use in 1930s and 1940s Germany. The term 'parasite' took on the meaning the Nazis ascribed to it relatively late, through Victorian discourses on 'degeneration' (Lankester, 1880; cf. Pick, 1993). My usage of the term in this chapter and throughout this book, grounded in the Greek ritual of the *pharmakos*, in the ancient Megarian account of the origins of comedy and in a fragment from Epicharmus, thus operates at a rhetorical and etymological distance from these later uses of the term.
3 This is a question posed and tackled, in varying ways and with varying responses, by scholars working in the fields of international political economy (e.g. Strange, 1996); global governance (e.g. Barnett and Duvall, 2005; Held and McGrew, 2002); liberal cosmopolitanism (what John Ikenberry calls 'Liberal Internationalism 3.0' (Ikenberry, 2009); and so-called 'New Wars' (e.g. Kaldor, 1999), among many others.
4 Gurs, located on the French side of the Pyrenees, was built by the French government in 1939 primarily in order to intern Spanish refugees who had crossed the border after the end of the 1936–1939 Civil War. Even

before the German invasion of 1940 the camp was being used to detain fleeing Jews from Germany and elsewhere (including, briefly, Hannah Arendt), a role which expanded after the establishment of Pétain's client state in the south of the country. By 1942, the camp was functioning as a transit point from which Jews arrested in southern France could be sent to extermination camps in the East, primarily Auschwitz-Birkenau. Almost 4000 non-French Jews (including Rosenthal himself) were killed in this way. Another 1100 or so died within Gurs itself, primarily from illnesses like typhoid and dysentery whose spread was exacerbated both by overcrowding and by the lack of basic resources like food, water and sanitation (Megargee, 2018, vol. 3: 150–153).

5 On the camp, see Edkins and Pin-Fat (2005); Puggioni, 2005; Neal, 2006; Huysmans, 2008. All of this literature acknowledges (without necessarily following) the work of Giorgio Agamben, especially the first volume of his *Homo Sacer* series (1998). On the relationship between visual media and international relations, meanwhile, see – among much else – Bleiker (2018). On popular culture, see Weldes (2003); Grayson, Davies and Philpott (2009). On comics, see Hansen (2011; 2017); Wedderburn (2019); Redwood and Wedderburn (2019).

6 One might say that Adorno's statement regarding the barbarity of writing poetry after Auschwitz has achieved fame and notoriety at the expense of poetry written in Auschwitz (Adorno, 1997: 34; cf. Nader, 2007). It is notable, in any case, that very little contemporary documentation of the wartime genocide has anything more than a specialised audience. Anne Frank's diary is probably the sole exception, though Charlotte Salomon's extraordinary and almost uncategorisable artwork *Life? Or Theatre?* has begun – rightfully, if belatedly – to attract serious academic and curatorial attention. Cf. Pollock (2018).

7 Laharie (2008). For examples of artwork from within the camp system more generally, see Benvenuti (2016). Secondary reflections on some of this work can be found in Carr and Mytum (2012). Of course, the variable material conditions within the camps, dependent on all sorts of factors ranging from their function to their geographical location in relation to supply and frontlines, played a key role in determining the possibilities available to detainees. Nevertheless, work survives from a wide variety of camps, including those with extermination facilities such as Birkenau.

8 Ellipses in original. All translations from *Mickey au Camp de Gurs* are my own, working off a facsimile of the original at the Mémorial de la Shoah, Paris. Additional help has been given by Jessica Freeman-Attwood, to whom I owe my thanks. Any remaining infelicities or mistakes are mine (Rosenthal, 1942a).

Aesthetic parasitism 111

9 The introduction of fictional characters into historical events, meanwhile, is a hallmark of comic-book fiction. One particularly egregious example is the 1991 Captain America comic from Marvel's counterfactual-historical 'What If …?' series in which Captain America, placed at the head of the D-Day invasion, leads the Allied forces through Western and Central Europe at such speed that they are able to liberate Auschwitz ahead of the advancing Soviet forces.
10 Mickey tells the clerk that his 'father' is Walt Disney, and that he has no mother at all. It should be noted in this context that 'Jewishness' is traditionally matrilineal. Whether Rosenthal was aware of Walt Disney's own (now well-documented) anti-Semitism is a matter of speculation.
11 Nussbaum painted his self-portrait while in hiding in Belgium. In 1944 he was discovered by German agents and sent to Auschwitz, where he was killed. His painting thus derives from a time of informal concentration in which he was outside the camp system, but nevertheless tightly enclosed, hidden from view only by the generosity, good will and bravery of his Belgian friends. This constraint is implicit within the backdrop that he gives himself in his portrait: high, blank walls mirrored by a heavy, sinking sky, both rendered in charcoal grey.
12 For the story of Hurbinek, see Levi, 1987: 25–26; a commentary on this passage can be found in Shapiro, 2016: viii–ix. It would be unconscionable to cite Hurbinek's name without quoting the end of Levi's account, for reasons which the text itself makes abundantly clear: 'Hurbinek, the nameless, whose tiny arm – even his – bore the tattoo of Auschwitz; Hurbinek died in the first days of March 1945, free but not redeemed. Nothing remains of him: he bears witness through these words of mine.'
13 Rosenthal (1942b).
14 All translations from *Petit Guide à Travers le Camp de Gurs* are my own.
15 This is a strategy also pursued in the third of Rosenthal's strips (not discussed in detail in this chapter, entitled *La Journée d'un Hébergé* (*A Day in the Life of a Hébergé* [Resident]). The last panel of *La Journeé* depicts the hébergé lying in bed at the end of the day documented by the strip. The caption reads: 'But before you go to sleep, don't forget to thank Mr Minister-of-the-Interior who sent you here, and Mr Manager-of-the-hotel for his ceaseless care. And thank the good guards who protect you during your slumber … And he's out!' Rosenthal (1942c).
16 Gurs did, in fact, have a makeshift theatre, which staged fairly regular performances.
17 See Chapter 1.
18 Rosenthal must presumably have stolen or 'borrowed' the stamp, which throws up all sorts of mischievous (if hypothetical) images: the detainee

appropriating and wielding a tool and symbol of the sovereign; the censor himself unable to locate the stamp with which he performatively confirms his status (perhaps searching underneath the pile of letters he can no longer redact), and so on.

19 This is not altogether far-fetched. A number of camps and ghettoes issued their own 'money', known as 'Lagergeld'. Therisienstadt and the ghetto at Łodz are the best-known – but by no means only – examples of this phenomenon.

20 On Abbas al Aboudi, see Winsor (2018). The best initial port of call for Eaten Fish (real name Ali Dorani) is probably the website started by Australian cartoonist First Dog on the Moon in order to campaign for his safe passage from Manus. Available at https://eatenfish.com/ (accessed 29 June 2020). Behrouz Boochani tweets at https://twitter.com/behrouzboochani (accessed 29 June 2020). See also Boochani (2018).

4

Physical parasitism: ACT UP and the HIV/AIDS pandemic

Introduction

The devastating spread of HIV/AIDS over the last forty years has been of such magnitude that it has become a constitutive part of the contemporary global imaginary: as Jean Comaroff claims, 'it is impossible to contemplate the shape of late modern history ... without the polymorphous presence of HIV/AIDS, the signal pandemic of the global here and now' (2007: 197).[1] For Comaroff, HIV/AIDS cannot be understood in purely scientific terms. It has overwhelmed the medical language, discourses and practices originally sent to tame and subdue it, setting off 'an avalanche of mythmaking', in Comaroff's words, or an 'epidemic of signification', in Paula Treichler's (Comaroff, 2007: 198; Treichler, 1987). HIV/AIDS has 'rewrit[ten] the global geopolitical coordinates within which we think and act': it has contributed to the production of new forms of community, new affinities and antagonisms, new dynamics of (in)security, and new techniques of governance (Comaroff, 2007: 198).

It is, in part, for this reason that Cindy Patton talks not about the discovery but about the 'invention' of AIDS (1990). Patton, like Comaroff and Treichler, does not consider HIV/AIDS to be the passive object of science. The pandemic straddles questions of geography, class, race, gender and sexuality; it provides some with a prominent speaking role and keeps others forever in the wings. This recognition demands that attention be paid to the political as well as the medical dimensions of HIV/AIDS. Within International Relations (IR), a number of scholars have thus sought to understand the implications and consequences of the pandemic not only for global health policy, but also for practices of global governance and security (e.g. Elbe, 2006; McInnes, 2006; Harman, 2010).

In addition to studying the politics of HIV/AIDS, however, one might also consider the pandemic in *bio*political terms, interrogating the ways in which attempts to manage its incidence and transmission exert 'power ... over [wo/]men insofar as they are living beings' (Foucault, 2003b: 247). For Stefan Elbe, the securitisation of HIV and AIDS by the United Nations (UN) Security Council has enabled the enactment and extension of a 'biopolitical economy of power' that has shaped and informed global health policy (2005: 404). Yet it is not just here, within the high-political sphere of transnational organisations, that a biopolitical framework might be used to shed light on how the crisis has been governed, understood and experienced. As Patton explains:

> [understanding] the politics of sex and germs ... is essential to successfully connect individual experiences with the social and political structures that impede attempts to cope with AIDS at every level.
> *(1985: 17)*

For Patton, there is a biopolitics of HIV/AIDS that must be engaged if one is to understand the ways in which the virus and syndrome (and the experiences of those who live with them) intersect with broader, transversal systems of power and governance. Moreover, this understanding is in turn a *sine qua non* for any sensitive, inclusive and effective response to the pandemic: one cannot address HIV/AIDS as a health crisis without also engaging its social, political and biopolitical manifestations.

While Elbe sees the biopoliticisation of HIV and AIDS as a consequence of their incorporation into transnational security discourse in the early 2000s, in this chapter I will show how such dynamics were in operation from the early 1980s, as part of the processes by which AIDS was first constituted as an object of medical and political concern. The development of HIV/AIDS discourse is thus inextricable from biopolitical mechanisms dividing a 'healthy' population to be protected and secured from the 'diseased' or 'sick' against whom such protective measures are required. Abjected from the population as a whole, those constituted as carriers or vectors of

HIV/AIDS have often been made the object of punitive and violent political and biomedical strategies.

Having established the biopolitical implications of HIV/AIDS policy in the United States in the 1980s and early 1990s,[2] I turn to ask how people living with HIV/AIDS engaged with these techniques of governance: how they 'target[ed] AIDS as a political crisis' rather than merely a medical one, and how in so doing they made parasitic claims to agency and subjectivity. In making such claims – often, though not exclusively, through humour – these people and groups sought to traverse, destabilise and problematise the biopolitical divisions and boundaries by and through which their bodies were governed. Their methods in so doing often focused on the physical recontextualisation of queer bodies, bodies with AIDS or bodies perceived to be such into the very spaces effecting those bodies' biopolitical abjection. By occupying the offices of the National Institutes of Health and the Food and Drug Administration, or by staging a carnival outside (and inside) New York's Catholic Cathedral, AIDS activists enacted and performed an encounter, often sustained through humour, between a particular ethicopolitical vision of 'health' (as heterosexual, as 'family-oriented', as 'respectable', as white) and the bodies against which that vision was defined. This is what I call 'physical parasitism': the physical recontextualisation of abject bodies into the social or material spaces producing or symbolising their abjection.

The chapter proceeds in three sections. The first considers the ways in which the AIDS crisis in the United States – from its very moment of emergence – was incorporated into a biopolitical apparatus that functioned as the extension of an epidemiological discourse nominally tasked with 'discovering', naming and providing objective knowledge about the syndrome. The second introduces the AIDS Coalition to Unleash Power (ACT UP), a local and international activist organisation that worked (and continues to work) to fight the pandemic, and outlines the terms of 'physical parasitism' in the context of HIV/AIDS. The third and final section discusses a number of ACT UP actions, focusing in particular on the 1991 stunt by ACT UP's Treatment Action Guerrillas (TAG) in which they placed a giant inflatable condom over the house of the notoriously homophobic US Senator Jesse Helms.

HIV/AIDS, biopolitics, epidemiology

According to Stefan Elbe, HIV/AIDS 'marks an important contemporary site for the global dissemination of a biopolitical economy of power revolving around the government of "life"' (2005: 403). Elbe argues that the creeping securitisation of HIV/AIDS around the turn of the millennium indicates an expansion of the traditional concerns of security discourse: 'no longer confined to defending sovereignty, territorial integrity, and international law ... population dynamics – including levels of 'disease' – have now become strategically significant as well' (2005: 406). As a 'strategically significant' concern, HIV/AIDS has demanded a twofold political response. First, agencies like the Joint UN Program on HIV/AIDS and the World Health Organization are required to observe, gather data and produce knowledge about the epidemic. Second, they intervene on the basis of this knowledge, either by themselves or in tandem with other international organisations, states and non-governmental organisations, in order to manage and administer the epidemic effectively (Elbe, 2005: 407; UN S/PV.4087; UN S/RES/1308).

Crucially, however, Elbe also notes that the knowledge produced about HIV/AIDS functions biopolitically insofar as it differentiates between groups within the general population and tailors a variable response accordingly: it 'generate[s] new sub-populations by singling out specific risk groups that need to be targeted [for intervention]' (2005: 407). In so doing, HIV/AIDS discourse enacts various distinctions – between the 'healthy' and the 'sick', the 'safe' and the 'at-risk', the 'Western' and the 'African' and so on – that might 'hypothetically ... give rise to a new biopolitical racism'[3] operating through the very security institutions and practices ostensibly tasked with protecting people from the virus (2005: 410). Elbe identifies three ways in which this 'hypothetical' racism might come to disadvantage people with HIV/AIDS: through quarantine, through the outright refusal of treatment to those in need of it and through the selective administering of treatment to some groups at the expense of others. All of these options function as part of a biopolitical rationality that, having demarcated a division between the 'healthy' population on the one hand and the 'sick' on the other, seeks to secure the former from the threat of infection by the latter. People living with HIV/AIDS, then, might for Elbe 'hypothetically' be abjected from the population to be secured, in the process legitimising measures that expose them to the increased risk – or even certainty – of death.

Elbe's analysis explores the ways in which HIV/AIDS has been – and might continue to be – (bio)politicised at the highest level of international and transnational politics. Yet the Security Council's adoption of a 'broader security agenda' encompassing HIV/AIDS in 2000 did not emerge *ex nihilo*: while Elbe highlights the potentially racist measures that could result from the incorporation of HIV/AIDS into international security discourse, it is not only in this high-political context that biopolitical lines of division are produced (cf. Evans, 2010: 416–417). The classification of populations into separate groups (and the consequent legitimisation of targeted security, administrative or control measures) is a technique that can also be understood as the extension of an epidemiological discourse that in no small part has established and defined what HIV/AIDS signifies in the contemporary world (Patton, 1996; Waldby, 2004: 8). Biopolitics does not necessarily materialise with a securitising speech act, then, but is also integral to how HIV/AIDS has been biomedically constituted from the very moment at which it was first perceived. To take the January 2000 meeting of the UN Security Council as a starting point, as Elbe does, thus potentially obscures the ways in which biopolitical techniques might have operated as part of the discourses and logics that produced the virus as an object of scientific and political concern in the first place.

In this section I will therefore show how all three of Elbe's 'hypothetical' biopolitical security responses to HIV/AIDS – quarantine, refusal of treatment and selective treatment to some demographics but not to others – were in operation from the very start of the epidemic. These measures represent an extension of the epidemiological discourse that 'discovered', named, defined and claimed to 'know' HIV/AIDS during the 1980s and beyond. From the beginning, then, HIV/AIDS has been produced as an entity from which the health of a 'general population' must be secured by estranging or abjecting certain other demographics from that population (Foucault, 1998: 138; 2003b: 241). I will first discuss how epidemiological logic might lend itself to a biopolitical approach to the management of health and sickness, before considering each of Elbe's three 'hypothetical' security measures in turn in order to show how it actually *did* so in the United States from the very start of the crisis.

Epidemiology and biopolitics

Despite its popular associations with apocalyptic visions of contagion, uncertainty and fear, in etymological terms the word 'epidemic' simply means 'more cases than expected of a particular illness'. An epidemic is thus an irregularity: a departure from whatever is considered to be the typical, usual, 'natural' or 'normal' rate of infection. As the study of epidemics, however, epidemiology is concerned not merely with detecting curiosities in the medical record, but also with ascribing causes, identifying segments of the population more at risk than others and prescribing measures for control and containment. Heyward and Curran, two Centers for Disease Control (CDC) scientists involved in the epidemiological study of HIV/AIDS throughout the 1980s, define their field of enquiry as follows:

> The discovery of the epidemic, the enumeration of the varied manifestations of HIV infection and the analysis of the circumstances that made it possible for such an infection to spread have been missions assigned to epidemiology: the study of the occurrence and distribution of disease ... [enable] epidemiologists [to] ... identify the population groups that are at greatest risk of acquiring AIDS and thereby develop strategies for the prevention and control of the disease.
>
> *(1988: 72)*

Epidemiology is thus the biopolitical science *par excellence*, for three reasons. First, it takes as its object of study biological life: in particular, health and sickness (cf. Foucault, 1998: 139). Second, by attempting to work out the occurrence and distribution of disease, epidemiology by definition operates at the level of the population rather than the individualised, compartmentalised body of disciplinary power (cf. Foucault, 2003b: 245; 1991). And third, epidemiology not only produces knowledge about the prevalence, distribution and spread of certain diseases within certain populations, but also seeks to act upon this knowledge in order to 'control' any outbreaks and secure a particular, 'normal', 'natural' or 'optimal' state of life (cf. Foucault, 2003b: 246).

The measures taken in order to achieve these goals can take any number of forms: for example, though one might choose to 'control' or 'manage' a hereditary condition by providing appropriate treatments, funding additional research and so on, one might also choose to do so through enforced sterilisation, or even euthanasia. It is at the level of ethics and politics that the decision between these different avenues must be made: both are epidemiologically valid, and both have been advocated for by epidemiologists at different times and in different places.[4] The epidemiological identification of certain groups at 'high risk' of infection or illness thus maps neatly onto a biopolitical logic that seeks to abject certain groups from a general population in need of protection. In order to manage and control a disease, an epidemiological rationality may well demand the management and control of demographics deemed to be infected or at risk of infection.

Catherine Waldby notes precisely this conflation of condition and person-living-with-condition in the context of HIV/AIDS. She begins her book *AIDS and the Body Politic* by observing the militaristic character of epidemiological language and rhetoric: diseases 'infiltrate' or 'attack' bodies that 'battle' against them, backed up by a scientific establishment that 'fights' or 'combats' the spread of illness through the development of vaccines or cures (2004: 1, 16–17). While scientific and biomedical discourses tend to place themselves on one side of the metaphorical battlefield and the virus itself on the other, however, Waldby sees things differently: the sexualised, gendered and raced elements of both HIV/AIDS discourse *and* the epidemiological knowledge that has in part constituted it as an object of concern muddy and confuse any attempted distinction between the virus itself and those bodies or groups perceived to carry it (2004: 3–4). For Waldby, HIV/AIDS cannot be thought of as separate from these bodies and groups: as such, she claims, the so-called 'war against AIDS' can often be seen to take the form of a war against people living with AIDS, or against groups perceived epidemiologically to be at high risk of contracting the HIV virus (2004: 8–13). Max Navarre, a founding member of the PWA [People With AIDS] Coalition, exasperatedly testifies to precisely this: 'I am a person with a condition', he insists. 'I am not that condition' (1987: 143).

In the case of HIV/AIDS, then, efforts to soften the impact of the crisis on affected communities and care for those affected by the disease have co-existed with epidemiological-biopolitical practices that have marginalised and dislocated people living with AIDS – or people perceived to be 'carriers' or vectors of the HIV virus, regardless of their actual status – from a population whose continued 'health' or 'security' must be assured. In so doing, certain attitudes and practices are legitimised that muddy the distinction between condition and person-with-condition and in so doing increase the risk of sickness and/or death for those perceived to be carriers, or vectors of infection. These measures for 'controlling' the epidemic can be seen to include the three biopolitical responses identified by Elbe as 'hypothetical' consequences of the securitising discourse of the UN. I will look at each, briefly, in turn, before moving on to consider how people with HIV/AIDS themselves 'operated' within and on this biopolitical terrain.

Quarantine

The logical outcome of testing is a quarantine of those infected.
(Helms quoted in Crimp, 1987a: 8)

Senator Jesse Helms' call for a quarantine of all people recording a positive HIV test neatly illustrates the way in which an epidemiological concern with the prevalence and administration of disease within a population can complement biopolitical measures differentiating between particular demographic groups. Quarantining people with HIV was a not-uncommon suggestion for managing the epidemic throughout the 1980s, supported by conservative politicians such as Helms and William Dannemeyer (Meyer, 2003: 138; H.R.5638; H.R.345), as well as by pressure groups claiming to represent 'family values'[5] and on occasion the popular press (cf. Patton, 1985: 85). For these voices, and others like them, the 'logical outcome' of epidemiological investigation into HIV/AIDS was to abject people recording positive test results from society altogether. Such measures sought rhetorically, socio-politically and physically to dislocate people living with HIV from a general, 'healthy' population perceived to be placed at risk by the mere presence of the virus within communities.

Helms' calls for a quarantine of people with HIV/AIDS did not lead to widespread 'AIDS camps', though they did exist:

HIV-positive Haitian asylum seekers were kept in Guantánamo Bay for as long as eighteen months while their applications were processed (Paik, 2013; *AUOHP* interview with Betty Williams). Yet even if an official, universal quarantine was never enacted in law, its spectre hung over the lives of American people who had tested positive for HIV throughout much of the first decade of the crisis. The association between punitive measures like these and a positive test result cultivated a deep suspicion towards testing itself – a mistrust exacerbated by the persistent possibility that the anonymity of those getting tested or the confidentiality of their results might be conceded or compromised. People living with HIV/AIDS themselves were consistently firm in their calls for the federal government to guarantee confidentiality and/or anonymity, a demand made in a number of documents and statements including the 1983 'Denver Principles', the 1985 'Patient's Bill of Rights' and a 1990 ACT UP handbook (PWA Coalition, 1987a, 1987b; ACT UP, 1990). Yet despite this pressure, legislation introduced on the subject tended to recommend the opposite: that results be passed to state or federal health officials.[6] As a result, Gay Men's Health Crisis (GMHC), one of the earliest and most important HIV/AIDS-related pressure groups and care-providing organisations in New York City, was sufficiently concerned about the prospect of quarantine to advise people *not* to test themselves for HIV at all (Epstein, 1996: 242).

In this way, the threat of a mass quarantine impacted upon the experiences of people with HIV/AIDS or those perceived to be at high risk of contracting the virus even without such a measure being explicitly and formally enacted. Even if quarantine itself was never formally enacted on a large scale, however, 'quarantine logic' – the attempt to enact an impermeable boundary between those perceived to be 'contagious' and an 'innocent', 'healthy' population – was widespread. HIV-positive children were prevented from enrolling in or attending schools. Activists taking part in AIDS-related actions were met by policemen wearing masks and bright yellow rubber gloves (Crimp with Rolston, 1990: 20; Patton, 1990: 131). And in its verdict on the case of Edwin Meese, the Justice Department affirmed that employers could sack employees with HIV/AIDS if they feared there might be the possibility of the disease spreading – regardless of whether such fears were grounded in an understanding of how the virus was actually transmitted or not (Bersani, 1987: 201; Crimp with Rolston, 1990: 33).

Measures like these, in common with the calls for a mass quarantine, constituted people with HIV/AIDS (or those perceived to carry the virus, like gay men, intravenous drug users, sex workers, Haitians, Africans and so on) as threats who had to be kept at a remove from the 'healthy', uninfected population. Importantly, none of these responses displayed any interest whatsoever in the health or well-being of people living with HIV/AIDS themselves. Instead, they were concerned with creating impassable boundaries between 'healthy' and 'sick', in order to ensure that an 'innocent' population without AIDS could not be endangered by those perceived to be harbouring the HIV virus.

Refusal of treatment

> Remember 1988, 1990, 1992 – NYC literally had hospital gridlock, and that was when they were keeping people out on hospital gurneys in the hallways. That was when people were not being fed, bathed or touched. It was horrendous. You can't imagine what it was like to be black, gay, a drug user, transgender, and dying from AIDS.
>
> (Cyler, 2002: 355)

In epidemiological terms, to refuse to treat people living with HIV/AIDS can be read as an attempt to manage the epidemic by allowing the infected population to die off, in so doing rendering the virus itself extinct. Implicit within this logic, of course, is the assumption that the 'healthy' population would be better off *without* the sick. In harmony with the rationale for quarantine, then, to refuse treatment is to refuse to place any value in the well-being of people living with HIV/AIDS, instead 'let[ting] them die' in order to secure a 'healthy' population from which they have been dislocated and of which they are not – and cannot be – a part.

One can identify three ways in which a logic of refusal was in operation during the early years of the HIV/AIDS crisis. Keith Cyler's testimony at the beginning of this section describes the first of these, namely the outright denial of treatment by medical professionals. In addition to the experiences reported by Cyler, Tamar W. Carroll reports that some people with HIV/AIDS didn't even get as far as the hospital corridor: a number of private hospitals in New York City refused to admit AIDS patients altogether, while the company Galaxy Carpet Mills denied medical insurance benefits to any person with HIV/AIDS in its employ who had contracted the virus 'voluntarily' (2015: 139, 160, 234).

Yet while some people with HIV/AIDS were literally and directly refused treatment on the 'frontline' of the healthcare system – left to lie on gurneys in corridors or at home, remaining unfed, unwashed, untouched and/or uninsured – others were refused support more indirectly by the political apathy, passivity and silence in which the epidemic drifted. Often presented as a disease that only affected already marginalised groups like homosexual men, drug users and people of colour,[7] HIV/AIDS was able to be presented to an implicitly straight, white public as a marginal issue. As such, Ronald Reagan was able to disregard the HIV/AIDS crisis throughout the entirety of his first term in office, first mentioning the condition publicly in a news conference in September 1985, over four years after the June 1981 CDC report, three after the term AIDS had been coined, and after more than ten thousand people had died in the United States alone.[8]

Reagan's reticence was not unique. As Deborah Gould says: 'In the early years of the AIDS epidemic, both parties [Republican and Democrat] at all levels of government responded to the health crisis with a deafening silence' (2009: 11). It is this 'deafening silence' that causes Randy Shilts to argue in ... *And the Band Played On*, that 'by the time America paid attention to the disease, it was too late to do anything about it ... the first five years of AIDS in America is a drama of ... needless death' in which it was hoped the crisis would disappear, as if by magic, all by itself (1988: xxi–xxiii).

Even when measures were taken to provide resources and support to help respond to the epidemic, however, certain conditions could be attached that made it more difficult for certain groups to obtain the information or treatment they needed, and this can be seen to be a third way in which the response to HIV/AIDS operated according to a biopolitical logic of refusal. In 1987, for example, a federal appropriations bill was tabled earmarking almost a billion dollars for AIDS research and education – by far the most financially significant statement of political support for the fight against the epidemic up to that point (H.R.3058; Crimp, 1987b: 259).

However, Senator Jesse Helms introduced an amendment designed to restrict the ways in which this federal money could be used:

> Purpose: To prohibit the use of any funds provided under this Act to the Centers for Disease Control from being used to provide AIDS education, information, or prevention materials and activities that promote, encourage, or condone homosexual sexual activities or the intravenous use of illegal drugs.[9]

Because much of the preventative work being done at the time by organisations like the Shanti Project in San Francisco and GMHC in New York City involved working *with* gay men and drug users, through promoting safer sex practices, establishing needle exchanges and so on, this amendment – passed ninety-four in favour to two against – had the effect of refusing support to the very people and organisations already working to reduce the rate of infection through the dissemination of 'information … materials and activities', and whose efforts had in many cases already been shown to have been successful in slowing the rate of infection.

While Helms' amendment might not have directly refused treatment to people with HIV/AIDS, then, it nevertheless – in its refusal to 'condone' homosexuality or drug use – sought to expel or displace these groups from the broader population. It did this by rendering certain practices invisible and unspeakable: ideas about how a gay man might face the AIDS crisis *as a gay man*, for example, were silenced. Gay and/or drug-using people with HIV/AIDS could only receive support by accepting 'education' or 'prevention materials' that refused to acknowledge or 'condone' their practices. They could not receive – were refused – help, material or education as gay men, or as drug users. In this respect the Helms Amendment, just like the political silence that preceded it, represents a biopolitical refusal of treatment by, in Cindy Patton's words, 'criminalis[ing] messages in dissident vernaculars', and in so doing silencing or rendering invisible the voices and experiences of a large number of people living with HIV/AIDS (Patton, 1990: 55).

Selective treatment

The type of conditional support for people with HIV/AIDS characteristic of Helms' amendment, as well as similar measures such as Section 28 in the United Kingdom, can be seen to signify not only a refusal of education and/or treatment but also its selective availability. In making funding for preventative materials and education programmes available to, say, a family organisation advocating abstinence, but not a community group trying to set up a needle exchange, or a health organisation hoping to distribute condoms, Helms' amendment illustrates the ways in which a biopolitical response to AIDS might attempt to organise its administration of a particular epidemic along particular normative lines. Such measures function by drawing boundaries or limits that preclude some people from receiving treatment or support while granting that right to others.

Perhaps the most consequential instance of epidemiological-biopolitical selectivity can be seen in the way in which the epidemiological 'discovery' of AIDS assumed certain demographic associations and correlations which framed the classification and demarcation of what AIDS actually was, and which thus determined who could have access to medical and social support, and who could not. AIDS was given an official 'definition' by the CDC in 1982, and it was this definition that guided not only diagnoses, but also treatment, medicine and welfare (which was in most cases covered by insurance only after such a diagnosis had been made). Yet certain biomedical concerns – in particular, the initial epidemiological focus on gay men – served to ensure that treatment and support was not universally available.

Until 1991, to be diagnosed with AIDS required not only seropositive status, but also the presence of certain opportunistic infections. These illnesses, however, had been chosen in the wake of epidemiological investigations with a specific demographic emphasis: as Marion Banzhaf observes, 'the [CDC] definition had been arbitrarily developed through an observational, systematised collection of diseases that were being seen in gay men alone' (*AUOHP* interview with Marion Banzhaf, 74). This meant that much more was known about the experiences of men with AIDS than those of other demographics, for whom the 'official' disease profile associated with the syndrome was frequently unrepresentative.

This had grave consequences: in women, for example, AIDS often leads to gynaecological infections, including cervical cancer (Shotwell, 2014; *AUOHP* interviews with Terry McGovern, 24–26;

with Maxine Wolfe; 81–97; with Heidi Dorow, 44–57). However, it was not until 1993 that such infections were added to the official CDC definition (Carroll, 2015: 151). This meant that many American women with AIDS during the 1980s and early 1990s faced a great deal of difficulty in receiving a diagnosis, which in turn made it impossible to access medical, social and financial support. As a result, they died far more quickly than men: as Banzhaf argues, with a focus on social welfare provision, 'If you got an AIDS case definition, you were entitled to benefits, social security disability benefits – and without that AIDS case definition, you didn't have that, and it could literally mean the difference between life and death' (*AUOHP* interview with Marion Banzhaf, 75). The same was true of medical care: without a diagnosis, insurers would not pay for treatment, and this inevitably hugely disadvantaged the women with AIDS who were not displaying the official CDC symptoms (Carroll, 2015: 133). The epidemiological focus on certain population groups, in other words, perpetuated the invisibility and silence of those groups not considered to be affected by the disease, in such a way that their risk of death increased.

Even after diagnosis, treatment and support were heavily dependent on other factors, including class and race. In October 1988, *Scientific American* reported that as many as one in five HIV/AIDS patients had no health insurance at all, while four in ten relied on Medicaid, a proportion four times the national average (Fineberg, 1988: 133–134). Those without comprehensive insurance or the means to afford it, or who needed access to medicines at an earlier stage in the development of their condition than their insurers would allow, were thereby in effect denied treatment. This situation was hugely exacerbated by the crippling cost of the drugs – AZT, the first drug for AIDS made available, was priced at eight thousand to ten thousand dollars per year – as well as the uneven provision of healthcare.[10] As Donald Grove stated in his plenary speech at the ACT UP ten-year anniversary conference, 'When AZT was all the rage, it began to look as though it might actually be contributing to mortality among men of colour – but then the studies came out which showed that it wasn't AZT which was lethal, it was the shitty healthcare which existed for people of colour in their communities' (1997).

These economic divisions were (and are) amplified on a global scale: as Steven Epstein asks, 'in countries that spent only a handful of dollars per capita on health care in a year, what, then, was the likelihood that *any* antiretroviral therapy developed in the West would actually see widespread use?' (1996: 325, emphasis in original). The global (un)availability and (in)accessibility of AIDS treatment and HIV prevention materials continues to be an issue with devastating consequences for millions of people. The dynamics of in- and exclusion on which biopolitical 'racism' depends are thus multiple and transversal – apparent in the global governance of HIV/AIDS as well as in the American-centric epidemiological discourses through which the virus and syndrome have been produced as objects of concern. In both instances, the emphasis is on preserving, maintaining or fortifying a particular vision of 'life' defined not only by the protection of physical health but also by particular gendered, raced and sexualised norms. 'Health', in other words, comes to look like a straight, white, 'family man' (cf. Haraway, 2013; Patton, 1990; Waldby, 2004).

ACT UP, physical parasitism and humour

ACT UP

By the mid-to-late 1980s, AIDS-related illnesses had claimed thousands of lives. Urban communities in the United States, especially but by no means solely those of gay men and drug users in the big coastal cities, were being devastated. The threat of quarantine lingered, and prospects concerning the development of new medicines, the improvement of care facilities and the allocation of additional resources to help combat the epidemic looked bleak. Activist Vito Russo, speaking at a rally in Albany in May 1988, delivered a speech that encapsulated the mood of many:

> Living with AIDS is like living through a war which is happening only for those people who happen to be in the trenches. Every time a shell explodes, you look around and you discover that you've lost more of your friends – but no-one else notices. It isn't happening to them. They're walking the streets as though we weren't living through some sort of nightmare … [Actually,] it's worse than a war. Because during a war, people are united, in a shared experience. This war has not united us, it's divided us. It's separated those of us with

AIDS and those of us who fight for people with AIDS, from the rest of the population.
(Original footage of this speech can be found in Wentzy, 2002)

Russo's sense of invisibility, his sense that AIDS-related deaths were going unnoticed and uncared for, his sense of being 'separated' as a person living with HIV/AIDS from 'the rest of the population', all indicate the social and emotional consequences not only of the biopolitical abjection of people living with HIV/AIDS from society more broadly, but also of the invisibility attendant upon that dislocation ('no-one else notices. It isn't happening to them'). It was in this context that ACT UP was formed. On 10 March 1987, writer and activist Larry Kramer spoke at the New York Lesbian and Gay Center, calling for a new movement that would noisily and angrily place AIDS in the public consciousness and on the political agenda (Hubbard, 2012). ACT UP had its first meeting that same week, and by the end of the month had adopted its name and slogan: 'ACT UP! Fight back! Fight AIDS!' (*AUOHP* interview with Ron Goldberg, 59).

Proclaiming 'Silence = Death' on its placards, ACT UP asserted that the abject 'separat[ion] ... from the rest of the population' noted by Russo was not only emotionally unbearable and politically unconscionable, but also contributed to the deepening of the crisis in medical terms. The group thus understood HIV/AIDS as a biopolitical problem: as a site at which biomedical and political dynamics intersected and intertwined in such a way that 'silence' and 'death' were equivalent. The abjection of those living with HIV/AIDS from 'the rest of the population' was thus not merely a problem of (in)equality, inclusion and/or (in)justice: it was also key to producing the conditions necessary for the epidemic to perpetuate itself, or worsen.

A crucial part of ACT UP's strategy for combating HIV/AIDS was thus to problematise and destabilise the forces working to 'inscribe and reinscribe the ineluctable ... difference that reassure[d] a shifting "general public" that it [wa]s not subject to [the virus or syndrome]' and could therefore safely ignore the crisis ('they're walking the streets as though we weren't living through some sort of nightmare') (Patton, 1990: 55; see also Watney in Michaels, 1990: 16). By challenging these boundary-drawing practices – practices that constituted people living with HIV/AIDS as dangerous and contagious others, lingering threateningly outside the biopolitically constituted borders of 'healthy' or 'normal' society – the group also sought to transform what it meant to live with the virus or syndrome, or to be a member of a so-called 'high-risk population'.

ACT UP thus worked to produce the person living with HIV/AIDS as a visible, audible subject – and in particular, as a subject who could participate in, influence and frame biomedical, political and popular discourses concerning her own condition, including those that contributed to the formulation and development of strategies for its prevention and treatment.[11] This insistence on the involvement of people living with HIV/AIDS in the medical and political decisions that affected them demanded the re-evaluation not only of what it meant to live with the virus or syndrome but also of the biopolitical logic by which the contagion of the abject 'person with AIDS' had hitherto been produced.

ACT UP's readiness to 'fight back', then, signified an intention to ensure that the person living with HIV/AIDS could emerge from the obscure and silent realm in which she had previously dwelled, and come instead to occupy an entirely new subject position. To refuse 'silence' was therefore a key part of ACT UP's strategy for resisting 'death': it opened up the space from which the group could 'operate' on a political terrain previously defined by their inaudibility and invisibility; by their biopolitical dislocation from the population more generally.

Physical parasitism

ACT UP demanded the 'resignification' of what it meant to live with HIV/AIDS. As Judith Butler says, speaking of the reclamation of the word 'queer' in the context of the HIV/AIDS epidemic:

> this is the politicization of abjection in an effort to rewrite the history of the term, and to force it into a demanding *resignification* [emphasis added]. Such a strategy, I suggest, is crucial to creating the kind of community in which surviving with AIDS becomes more possible, in which queer lives become legible, valuable, worthy of support, in which passion, injury, grief, aspiration become recognized without fixing the terms of that recognition in yet another conceptual order of lifelessness and rigid exclusion.
>
> *(2011: xxviii–xxix)*

What was at stake in ACT UP's desire to 'fight back', then, was not simply a rearrangement of a pre-existing hierarchy; a reshuffle of where at the table particular people or groups got to sit. Rather, it was about 'resignification': about enlisting the very terms or identities that effected a particular inscription of abject illegibility or dislocation ('queer', 'person with AIDS') in the service of resisting it. Yet how was this resignification effected? Butler continues:

> The increasing theatricalisation of political rage in response to the killing inattention of public policy-makers on the issue of AIDS is allegorized in the recontextualisation of 'queer' from its place within a homophobic strategy of abjection and annihilation to an insistent and public severing of that interpellation from the effect of shame. To the extent that shame is produced as the stigma not only of AIDS, but also of queerness, where the latter is understood through homophobic causalities as the 'cause' and 'manifestation' of the illness, theatrical rage is part of the public resistance to that interpellation of shame.
>
> *(2011: 178)*

Butler here notes the extent to which the discursive 'recontextualisation' of such signifiers as 'queer' (or 'person with AIDS') was effected by the theatrical tactics used in specific actions by groups like ACT UP to achieve their goals. ACT UP member Maxine Wolfe describes the group's approach:

> There was this whole idea that you would do what you had to do to get in somewhere, and that you would get into it; you wouldn't be on the outside looking in, asking people to take your leaflet but you would be demanding that people pay attention to what you had to say and taking over spaces where people would not expect that you could get in.
>
> *(Quoted in Somella, n.d.; see also Gould, 2009: 197–198; Greenberg, 1992; Sawyer, 2002; Strub, 2008; and the AUOHP interviews with Maria Maggenti, 7, 19 and with Larry Kramer, 17)*

ACT UP actions, then, involved not simply the discursive 'recontextualisation' of the word 'queer' or the phrase 'people with AIDS', but also the physical recontextualisation of queer bodies or the bodies of people living with HIV/AIDS into the very spaces that had previously worked to produce their abject silence and invisibility. The first ACT UP action, on 24 March 1987, involved a sit-in on Wall Street to protest pharmaceutical profiteering at the expense of people living with HIV/AIDS: three hundred to four hundred bodies, many queer, many living with HIV/AIDS, 'recontextualised' themselves within the deeply homophobic centre of American finance, presenting themselves at the symbolic heart of a money industry that they believed saw people living with HIV/AIDS as consumer-contributors to a balance sheet, rather than as living people with particular needs and desires (*AUOHP* interview with Michael Petrelis, 25–29; see also Sellars, 2016). Subsequent actions functioned according to a similar logic, including the occupations at the National Institutes of Health (*AUOHP* interviews with Brian Zabcik, 35–60; with Mark Harrington, 43–45, 55), the Food and Drug Administration (Eigo et al., 1988; see also *AUOHP* interviews with Maria Maggenti, 18; with Gregg Bordowitz, 21–32; with David Barr, 32–38), the Fifth International AIDS conference in Montreal (*AUOHP* interviews with Peter Staley, 53–54; with Mark Harrington, 51–57) and New York's St Patrick's Cathedral (DIVA TV Collective, 1990; see also *AUOHP* interviews with Victor Mendolia, 16–24; with Tom Keane, 16–27). Perhaps most movingly, on 11 October 1992, a number of ACT UP activists scattered the ashes of loved ones dead from AIDS-related illness over the fence onto the lawn of the White House (Wentzy, 1992; see also *AUOHP* interview with David Robinson, 58–64).

Although these actions had different targets, different strategic aims and any number of tactical idiosyncrasies, they nevertheless exemplify what I call 'physical parasitism', referring to the physical recontextualisation of queer bodies, bodies with AIDS or bodies perceived to be such – including the burned ashes of bodies dead from AIDS-related illness – into spaces that had previously produced and/or symbolised their abjection from political, biomedical or popular discourse and decision making. Such recontextualisations demand the resignification of the bodies in question, posing a performative challenge to the illegibility, invisibility or inaudibility of people with AIDS and insisting that their subjectivity, agency and identity be recognised.

These recontextualisations also effected, in Butler's words, an 'insistent and public severing' of people living with HIV/AIDS from any effect of shame or guilt, producing as they did subjects who did not hide away, but who could instead publicly – even theatrically – stage and perform their desires and struggles, as part of 'kiss-ins' or 'die-ins', for example (cf. Butler, 2011: 178). Mark

Lowe Fisher, writing shortly before his death to request a public, open-coffin funeral in front of the White House, rationalised this macabre but powerful recontextualisation of his own (dead) body in precisely these terms: 'we are dying because of a government and a healthcare system that couldn't care less. I want to show the reality of my death, to display my body in public. I want the public to bear witness. We are not just spiralling statistics, we are people who have lives, who have purpose, who have lovers, friends and families' (quoted in Wentzy, 2002).

In this action, and in others like it, ACT UP enacted encounters between their own abject bodies and the 'normal' or 'healthy' population from which they had been excluded. Moreover, by intruding into such spaces, ACT UP activists made performative claims to political selfhood. Rather than accepting their assigned status as passive or silent victims of the disease, ACT UP instead sought to force open cracks in the biopolitical strategies of control through which they and their condition were governed. In the process, they enacted alternative subjective spaces in which people living with HIV/AIDS could 'operate' productively and creatively in the political processes surrounding the crisis.

In sustaining these parasitic encounters, ACT UP drew on an extremely broad emotional and affective register. For example, the sorrow and grief evident in the public funerals and ash-scattering actions were frequently shot through with rage, as evidenced by the group's slogan that they were 'united in anger'. It is perhaps for this reason that the role of humour in ACT UP's activism has been frequently glossed over or overlooked. A number of ACT UP activists have bemoaned this oversight, noting the importance of laughter, humour and comic practice to the movement's tactics and day-to-day operating (Greenberg, 1992). As Alan Klein testifies: 'the other thing that ACT UP gave all of us was ... a whole lot of humour. Nobody ever talks about the humour' (*AUOHP* interview with Alan Klein, 33).

For some, this was a way to consolidate internal solidarity and relieve the burden of pain, anger and loss that accompanied so much of the group's work. According to Douglas Crimp, for example, 'ACT UP's humour is no joke. It has given us the courage to maintain our exuberant sense of life while every day coping with disease and death, and it has defended us against the pessimism endemic to other left movements, from which we have otherwise taken so much' (Crimp with Rolston, 1990: 20). This assessment is echoed by other former members of the group, including Ron Goldberg, Tom Keane, David Robinson, Jeanne Kracher and Maxine Wolfe (*AUOHP* interviews with Ron Goldberg, 48; with Tom Keane, 32–33; with David Robinson, 28; with Maxine Wolfe, 111; Jeanne Kracher quoted in Gould, 2009: 196–197). Yet for others, humour was also an important component of the group's tactical approach: as Anna Blume claims, the group was always looking for 'the freshness of irreverence' in its actions (*AUOHP* interview with Anna Blume, 16–17). Benjamin Shepard similarly asserts that a key component of ACT UP's approach was its recognition of 'the subversive effectiveness of a joke' (2002: 13), while Deborah Gould, meanwhile, acknowledges not only that 'the movement was awash with campy humour', but also that this humour spilled outwards and was projected beyond the group through their actions and demonstrations (2009: 196–197). As such, 'ACT UP's direct action and protests frequently combined the serious with the humourous … ACT UP's street theatre often included scathing and comical satires of people we were targeting, along with lots of drag, sexual innuendo, and jokes … participants sometimes injected queer sensibilities and humour into the most unreceptive of places' (2009: 197–199).

This comic 'street theatre' took many forms. At an October 1989 demonstration in Chicago, activists wheeled out a 'Freedom Bed', on which a series of people, couples and groups would perform safer-sex skits and sketches, all the while fighting off the occasional intrusion from co-performers in costume as Supreme Court justices or anti-gay, AIDS-inactive political figures such as Senator Jesse Helms, President George (H.W.) Bush and others (Gould, 2009: 197). For a more extended period in the early 1990s the Church Ladies for Choice, a (mixed-gender) drag troupe made up mostly of ACT UP members, counter-protested far-right abortion clinic protests. The Church Ladies, always dressed in Sunday best, aimed both to undermine the 'realness' of the earnest anti-abortion groups next to whom they stood, as well as to provide support to women trying to enter the clinics in question by helping them through picket lines (Carroll, 2015: 169–171; Cohen-Cruz, 2002; *AUOHP* interview with Steve Quester, 17, 33–35). At the December 1989 'Stop the

Church' action against Cardinal John O'Connor, disruption within the church coincided with a costumed parade outside, including a twenty-foot, helium-filled rubber emblazoned with the slogan 'Cardinal O'Condom' and clowns throwing regular condoms like confetti, while bearded activist Ray Navarro interviewed participants for ACT UP's in-house DIVA TV in costume and character as Jesus (France, 2012; Stoller, 1998: 126–127). Graphic design collective Gran Fury made good use of puns and innuendo in their slogans and on their placards, highly visible at almost every ACT UP action ('Know Your Scumbags'; 'Men: Use Condoms or Beat It'), while the group's contribution to the June 1987 Stonewall anniversary parade was a float parodically decked out as a quarantine camp, complete with guards in gloves and masks and a laughing Ronald Reagan behind the wheel (Crimp with Rolston, 1990: 34–35; *AUOHP* interviews with Maria Maggenti, 16; with Bill Dobbs, 26–27).

It is these actions, and others like them, that lead Adrienne Christiansen and Jeremy Hanson to analyse ACT UP *in toto* through a 'comic frame' (1996). Not all of ACT UP's actions can comfortably be seen through this lens – it is unclear how Christiansen and Hanson would incorporate the ash-scattering action within their evaluation, for example. Nevertheless, it is clear that humour played an important role in both the group's internal dynamics and its tactical methodology. An important question to ask, then, is *how* humour might relate (or not) to the recontextualising and resignifying practices constitutive of physical parasitism. In order to answer this question I will look at a particular action, namely the 1991 stunt in which members of ACT UP's TAG draped a huge inflatable condom over the house of Senator Jesse Helms.

Jesse Helms and the condom

> If they would keep their mouths shut, and go about their business – whatever their sexual orientation is – nobody would ever say a word and we wouldn't know anything about them. But no, they march in the streets.
>
> *(Quoted in France, 2012)*

> this tiny criminal band [in the Senate] debates whether these ... audiences can withstand the shock of seeing, or hearing about, or in any

way encountering the terrible satanic device that dare not speak its name: the lowly condom ... The condom has come to be the one sayable thing in a sea of silence, the one do-able intervention in a world of apparent impotence.

(Treichler, 1987: 50–52)

In his call to quarantine people with HIV/AIDS, in his 1988 amendment to the Departments of Labor, Health and Human Services, and Education and Related Agencies Appropriations Act refusing federal funds to any group 'promot[ing], encourag[ing] or condon[ing]' homosexuality, and in his constant and open hostility to gays and lesbians, Jesse Helms was a prominent and powerful thorn in the side of the AIDS movement. In 1991, fed up with Helms' 'consciously stubborn, scornful stance on AIDS policies', the TAG – a new medicine- and drug-focused subcommittee within ACT UP that would eventually disaffiliate itself and operate independently as the Treatment Action Group – decided to target Helms for its very first action (Allen, 2006). Peter Staley, leading TAG, dreamed up the idea of draping an enormous inflatable condom over Helms' house in Arlington, Virginia, and the group set about making plans to execute his proposal.

The reasons behind the action were multiple. First, the condom was symbolic: the so-called 'Helms Amendment' had thwarted contraceptive distribution schemes by denying them federal funding, and so the action sought to bring condoms back into the public eye as an effective method of preventing the transmission of HIV. In this respect (and others), the humour and absurdity of the image was key: for Staley, 'one of the best tools an activist can use is humour. If you can get folks laughing at your target's expense, you diminish his power. I wanted the country to have a good laugh at Helms' expense. I wanted his fellow senators to have a little chuckle behind his back. And I wanted Senator Helms to realise that his free ride was up – if he hit us again, we'd hit back' (2008).

In addition, however, the condom also served as a handy icon for a more positive message: that of safer sex. Discussing the action, activist Jim Serafini stated his hope that the condom's prophylactic qualities might help neutralise and contain Helms himself: 'We need protection against Helms' bigotry and ignorance. Condoms have worked pretty well in protecting against HIV, so we decided to try one on the senator' (quoted in Allen, 2006). Something approaching this sentiment was stencilled onto the condom in large capital letters: 'A CONDOM TO STOP UNSAFE POLITICS. HELMS IS DEADLIER THAN A VIRUS'.

If Helms wanted to secure his own world from intrusion by gays, lesbians, people with HIV/AIDS and their allies, then the condom sought humorously to invert the polarities of who needed protection from whom. If Helms wished to be at a remove from the people he described simply as 'them', then the condom would grant him his wish – but with the caveat that *he* would be the one hushed up and confined, rather than the people he sought to silence from the Senate floor. Trapped within an impermeable latex membrane, his ideas left with nothing to do except to swim fruitlessly round in circles until they expired, the image of Helms within the condom carried a number of messages that resignified the antagonistic relation that existed between him and HIV/AIDS advocates and activists like ACT UP and TAG.

The action itself was well rehearsed, and went smoothly: on a sunny September morning, seven activists emerged from a van and got to work – two climbed atop Helms' roof and began unfurling the condom, while others moved the generator into place and hammered pegs into the ground onto which the condom could be secured (Hilferty and Huff, 1991). Within a couple of minutes the condom was in place and inflated, sheathing the entirety of Helms' home and displaying the slogan. Assembled photographers and journalists looked on, having been informed in advance of what was going on, interspersed with Helms' bemused neighbours. The stunt was featured that night on local and national news outlets, and while Helms scornfully mentioned the incident on the Senate floor, he did not press charges (Allen, 2006; Staley, 2008).

The action's appeal to humour can be seen to have functioned in three – connected – ways, all of which helped to recontextualise and resignify HIV/AIDS, people living with HIV/AIDS and the 'lowly' condom itself. In so doing, the action carved open space from which the activists could 'operate' on and with the biopolitical terrain within which the HIV virus had been constituted as an object of political concern, engaging the abjection and objectification that Helms himself had sought to impose upon lesbians, gays and people living with HIV/AIDS ('if they would keep their mouths shut').

First, the absurdity and humour of the action served to exaggerate the unexpected and dissonant presence of the activists, as well as of the condom itself ('the terrible satanic device that dare not speak its name'). The action recontextualised the condom in two ways: symbolically, by resignifying it as a device for safer thinking about AIDS, but also physically, by sheathing in condom-shaped canvas the house of one of the most fervently homophobic politicians in America; a man who advocated quarantine and who consistently voted to against measures that might have supported people living with HIV/AIDS. Though such an inharmonious intrusion into a particular space (in this case, a private, domestic one) might appear to run the risk of encouraging rancour from those to whom the action is addressed, the use of humour also served the purpose of defusing hostility. Notably, all three primary accounts of the action – by TAG members Allen, Staley and Sean Strub – note that upon arriving, the police found the sight visibly amusing, serving to defuse the conventional, hostile frame of police-activist interaction. As Allen reflected: 'The key to a good demo of this sort is to break the rules enough so people can't help but pay attention to what you're doing, but not ... to the point where people hate you once they start paying attention to you' (Allen, 2006). The provocation of laughter, then, served both as a force multiplier – a way of amplifying the 'noise' generated by the recontextualised symbol and/or body – as well as a way of sustaining the activists' dissonant, parasitic presence, even if only briefly. In the case of this particular action, its absurdity also served to generate media coverage and disseminate the image of the 'condomised' house across the nation, albeit mostly fleetingly and – in some cases – trivially.[12]

Second, the action also contributed to the group's broader goal of resignification. Helms, through his amendment as well as through what he had said on the Senate floor, had attempted to silence both people with HIV/AIDS – who he thought should 'keep their mouths shut' – as well as those seeking to distribute condoms or information about safer sex, who in many cases could no longer receive public money as a result of his legislative interventions. The action, however, recontextualised both people with HIV/AIDS and the condom itself out of the abject void into which Helms had worked to cast them and into a space where they could claim political subjectivity and agency. The stunt, like ACT UP's other actions, performatively constituted activists – and by extension perhaps, people living with HIV/AIDS more widely – as particular types of subject: non-silent, capable of shaping and influencing the political and biomedical management of their condition. In so doing, their action also humorously resignified Helms himself, now symbolically sheathed by a prophylactic that could ensure his dangerous ideas could not be transmitted, while also making the point – the very point that the Helms amendment had silenced – that this containment and protection is precisely what a *real* condom does with the virus.

Third, in performing this comic recontextualisation and resignification, the action also 'operated' on and with the biopolitical-epidemiological terrain upon which the HIV/AIDS crisis had been constituted as an object of scientific, political and popular concern. In refusing to 'keep their mouths shut', and in publicly challenging the ban on federally funded gay sex education, the activists aimed to draw attention to policies and attitudes that Mark Allen described as 'a viable threat to our well-being' (2006). The humorous sensibility behind the action – the intention to produce laughter amongst Helms' peers in the Senate as well as a nationwide audience on TV – served to engage with this abjection in a way that might have been less compelling and more difficult had more 'serious' methods been used. In Allen's words: 'it was an injustice that we felt powerless to meet at Helms's own level so, using a colourful stunt that could work through the media, we recontextualised our defence into a viable communicative form that was readable on many levels' (2006).

The extent to which this stunt was a 'success', however – not to mention what 'success' in this context actually entails – is of course open to debate. For those who participated in the action, it made a powerful statement that, in however brief or small or pithy a way, recontextualised and resignified the fact of living with HIV/AIDS in the face of an overwhelming apparatus of which Helms was a small but not insignificant node. In so doing, it perhaps provides an example of how ACT UP's appeals to humour – including but not limited to this particular action – might have functioned both to cultivate internal cohesion, solidarity and positivity, and as a way performatively to make public claims to political identity, subjectivity and agency.

Don't think being slightly absurd isn't a viable form of real communication: it's often a very powerful one, and sometimes your only viable option when faced with the abyss.

(Allen, 2006)

Conclusion

The importance of humour to ACT UP's way of operating throughout the 1980s and early 1990s can be seen not only in the condom action, but also in numerous other interventions, such as the 'Freedom Bed', the Church Ladies for Choice, the Stop the Church parade, the Stonewall Anniversary Parade float and a number of placards, chants and songs. These actions, though diverse, all make appeals to humour as part of a broader attempt to resignify what it meant to live (and die) with HIV/AIDS in the context of a biopolitical apparatus working to abject people living with HIV/AIDS from a 'healthy' population to be secured from the virus and syndrome. One way in which ACT UP activists sought to effect this resignification was through what I have called 'physical parasitism': the recontextualisation of abject bodies (queer bodies, bodies with AIDS or bodies perceived as such) into the very spaces working to produce their abjection.

ACT UP's actions were often compelling and in many ways startlingly effective: as Larry Kramer has said, when asked which treatments in particular ACT UP helped to make available to HIV-positive Americans, 'All of them. I have no doubt in my mind. Those fucking drugs are out there because of ACT UP. And that's our greatest, greatest achievement – totally' (*AUOHP* interview with Larry Kramer, 27). In relation to the group's appeals to humour and its role in their work more generally, however, three points need to be made.

First, it is important to note that the group did not always choose to adopt a comic register. The 'ashes action' of 1992, for example, might tentatively be read as a 'parasitic' recontextualisation of the (cremated) bodies of people dead from AIDS-related illness into a space hitherto symbolic of their abjection (namely the White House lawn). This recontextualisation not only produced the bodies in question as particular types of body – grieved bodies, loved bodies, visible bodies – but also demanded a resignification of what it meant to live and die with AIDS. However, it was not humour or the production of laughter that framed or sustained this demand for resignification. In this instance, then, it is possible to see one way in which the parasitic way of operating outlined in Chapter 2 exceeds the category of 'humour' or 'comedy'.

Second, the strategic usefulness of the kind of 'street theatre' practised by ACT UP was dependent on many other variables, not all of which were entirely (or even at all) under the control of the participants. The efficacy of the condom action, for example, was dependent on media coverage which the group could not in and of themselves guarantee, while different policing strategies may well have affected the impact of actions like Stop the Church or the 'Freedom Bed'. It is thus important to remember that the impact of these actions was delimited by the political terrain into which they intervened.

Moreover, theatrical actions like these – just like any joke – can become stale. As Staley himself acknowledged, after the condom action, 'we were becoming a broken record ... the public would see the images and just say, "Oh, it's another AIDS demonstration". They wouldn't know the issue ... They wouldn't stop and say, "Oh, my god ..." We had really lost a lot of our uniqueness and the ability to get our message out – and therefore we lost the ability to effect change' (Treatment Action Group, 2002). Shortly after the condom action, TAG split from ACT UP and became the Treatment Action Group, a lobby, advocacy and pressure group working far more cooperatively with the established, institutionalised networks of medical, scientific and political power. According to Staley, at the same time that direct action like the condom stunt ceased to be effective, 'the "inside" work that T+D [Treatment and Data, a precursor to TAG] had gotten so good at ... was becoming a well oiled machine. There was no door that was closed to us anymore' (Treatment Action Group, 2002).

TAG's split from ACT UP marked the extent to which it was felt that the group's humorous, confrontational techniques and practices had lost their efficacy: instead, TAG adopted the 'serious' register of the medical and political establishments and embedded itself within the system that had previously worked to silence and abject them. Yet one might also say that it was – in part – thanks to ACT

UP's attention-grabbing comic street theatre that the doors through which a group like TAG could walk were open.

Third, ACT UP's local focus has served to obscure the global dynamics and consequences of HIV/AIDS. In 2012, Larry Kramer claimed that 'the government didn't get us the drugs, no-one else got us the drugs. We, ACT UP, got those drugs out there' (quoted in France, 2012). This is clearly a powerful victory, and one which has had far-reaching and life-saving consequences. Yet these drugs are far from universally available: as a result, roughly a million-and-a-half people continue to die from AIDS-related illnesses each year, mostly in the global South (UNAIDS, 2016: 2–3). The metaphorical doors may have been open to the mostly male, mostly white, mostly university-educated and entirely American TAG, but they continue to be closed to millions in the global South, for whom access to AIDS medication – or even to preventative measures like condoms – may still seem a long way off (Mbali, 2013). As Mark Harrington acknowledges: 'Treatment activists have won many victories which have extended health and life for thousands of people with HIV, but we have had virtually no impact on AIDS in the developing world, where 80 percent of cases occur' (1997: 283).

Despite ACT UP's successes, it must nevertheless be acknowledged that HIV/AIDS is no less a crisis now than it was then, and that many of those living with the virus or exposed to it remain entirely abjected from the medico-political apparatus that governs and administers the pandemic. States who wish to develop generic versions of HIV/AIDS drugs have been (and continue to be) frustrated by intellectual property laws and aggressive legal action on the parts of pharmaceutical companies. Even amongst the generic drugs that are available, wide variability in price and effectiveness means that distributing them remains a challenge (Boseley, 2016). Those denied treatment in these ways – overwhelmingly in the global South – are biopolitically abjected from a (wealthy, Western) population whose health is deemed to be important enough that medicines *can* be made available. As the South African satirist Pieter-Dirk Uys commented in 2002, 'in the old South Africa we killed people: now we're just letting them die' (quoted in C. Campbell, 2003: 188; cf. Foucault, 1998: 138; 2003b: 241). Didier Fassin quotes a South African person with HIV/AIDS expressing a similar sentiment:

> Most people with HIV are unskilled, uneducated, unemployed. We have no value, we just cost. How will the government benefit from us? The more numerous we are the more problems we cause. If they can get rid of us, there will be less unemployment, less crime, fewer problems. Let them die, they say.
>
> *(2008: 154)*

Although the denialism that marked the Mbeki administration's (non-)response to the HIV/AIDS epidemic is no longer as prominent as it was, universal access to treatment remains an unfulfilled ambition, both in South Africa and more generally around the world. The 2016 International AIDS Conference in Durban focused on this problem, gathering around the theme 'Access Equity Rights Now'. However, equity still seems a long way away. Despite ACT UP's successes on behalf of American and Western people living with HIV/AIDS, both silence and death continue to define the experiences of millions of people living (and dying) with the virus and syndrome. While ACT UP's jokes may have become stale, then, the problems they sought to address have not.

Notes

1 I am writing this footnote in June 2020, in the middle of another pandemic that may well supplant HIV/AIDS as 'the signal pandemic of the global here and now'. Notwithstanding COVID-19, however, Comaroff's sense of HIV/AIDS' centrality to twentieth- and twenty-first-century global narratives about health and sickness remains valid.
2 While acknowledging with Sawyer (2002: 102) that 'a virus recognises no national borders', this initial geographical focus on the United States is nevertheless important because it is from there that much of the epidemiological discourse that initially produced and constructed HIV/AIDS as an object of biopolitical concern derived.
3 The term 'racism' is taken from Foucault's earliest writing on biopolitics in his 1975–1976 lectures (2003b: 254–263). Though Foucault here explains what he means by biopolitical 'racism' with reference to the colonial project on the one hand and Nazi Germany on the other, in his course of 1978–1979 he discusses biopolitics' immanence within a liberal governmentality exemplified as much by neoliberal economic theorists as by nineteenth-century colonial patricians (2008: 21–22). In other words, 'biopolitics' comes to signify a range of mechanisms, technologies and techniques of governance which appear to exceed 'racism'

as understood in Foucault's initial explorations of the subject. In the case of HIV/AIDS, the importance of acknowledging the ways in which a biopolitical analysis might engage with questions of gender, sexuality and class in addition to those of race is made particularly acute by the wealth of queer and feminist writing on the subject (cf. Saalfield and Navarro, 1991; Patton, 1994; Schneider and Stoller, 1995; Haraway, 2013). I use 'racism' in this chapter to indicate a principle of differentiation that sits at the intersection of all these boundaries.

4 In *Women, Race and Class*, Angela Davis discusses the enforced sterilisation of (mostly) poor, black women deemed physically or socially 'unfit' in the United States throughout the early-to-mid twentieth century (Davis, 1983).

5 E.g. an American Family Association petition from winter 1983: 'Dear Family Member, Since AIDS is transmitted primarily by perverse homosexuals, your name on my national petition to quarantine all homosexual establishments is crucial to your family's health and security', quoted in Patton (1985: 85).

6 Mandatory disclosure laws were introduced in South Carolina; numbers testing halved as a result (Powers, 1991: 240). William Dannemeyer, meanwhile, sponsored a bill in 1989 that mandated compulsory, non-confidential testing for prisoners and prospective marriage partners, amongst others, and the maintenance of a database of those receiving a positive result. It was not passed. H.R.3102.

7 See, for example, the notorious *Cosmopolitan* piece entitled 'Reassuring news about AIDS: a doctor tells why you may not be at risk' (Gould, 1988; see also *AUOHP* interview with Maria Maggenti, 25–26; Carlomusto and Maggenti, 1988).

8 Douglas Crimp claims that Reagan's first public reference to AIDS was in 1987, but this press conference in fact precedes it by almost two years. I can find no evidence of any mention of the crisis by Reagan between 1985 and 1987 (Crimp with Rolston, 1990: 33; Reagan, 1985).

9 S.Amdt.963 to H.R.3058. In the end, a handful of small changes were made to Helms' amendment, and the text ultimately voted through read as follows: 'none of the funds made available under this Act to the Centers for Disease Control shall be used to provide AIDS education, information, or prevention materials and activities that promote or encourage, directly or indirectly, homosexual sexual activities' (see also Crimp, 1987b: 264).

10 Initially, AZT was prescribed only to patients who had developed AIDS; HIV-positive patients whose condition had not developed to that extent had no access to the medication unless they could pay for it themselves (Epstein, 1996: 117, 199).

11 The principle that people living with HIV/AIDS should have a stake in the decision-making processes that concerned their condition had, of course, been a pillar of AIDS activism since the 1983 Denver Principles (Crimp with Rolston, 1990: 78; Goldberg, 1998).

12 'The story was reported on the major news channels very briefly, usually with a "what a crazy world!" kind of angle at the end of the program. How could we really expect any serious comments from talking heads considering the tactics we used? Back then news outlets weren't exactly hungry for wacky political action stories with homo-centric leanings' (Allen, 2006).

5

Parodic parasitism: clowning and mass protest

Introduction

Since the late 1970s, economic and political measures including marketisation, privatisation, deregulation and flexibilisation have been continuously recommended as the means by which 'a much more deeply integrated and vibrant world' might be achieved (Griffin, 2015: 212–213; see also Nsouli, 2007; Critchley, 2012: 94–102). The principles underpinning these policies have coalesced into an orthodoxy that proclaims market-led globalisation as an agent of irresistible historical progress. From this perspective, the expansion of market rationality into social, cultural, governmental and international areas of life has enabled a path towards global 'integration' to be both cleared and followed (Nsouli, 2007).

A cacophony of critical and dissenting voices have exposed and explored the limits of this supposedly 'integrated' world, emphasising the states and peoples it has left behind, and the violence and inequity underpinning its vision of global interconnection (e.g. Applebaum and Robinson, 2005; Archibugi, 2004; Doyal, 2010; Fisher, 2009; Gill, 1995; Hurrell and Woods, 1995; Saurin, 1996; Scott, 1997). In addition to this enormous academic literature, however, activists and other popular movements both in the 'West' and the 'global South' have challenged the apparent hegemony of market capitalist ideas, practices and institutions. In Larry Bogad's words, these people and groups have worked 'to oppose the disastrous effects of corporate globalisation while building progressive, constructive, and dialogical connections between the people of the world' (2016: 114).

This loose coalition of groups and blocs – usually described using one of a number of names, including the 'global justice movement' (e.g. Bogad, 2016), the 'movement of movements' (e.g. Harvie, Milburn, Trott et al., 2005; Klein, 2002) or less charitably the 'anti-globalisation movement'[1] – has two intertwining and mutually constitutive purposes. On the one hand, it seeks to challenge the violence that sustains a system in which a handful of national governments claim a global mandate for market-led programmes of development (cf. Blair, 2005). On the other, it attempts to create alternative modes of association and affinity that reach across borders even as they prioritise people's immediate and specific needs.[2] The aim is not to oppose market-led globalisation by doubling down on existing local or national identities, but rather by creatively enacting new alliances and associations both locally and across borders, in ways that elude the disciplinary demands of capital.

In pursuing these goals, many within the movement have looked beyond traditional methods of mass protest in favour of a playful aestheticism and theatricality: what the Trapese Collective call 'cultural activism' (2007; cf. Özden Fırat and Kuryel, 2011a). Cultural activism is located 'where art, activism, performance and politics mingle and interact'; it denotes the incorporation of spectacular elements such as costume, music, street art, theatre, dance, sculpture and puppetry into political action (Trapese Collective, 2007: 172).[3] In so doing, cultural activism foregrounds performance, creativity and imagination as powerful methods of protest and dissent, capable of opening the necessary subjective and intersubjective space from which to 'question the dominant ways of seeing things' (Trapese Collective, 2007: 173). In the context of the 'global justice movement', the sights and sounds produced by cultural activists might therefore be read in two ways. First, in terms of whether and how they fashion a certain affective solidarity or camaraderie among participants. And second, in terms of whether and how they open up cracks or interstices from which to question or contest neoliberal orthodoxy (Özden Fırat and Kuryel, 2011a).

Prominent among the broad palette of practices encompassed by the term 'cultural activism' are those modelled on the tradition of carnival (Notes from Nowhere, 2003: 173–183; Bogad, 2016: 111–154; de Goede, 2005; Özden Fırat and Kuryel, 2011b; Shepard, 2005; Jordan, n.d.; cf. Grindon, 2004). The parallels between late-medieval/early-modern carnival and the 'Carnival of the Oppressed' held in Ogoni, Nigeria in 1999, the 'Carnival against Capitalism' held in London at the same time and the 'Carnival for Full Enjoyment' held in Edinburgh in 2005 should not be overstated (Wiwa, 2003; Schlembach, 2016: 124–128; Hodkinson and Chatterton, 2006: 307). Nevertheless, it remains true that comic and/or ludic practices, including but not limited to carnival, have been particularly important to many of those who have resisted the global prioritisation of capital over people over the past two decades. Groups such as the Yes Men, Billionaires for Bush and the Space Hijackers, among many others, have all sought to engage neoliberal dynamics, logics and practices with wit, verve and irony (Ollman, Price and Smith, 2003; Bogad, 2016: 255–263; Rossdale, 2019). Whether accepting responsibility for the Bhopal disaster in character as an executive of Dow Chemical, stuffing fake banknotes into the pockets of riot cops in order to thank them for suppressing dissent, or buying a second-hand armoured vehicle and trying to sell it at an arms fair, these groups have all placed humour at the heart of their tactical methodologies.

In this chapter, I examine the Clandestine Insurgent Rebel Clown Army (CIRCA), a group operating in the context outlined previously. In particular, I interrogate their use of parody in order to occupy, appropriate and undermine established, hegemonic subject positions. This is what I call 'parodic parasitism', referring to the ironic performance of specific, existing subjectivities in order to decentre or 'make strange' their privilege (de Goede, 2005). In the case of the Clown Army's parodic militarism, this tactic was designed to highlight the violent practices that enable global capitalism to operate on a day-to-day basis, including the policing of dissent during the mass protests in which the Clown Army took part.

The clown is a quintessential comic subject, intimately involved with processes of social reproduction yet also aloof from society itself (Zijderveld, 1982: 16–17). CIRCA transplanted this subject into (or onto the threshold of) specific political spaces: the police line, the kettle, the occupation, the roadblock, the 'global justice' march and so on. Imitating the militaristic rituals, symbols, practices and knowledges by and through which neoliberal order is maintained and secured, the Clown Army enacted and sustained encounters with the *actual* army (and/or the police) that asked questions of their claims to legitimacy. Drawing on Michel Foucault's examination of the grotesque in his *Abnormal* lectures, as well as on Judith Butler's writings on parody, I will argue that CIRCA's parodic militarism thus worked to problematise the violent forces working to sustain neoliberal hegemony by rendering them clownish or grotesque in their own right.

My argument proceeds in three stages. First, I explore Michel Foucault's ideas about 'grotesque' or 'Ubu-esque' power. Foucault posits a dislocation between power and legitimacy that he explicitly describes as clownish. While Foucault suggests that this dislocation is a necessary part of power's self-image, however, I argue that power's buffoonish, grotesque qualities are not always immediately apparent, but must sometimes be *made* so. Second, I draw upon Judith Butler in order to make the claim that parodic performance can provide an intervention of this sort (though it will also be acknowledged that this is not a function that it performs either unproblematically or by default). I build on Butler's analysis in order to outline the terms of 'parodic parasitism'. Third, I turn to look at CIRCA, and their parodic performances at mass protests in the early 2000s.

If the clown or fool is traditionally thought of as a liminal figure, enacting a troubling and destabilising presence at the boundaries and limits of order, then CIRCA's parodic militarism interruptively operates at and across the physical and symbolic frontiers commonly enacted at mass protests (between 'order' and 'anarchy', 'police' and 'protestor' and so on). CIRCA's parodic clown-soldiers embody the 'imitation characterized by ironic inversion' that exemplifies the parodic impulse (Hutcheon, 2000: 6). In so doing, they performatively draw attention to the grotesque qualities that infuse and underpin the *objects* of their parody: by operating next to and often with the *actual* army and police, they drag them over the footlights and onto the stage, incorporating them into their clownish games.

I conclude by suggesting that parody parasitically intercepts the channels through which knowledge, identity, authority and agency are established, by presenting a recognisable thing in a recognisable manner. It is something like this intuition that underpins Linda Hutcheon's comment that 'parody has often been called parasitic' (2000: 3). While Hutcheon presents the epithet negatively, however, I want (tentatively) to reclaim and repurpose parody's parasitic qualities. In Hutcheon's terms, parody 'de-doxifies': by recontextualising the representations and relations through which order is produced, reproduced and naturalised, it also politicises them, opening space for critique and contestation (1989: 94–95; 2000: 6–8). To rephrase this in Foucault's terms, parody's ironic, imitative inversion might be said to reveal power's buffoonish or grotesque aspect. Yet if clownish modalities of governance can potentially retain their ability to operate effectively despite their manifest illegitimacy, as Foucault claims, then this suggests an important political limitation to the parodic mode of parasitism exemplified by CIRCA.

Grotesque power

Michel Foucault's notion of 'grotesque' or 'Ubu-esque' power posits a discourse, individual, group or system that is able to establish and demonstrate certain relations of domination despite being outwardly unsuitable for the task: 'I am calling "grotesque" the fact that, by virtue of their status, a discourse or an individual can have effects of power that their intrinsic qualities should disqualify them from having' (2003a: 11). Grotesque power is thus power invested in 'someone who [is] theatrically got up and depicted as a clown or a buffoon': a tyrant like Nero or Mussolini, or the eponymous protagonist in Alfred Jarry's *Ubu Roi* (Foucault, 2003a: 13; Jarry, 1968). It preserves its capacity to function – even 'in its full rigour and at the extreme point of its rationality' – despite the fact that it flows through delegitimised discourses, institutions or individuals (2003a: 13).

Foucault emphasises that grotesque power must be located 'in a place that is manifestly, explicitly and readily discredited'. The grotesque is not something hidden from view, but is freely and openly projected outwards from source. Indeed, this is key to its method: grotesque power is able to function effectively, despite its evident despicability, precisely because it is honest about the latter. It cultivates what Foucault would define in his 1980 lecture series as a logic of 'terror':

> Terror is not an art of government the aims, motives and mechanisms of which are hidden. Terror is precisely governmentality in the naked, cynical, obscene state.
>
> *(2014: 15)*

The grotesque modes of governmentality effective in the Roman Imperial court, in Fascist Italy, in Ubu's Poland and elsewhere do not hide their arbitrariness, their pettiness or their disproportionality. Indeed, the obedience they seek to inculcate is dependent upon their subjects' knowledge of their excess and immoderation: if one knows that the disobedience of a seemingly trivial command is likely to lead to death, then one is after all unlikely to disobey. This transparent admission of depravity – and the 'naked, cynical' terror it creates – are thus essential parts of grotesque power's functioning.

Although tyrants like Mussolini or Ubu might openly display their intemperance and decadence in order to ensure terrified obedience among their subjects, Foucault cites other examples of grotesque power in the *Abnormal* lectures that sit uncomfortably within this epistemological scaffold. For example, he discusses the judgements of the penal system – and especially the testimony of the psychiatric 'expert' – as paradigmatic examples of the grotesque, undifferentiated from the autocratic extremes of Nero or Mussolini (2003a: 35–36). Yet if the medico-legal authority wielded by the doctor or psychiatrist enables them to exercise power effectively, it is precisely because they refuse to acknowledge their arbitrariness, and claim instead to be the stewards of 'truth', 'science', 'legitimacy, or 'humanity'.[4] Indeed, in *Discipline and Punish*, published the same year as the *Abnormal* lectures were delivered, Foucault makes precisely this distinction: 'Everyone must see punishment not only as natural, but in his own interest ... The example is now based on the lesson, the discourse, the decipherable sign, the representation of public morality ... [In the penalty,] one will read the laws themselves' (1991: 109–110). Disciplinary power is characterised not by its grotesque materiality, but rather by its invisibility; it deals not in terror but in normalisation (1991: 187). As such, if the psychiatrist or the judge are clownish or grotesque, they are not so in the same way as the tyrant.

Foucault also identifies an 'administrative grotesque' in the bureaucracies of nineteenth- and twentieth-century Western government:

> Since the nineteenth century, an essential feature of big Western bureaucracies has been that the administrative machine, with its unavoidable effects of power, works by using the mediocre, useless, imbecilic, superficial, ridiculous, worn-out, poor, and powerless functionary.
>
> *(2003a: 12–13)*

Though Foucault does not point to a specific example, his description of the administrative grotesque inevitably brings to mind Hannah Arendt's portrait of Adolf Eichmann. Arendt represents Eichmann as a methodical man of limited creative or critical capacity; an unspectacular mandarin who subordinated his will to that of his superiors. Despite his personal mediocrity, however, the effects of the power that flowed across his desk and through his office were of an utterly cataclysmic scale. As Arendt makes clear, it is a vast web of bureaucrats (of which Eichmann is synecdochically emblematic), not a handful of psychopaths and supermen, that enabled industrial killing on the scale of the genocide that took place in wartime Europe (Arendt, 2006).[5]

For Foucault, the bureaucratic and imperial modes of governance are entirely equivalent: 'Ubu the "pen pusher" is a functional component of modern administration, just as being in the hands of a mad charlatan was a functional feature of Roman imperial power' (2003a: 12–13). Yet although Arendt's analysis in *Eichmann in Jerusalem* focuses on the same disparity central to the Foucauldian grotesque, between the effects of an action and the attributes of the people who perform it, it is not clear that the administrator and the autocrat are wholly equivalent. A figure such as Eichmann might have been 'manifestly, explicitly and readily discredited' sitting behind bullet-proof glass in an Israeli court – but it is unthinkable that he would have projected this persona from his Berlin office in 1943. In this context, he would surely have tried to embody legitimacy, authority and *gravitas*, rather than pantomimic extravagance.

If the psychiatrist or the bureaucratic functionary are clownish, then it is not in the same way as the tyrant or the autocrat. While grotesque power might sometimes project itself as despicable, clownish or ridiculous, in contexts in which its institutions, offices or people make claims to truth or legitimacy this is not automatically the case. The penal process presents the psychiatrist as a 'neutral' expert capable of delivering authoritative testimony or even judgement, while Eichmann no doubt presented himself as impeccably diligent and conscientious; a dedicated worker and a loyal servant to the Führer. There is little overtly or 'intrinsic[ally]' absurd about either figure: if they can be described as 'clownish', this is a quality that they do not project themselves, in the Ubu-esque manner. Foucault's statement that the place occupied by grotesque power is 'manifestly, explicitly and readily discredited' thus requires modification: grotesque power does not always make a ready spectacle of itself, but can also veil or obscure its contemptibility in claims to truth, moderation, naturalness, normality and/or justice.

'Clownishness' or 'grotesque-ness', then, are not ontological properties that a system of power relations (or a subject within a system) either does or does not possess. Rather, they are something performatively claimed or ascribed through the collage of signifying practices that accompany power's execution. To constitute a particular manifestation of power as grotesque, then, might require intervening to disqualify or discredit the claims to truth, normality, legitimacy or naturalness claimed by its discourses, institutions or offices. This intervention – potentially – opens up the same, grotesque discrepancy between the physiognomy of power on the one hand and its effects on the other, that is openly and willingly declared in a state of Ubu-esque terror.

Marieke de Goede calls this process of resignification 'the politics of making strange': an endeavour that 'begins by denaturalising, or *making strange*, political practices that appear as natural or common sense' (2005: 381, emphasis in original). To make something 'strange' therefore entails rethinking dominant discourses and practices by problematising the logics and assumptions that constitute them as 'natural', 'true', 'reasonable', 'just' or 'necessary'. For de Goede, the rationalities underpinning neoliberal financial practice are key sites at which this type of political undertaking can operate: if neoliberal globalisation is to be constituted as grotesque, in other words, then its claims to universality, justice and inclusion must first be problematised and denaturalised (2005: 381).[6] Only then can the arbitrary, grotesque and clownish qualities of its practice and procedure be brought into view.

Focusing on various practices of resistance which have sought to recontextualise the symbols and signifiers of financial exchange, de Goede emphasises imaginative, cultural practices as important vehicles for effecting these types of transformations (cf. Bleiker, 2000). Within this broad field, she is particularly interested in the appeals to humour and play made by activists and protestors drawing on the tradition of carnival. Quoting Bakhtin, de Goede argues that the appropriation of various images, practices and icons associated with capital has the potential to turn 'the symbols of power and violence ... inside out ... *all that was terrifying becomes grotesque*' (2005: 388, emphasis added).

If humour is of potential use in destabilising the received truths of neoliberal rationality and in so doing rendering its power-effects 'grotesque', it remains to be asked how precisely it might perform this function. By what means might the appropriation of certain signifiers or symbols reconstitute the meaning of their referent(s)? In the next section I will look at Judith Butler's writing on parody in order to explore precisely how humour might operate on or with grotesque manifestations of power. This will underpin my discussion of 'parodic parasitism', this book's third framework for understanding humour as a vehicle for performative claims to political subjectivity. I go on to interrogate how CIRCA's parodic militarism might have worked to render grotesque a security apparatus both buttressing global flows of economic exchange and seeking to exert control more immediately over the 'global justice' meetings (and surrounding protests) in which the Clown Army took part.

Parodic parasitism

In *Gender Trouble*, Judith Butler puts forward a performative account of gender, which she defines as a 'style of the flesh ... *a corporeal style*, an "act", as it were, which is both intentional and performative, where "*performative*" suggests a dramatic and contingent construction of meaning' (2006: 177, emphasis in original). Gender is not a given category that one can or cannot apply to particular subjects, but is rather something constituted through those subjects' practices: 'there need not be a "doer behind the deed" ... the "doer" is variably constructed in and through the deed' (2006: 181).

Butler is acutely aware, however, that gender's performative qualities are commonly obscured by a dominant discourse that constitutes 'male' and 'female' as stable and natural categories: pregiven, fixed; a canvas upon which the subject is painted. How, then, might one go about subverting the regime(s) of truth that institute, inscribe and sustain this discourse, in which one's masculinity or femininity functions as a pre-existing condition of personal, social – even human – being? How, in other words, might one render grotesque the logics and practices through which gender is constituted as 'natural', and in so doing draw attention to the contingency and contestability of its authority?

In order to answer these questions, Butler turns to drag culture, and in particular to its use of parody (2006: 174–190). Butler distances her understanding of drag from certain strains of feminist theory, which (she claims) tend to see it as 'degrading to women' (2006: 174). The implication here is that the drag artist's parodic 'womanhood' in some way debases women themselves: parody, in other words, takes a particular object (in this case, 'woman') as given, and then treats it with scorn. Butler, however, takes a different view:

> In imitating gender, drag implicitly reveals the imitative structure of gender itself – as well as its contingency ... In the place of the law of heterosexual coherence, we see sex and gender denaturalized by means of a performance which avows their distinctness and dramatizes the cultural mechanism of their fabricated unity ... The notion of gender parody defended here does not assume that there is an original which such parodic identities imitate. Indeed, *the parody is of the very notion of an original* ... gender parody reveals that the original identity after which gender fashions itself is an imitation without an origin.
>
> *(2006: 175, emphasis added)*

For Butler, the parody expressed in drag performances takes as its object not 'women' or 'men', but rather the very ideas of 'womanhood' or 'manhood'. The drag artist – illegible within either category's terms of belonging – upsets or 'makes strange' the epistemic and discursive regimes that constitute 'womanhood' and/or 'manhood' as natural, given and true. The gender identities imitated in the drag performance are thus denaturalised: recontextualised and resignified through the parodic appropriation of their key signifiers. In Butler's words, drag performances thereby function 'as imitations which effectively displace the meaning of the original ... [and] imitate the myth of originality' (2006: 176). By enacting an imitative, parodic performance of gender, drag nods towards the performative qualities of the so-called original itself. It thereby reconstitutes essentialist categories of identity as contingent and contestable effects of discourse and practice; things produced through action rather than the grounds of agency and subjectivity:

> Just as bodily surfaces are enacted as the natural, so these surfaces can become the site of a dissonant and denaturalized performance that reveals the performative status of the natural itself.
>
> *(2006: 186)*

For Butler, parody is a tool by which the prescriptive and violent power-effects of a particular referent can be questioned: it 'establish[es] that reality is not as fixed as we generally assume it to be' (2006: xxiii–xxiv; cf. Hutcheon, 1989; 2000). Parody, in short, makes strange the grids of intelligibility by and through which its object is known and understood. In so doing, it problematises the practices that produce, reproduce, sustain and secure a particular vision of 'truth' or 'order' by demonstrating their performative contingency. As such, 'there is a subversive laughter in the pastiche-effect of parodic practices in which the original, the authentic, and the real are themselves constituted as effects' (Butler, 2006: 186–187).

What is key for the purposes of this chapter is the way in which Butler sees parody as a way of ironically occupying a role, status or identity that is otherwise closed off to the parodist.[7] This is what I call 'parodic parasitism': the use of parody to make performative claims to hegemonic or privileged forms of subjectivity, in order to probe at the terms of belonging by which their hegemony and privilege are defined. Parody parasitically interrupts the channel(s) through which a particular object seeks to be understood, and in so doing shows that its 'truth' is not 'natural' or pre-given but rather performed in the same way as the parodic imitation. As such, parody dislocates power and order from the claims to naturalness or truth that often sustain them, in the process (potentially) rendering a particular manifestation of power discredited, theatrical, made up or 'grotesque'.

For Butler as for de Goede, the role of humour in this process is key. One might read Butler's call for laughter in *Gender Trouble*'s original preface in this light:

> How can an epistemic/ontological regime be brought into question? What best way to trouble the gender categories that support gender hierarchy and compulsory heterosexuality? Consider the fate of 'female trouble', that historical configuration of a nameless female indisposition, which thinly veiled the notion that being female is a natural indisposition. Serious as the medicalization of women's bodies is, the term is also laughable, and laughter in the face of serious

categories is indispensable for feminism. Without a doubt, feminism continues to require its own forms of serious play.
(2006: xxviii; cf. Irigaray, 1985: 162–163)

If laughter is 'indispensable' for feminism, as Butler suggests, it is because it indicates a 'consciousness of contingency' (Critchley, 2002: 10) that is itself indicative of an awareness that certain discourses and/or practices are not as natural or inevitable as one might previously have assumed. For Butler as for Foucault at the beginning of *The Order of Things*, laughter functions as an indication that a 'serious category' has been made strange: it expresses a realisation that particular power-effects can be (or have been) dislocated from their claims to truth, naturalness or necessity; that they have been made to appear ridiculous or buffoonish. Parodic imitation thus performatively opens space from which the received truth of the original can be questioned or contested.

As I will discuss in more detail presently, the clown is an exemplary parodist. Both alienated from society and nature and yet somehow also their obscure other side, the clown's imitative travesty of a 'normal' human being interrupts the logics and practices underpinning 'normality' as a category of behaviour and identity.[8] This function is embodied by the court jester, simultaneously 'a counterpart and touchstone to the follies and vanities of those around him' and a scapegoat who bears the folly of the king on his own shoulders (Amoore and Hall, 2013: 101; Welsford, 1968: 66–67). Both interpretations smear the apparently clean distinction between clown and sovereign, fool and not-fool. The logic by which the former is said to derive from a symbolic 'outside' or 'elsewhere' is destabilised by her uneasy presence within the latter's court – a presence that suggests the line separating the clown from offices of power (and those who occupy them) is more permeable than might have been imagined. 'Dost thou call me fool, boy?', Lear asks his clown. 'All thy other titles thou hast given away; that thou wast born with', comes the reply.[9] Here, the distinction between king and clown has blurred, and perhaps even collapsed entirely: legitimate power and its grotesque and clownish other side have come to resemble each other, to the point that it is not clear which is which. The fool has become a parodic travesty of kingship, the king a grotesque and laughable clown.

I turn now to look at CIRCA, a collective of clowns who took part in a number of mass protests in the early 2000s, including the series of actions surrounding the 2005 G8 summit in Gleneagles, Scotland. In their parodic imitation of the militarised forces sustaining the G8's authority as agents of neoliberal global governance, as well as the power dynamics more immediately at play between activists and police, CIRCA sought to open up and create space from which to question the naturalness or necessity of such arrangements. In this respect, the Clown Army's ironic performances of militarised political subjectivities sought to render the objects of their parody strange and grotesque, both by 'reveal[ing] the performative status of the natural itself' and by provoking 'laughter in the face of [otherwise] serious categories'. Given the ambivalence both of parody and of the grotesque, however, the political effects of CIRCA's method cannot be taken for granted.

CIRCA, parody and the neoliberal grotesque

The last twenty years or so have seen clowns become a common feature of protests around Britain, Europe and the world. The 2007 'No Borders' protests in England, the 2007 meeting of the G8 in Germany, the 2009 Copenhagen Summit on Climate Change, the 2010 meeting of the G20 in Toronto and the 2015 protests at both the European Central Bank headquarters in Frankfurt and the meeting of the G7 at Garmisch-Partenkirchen (among others) all saw clowns not only participating but featuring prominently (Amoore and Hall, 2013; Routledge, 2012: 447–448; Black, Weiss and Speciale, 2015; Lorenzetti, 2015; Elgot, 2015). In this section, however, I will look specifically at CIRCA, who initially formed for the 2003 visit to London of George W. Bush and who were the first group to use clowning tactically within the broader context of what became known as the 'global justice movement' (Bogad, n.d.; Jordan, n.d.; interview with Private Individual, August 2016).

CIRCA's members sought to be more than just activists in costume or fancy dress, making overt use of techniques drawn from traditions of performance including theatre, performance art and *bouffon* (Bogad, 2016: 166). To join the Army required the completion of two days' training in the 'methodology of rebel clowning', a mixture of practices from clowning and civil disobedience that aimed to instruct its participants not in the art of dressing or acting like a clown, but rather in *becoming* one: 'CIRCA's combatants don't pretend to be clowns, they *are* clowns, real clowns' (Klepto, 2004: 407, emphasis in original; Klepto and Up Evil, 2005: 245; Koogie, 2005: 128–129; interview with Theo Price, September 2016). To be part of the Clown Army, then, was to cultivate – and inhabit – an entirely different subjective space to that usually occupied by the 'activist' or 'protestor'.[10] CIRCA's clowning can thus be read as a performative, onto-political statement: the verb 'to clown', in the context of the Clown Army, did not just mean 'to do', but also 'to be'.[11] But 'to be' *what*? How should one understand the subjectivity of the clown?

The clown

The clown is an ambiguous figure. Deriving from an obscure realm beyond all frontiers of social and political propriety, 'a usurper with no right to be where [s]he is in the ordered world', she commensurately 'lack[s] … [an] ability to perceive, understand, or act in accordance with the order of things as it appears to others' (Willeford, 1969: 13, 26, 133). Like the *pharmakos*, then, she is unassimilable into the political sphere, an embodiment of all the chaotic forces against which a particular vision of order must be secured. Despite this, however, she is nevertheless most often found occupying a space within a particular culture's political inner sanctum, a strange, ambivalent presence at the right hand of the monarch (cf. Welsford, 1968: 74).

The clown thus parasites the socio-political space: not *of* it, she nevertheless remains in it, sustaining her dissonant presence by provoking laughter among those who truly belong. As such, she collapses (or straddles) the boundaries, the limits and the distinctions that demarcate and define not only her own otherness but also the order in which she resides, unsettling the 'comfortable identity references that we turn to for a purchase on the very possibility of politics' (Amoore and Hall, 2013: 95). The clown thus 'breaks down the boundary between chaos and order … [she] violates our assumption that that boundary was where we thought it was and that it had the character we thought it had: that of affirming whatever we have taken for granted and in that way protecting us from the dark unknown' (Willeford, 1969: 108; cf. Amoore and Hall, 2013: 102).

CIRCA's clowns explicitly sought to occupy this ambiguous, liminal subjective space – as their name suggested:

> We are circa because we are approximate and ambivalent, neither here nor there, but in the most powerful of all places, the place in between order and chaos.
>
> *(Quoted in Routledge, 2010: 394; 2012: 433)*

> [Clowns] inhabit a special place, an in-between space, a weird social no-man's land. The clown manages to be at the centre and the margins of society simultaneously ... This threshold space that the clown inhabits is powerful. It confuses the categories that the system imposes on us.
>
> *(Klepto and Up Evil, 2005: 248)*

This ambiguous 'threshold space' was precisely clowning's appeal as a mode of cultural activism in the context of mass protests more usually defined by clear, stark and implacable confrontations between police and protestor. To become a clown was thus a way to open up indeterminate subjective space in which to be creative, playful and critical with the relational terrain on which CIRCA operated. This terrain could be macro-political – high-political transnational meetings, mechanisms and systems of neoliberal governance, the 'War on Terror' – or it could be more locally focused, concerned with reconfiguring the ways in which activists on the ground interacted with each other, or with the security forces seeking to manage their collective presence and movement (Routledge, 2012: 439). In both instances, however, the group's parodic claims to militaristic forms of subjectivity were key to this reconfiguring, insofar as they enabled the Clown Army to make strange or render grotesque the objects of their parody.

CIRCA, clowning and parody

> The fool may be said ... to hunger after non-folly; he often even appears to desire incarnation as a non-fool. Just as silly as the fool's onslaught upon conventions are his attempts to learn what they are and to adapt himself [sic] to them. The pathos of many fool presentations lies in the fact that the fool is painfully unable to stop being a fool, though all of his [sic again] aspirations are for a place on the other side of the border.
>
> *(Willeford, 1969: 140–141)*

The clown always desires to enter the world of the non-fool, though her endlessly restaged attempts to adapt to custom and convention always fall laughably short. In performing this failure, however, the clown also draws attention to the performative elements at play in the 'original' towards which she aspires, positing a strange intimacy between herself and her non-foolish antagonist. Like the parasite, then, the clown oscillates ambiguously across the boundaries demarcating the 'normal', 'natural', 'reasonable' world from the obscure and abject void against which it is defined. To speak of the clown's presence within the spaces and channels of power as 'parasitic', however, is to obscure the specifically parodic qualities of her folly: whereas the parasite generally is understood as a 'noise – whether literal or metaphorical – intercepting or redirecting a signal, the clown can more specifically be understood as a noise that intercepts the signal in question by imitating it. One might therefore say, with Paul Routledge, that 'clowning sees through the pretensions of the social order and *becomes* that pretence in order to expose it' (2012: 433, emphasis added). As Amoore and Hall similarly note, '[clowns'] objects and antics are met with confusion, laughter and the call that they "have no place here", no place on the visible landscape of qualified civic and political life ... [yet] to be outside of the law, an outlaw, to have no place, places the clown in curious proximity to the king' (2013: 107–108).

Clowning parodically appropriates the symbols and signifiers of power in order to dislocate it from its claims to truth, right and/or legitimacy. In CIRCA's case, the most obvious of these signifiers was the group's parodic militarism, exemplified by its self-identification as an 'Army'. CIRCA adopted this label despite (and perhaps because of) their non-hierarchical structure and their non-violent approach to activism and protest. In so doing, they parodically appropriated the symbols and signifiers of a militarised political discourse that they argued functioned to uphold the interests of global capital under the banner of the 'War on Terror':

> We are an army because we live on a planet in permanent war – a war of money against life, of profit against dignity, of progress against the future. We are an army because a war that gorges itself on death and blood and shits money and toxins, deserves an obscene body of deviant soldiers.
>
> *(Quoted in Routledge, 2012: 433)*

CIRCA confronted the hegemonic (militarised) political discourse and practice of the war of terror and subverted it through creating an army of clowns ... Rebel clown logic used (deconstructed) army uniforms to associate itself with a culture of permanent war, and through that to the conventions to neoliberalism, wars for oil and the war on terror.

(Routledge, 2012: 433, 438–439)

This parodic militarism expressed itself in multiple ways. The most immediately visible was the 'deconstructed army uniform' or 'multi-form'. Each clown was given *carte blanche* to dress and accessorise as they wished within (broadly defined) military parameters. The resulting amalgams of military fatigues, face paint, colander-helmets, feather-duster bayonets and so on, combined with the group's rather idiosyncratic style of marching,[12] served to suggest a strange and inscrutable correspondence between the clowns and the object of their parodic performance.

The parodic logic behind the group's attire also informed a number of their actions. Klepto describes an action before the Gleneagles protests in which the Clown Army attempted to join the British Army at a recruitment centre in Leeds – in so doing, aiming to collapse entirely the distinction between themselves and the *actual* army to which they aspired by incorporating the 'parody' into the 'original' (Klepto, 2004; cf. Boyle, 2011: 202–203; interview with Theo Price). Inevitably turned down and turned away, the clowns continued to plead with the recruiters to let them join up, ultimately forcing the centre to shut down – at which point a CIRCA recruitment stand was erected outside in its stead (Boyle, 2011: 202–205). The Clown Army thus positioned itself as a doppelganger of the actual military, going so far as to supplant the 'original' or 'real' recruitment centre and offering itself as a like-for-like replacement. In the process, the often unquestioned strategies of everyday militarist discourses – the placement of recruitment offices within urban centres, the colourful advertising and promises of adventure and glamour in the waging of foreign wars and so on – were themselves dragged over the footlights and onto the stage, 'made strange', clownish and (potentially) grotesque.

Because parody is transitive – in other words, it requires a referent: one cannot simply parody, but must rather parody *something* – it sets into motion a playful and dynamic engagement with the 'original' it takes as its object. Like all clowns (and indeed like the parasite), CIRCA's parodic interruptions sought to expand the performance space, and to accommodate others not ostensibly part of the group. 'They're an army of clowns, we're an army of clowns. It's perfect' (Amoore and Hall, 2013: 93; cf. Koogie, 2005: 133). As the degrading and degraded double of the actual army, the Clown Army thus sought first to dissolve the distinction between themselves and the actual army, and second to coerce the latter onto the stage to participate in the performance – even if only by implication, as the complement to the clowns' own folly. As parodists, then, the Clown Army demanded participation from those they encountered, and especially from those ostensible non-fools whom they imitated.

CIRCA's participation in the demonstrations against the 2005 Gleneagles meeting of the G8 was arguably the Army's peak (it was certainly the Army's largest action, though some participants argued that earlier, smaller actions had perhaps worked better).[13] Nevertheless, the Gleneagles actions are comfortably the best-documented examples of CIRCA's practice (e.g. Bogad, 2011; 2016; Klepto and Up Evil, 2005; Koogie, 2005; Routledge, 2010; 2012), and remain notable as an example of the group's approach to parodic performance in the context of mass protest. These performances had two, parallel purposes. First, to 'make strange' the G8's apparently 'rational' discourse and rhetoric by drawing attention to their political, economic and environmental consequences. And second, to defuse or at least destabilise the oppositional or confrontational frames through which opposition to the summit was criminalised in the popular press. Paul Routledge draws attention to the first of these functions:

> Through the power of association – under the rubric of the 'War on Error' – rebel clown logic, combined with the performance of a clown army, parodied the War on Terror. The War on Error was a struggle waged against the political 'errorism' of Imperial wars (such as the war in Iraq); the economic 'errorism' of neoliberalism, and the environmental 'errorism' of over-consumption and fossil-fuelled economies.
>
> *(2012: 439)*

Larry Bogad, meanwhile, outlines the second:

> Our intent was to change the hegemonic discourse around the impending global justice demonstrations, reversing the rhetoric of criminalization and 'anti-social elements' to where we felt it better

applied, and making points about troubling policy issues while wearing the red nose.

(2016: 180; cf. Gorringe and Rosie, 2008: 699; Routledge, 2010: 389)[14]

These two goals came together in 'Operation HA.HA.HAA' ('Helping Authorities House Arrest Half-witted Authoritarian Androids'), one of CIRCA's main exercises at Gleneagles (cf. Routledge, 2005: 112, 117).[15] Aligning themselves with the police securing the perimeter of the conference zone, CIRCA sought to reinforce the impermeability of the barrier surrounding the meeting – but not, of course, without resignifying it. The fences and lines of riot police patrolling the perimeter of the conference zone, CIRCA claimed, *was* of crucial importance – not to keep protestors out, however, but rather to keep those within the congress *inside*, where they could do no harm to the world at large (Bogad, 2016: 178).[16] Meanwhile, police tactics aimed directly *at* the clowns were similarly interpreted as playful interactions, and thereby incorporated into the comic performance: kettles became playpens, while clowns filled their pockets with oddities and curiosities, all of which would have to be logged if they were subjected to a stop-and-search (Jordan, n.d.). McClish quotes a CIRCA activist describing the moment when a kettle formed and clowns tried to 'jump in willingly, turning the "police pen" into a "play pen", but then jump out again (or get stuck trying to get out) and plead with them to throw us back in' (2007: 107). Bogad, meanwhile, notes an occasion at a CIRCA action prior to Gleneagles where 'Colonel Klepto was arrested. When his pockets were searched and the contents itemized, the police had to go through the whole list of absurd objects, culminating in a wind-up toy of a wanking bobby' (2016: 167).

On an immediate level, then, CIRCA sought to undermine the confrontational dynamic often at work between activists and police by dragging the latter on stage to perform with the former, blurring the line between them in doing so. On a broader, symbolic level, however, Operation HA.HA.HAA worked to do the same with the G8 meeting itself, recasting and resignifying the conference site by suggesting that the security apparatus surrounding it was facing inwards rather than out, in so doing making it the focal point of a clownish display of military defiance. In both cases, however, CIRCA's clowning sought to detach particular power-effects from the epistemic and ontological grids of intelligibility buttressing their authority. By incorporating the nominal non-fools of the security apparatus within the clownish world of performances, games and jokes (and thereby dissolving or at least weakening the boundaries between the two), CIRCA's parodic militarism worked to constitute both the meeting of the G8 and the security forces patrolling its perimeter as laughable, ridiculous, clownish, absurd – and as such, at least potentially grotesque.

Conclusion

> Rebel clown logic is an associative logic, based on visual signs, wordplay and emotional resonance. It drew explicitly on key elements of clowning, attempting through playful confrontation to exaggerate and invert the social order, recontextualising it in order to reveal its absurdity, and invite others (such as the public) to reconsider it. Rebel clown logic was combined with the multiforms, clown faces, and clown manoeuvres in order to attempt to subvert the hegemonic logic and the taken-for-granted world articulated by the G8.
>
> *(Routledge, 2012: 438–439)*

By dislocating neoliberal discourses and institutions from the regimes of truth underpinning them, CIRCA's use of parody sought to render them 'grotesque', in the Foucauldian sense. Although Foucault theorises grotesque power as a mode of governance that openly displays its arbitrariness and immoderation, his examples – including the 'administrative grotesque' of someone like Adolf Eichmann and the medico-legal grotesque of the psychiatric expert – do not obviously fit this 'Ubu-esque' model. In order to be recognised as grotesque, therefore, some manifestations of power must first be detached from the regimes of truth that sustain them.

This is precisely what CIRCA sought to do with their appeals to what I have termed 'parodic parasitism', both at Gleneagles and elsewhere. Parody allows performative claims to privileged subject positions to be made – ironically – by those who would otherwise be closed off from making such claims. In so doing, it enacts an encounter between original and imitation that interrupts and interferes in the channels through which the former is understood and legitimised as natural, true, authoritative or normal. CIRCA's parodic recontextualisation of military symbols and signifiers thus operated by disrupting the grids of intelligibility through which a militarised neoliberal apparatus – symbolised both by the G8 itself as well as by the police and security operations outside the conference centre – was commonly understood.

For all of CIRCA's style and imaginative flair, however, it is clear that neither they nor the clown as an archetypal comic subject should be romanticised. The cultural activism of CIRCA and others (and the more conventional mass protests that took place in Edinburgh and elsewhere under the 'Make Poverty History' banner) did not stop the G8 summit going ahead, or even notably disrupt them beyond a traffic jam or two (Routledge, 2012: 448). Like all parasitic encounters, those between CIRCA and the security forces opposing them were fleeting and contingent, momentary juxtapositions and joint articulations rather than lasting reconfigurations.

This was partly by design: CIRCA's aims were openly fragmented and fragmentary, limitations that are arguably a constitutive part of clowning generally. However, this does not necessarily preclude their ludic (and/or ludicrous) encounters from effecting political change. For Michel Serres, the parasitic encounter is a necessary condition of transformation: 'parasites make history' (2007: 238). The history created in this way is not what Nietzsche calls 'monumental history': epoch-defining transformations, usually carried out by great men. Instead, 'the theory of the parasite brings us to miniscule evaluations of changes of state': brief oscillations between noise and signal, in which the possibility for change is first opened and prefigured (Serres, 2007: 194). Such brief encounters, exemplified by the performance-based cultural activism of the so-called 'global justice movement', offer the possibility – but only ever a possibility – of more lasting transformations.

The partiality and incompleteness of CIRCA's clowns represent an invitation to reconsider the claims to truth, naturalness, inevitability or justice that support and legitimise neoliberal discourses and institutions, including but not limited to their instruments of violence. The clown does not always or necessarily issue this 'invitation', and she cannot compel her audience to accept it: like the parasite, her interruption is conditional and contingent. This is particularly important in relation to grotesque manifestations of power, where a parodic intervention may be rhetorically and critically powerful without being politically effective: if, as Foucault suggests, grotesque power can operate at its maximum rate of efficiency despite being outwardly unsuitable to exercise command, then it seems necessary to conclude that the political effects of clowning – like the clown herself – remain limited or even ambivalent.

However, CIRCA's use of humour to make performative claims to particular subject-positions also helped to shape the immediate affective experience of mass protest for those involved (cf. Solomon, 2019). This demands a rethinking of the temporalities through which mass protest is often conceived. Strategic narratives (did the protest 'achieve' particular goals?) make little sense when faced with such momentary, fragmentary interruptions that seek to cultivate immediate affective and emotional resonances. To think about humour solely in relation to questions about transformation, change and history thus obscures its inextricability from the immediate, embodied and emotional experiences of those who practise it.

Notes

1 Less charitable because many of those protesting in (say) Seattle in 1999, in Prague in 2000 or in Gleneagles in 2005 were in many ways putting forward a profoundly global vision of society, in which the movement of people across borders would be unrestricted and world-scale problems such as environmental degradation and poverty tackled co-operatively across national divides. The term 'anti-globalisation' was therefore rejected by most of those within the movement (e.g. Graeber, 2002: 62–66), and its shortcomings are acknowledged in most academic writing that cites the term (e.g. el-Ojeili, 2005; el-Ojeili and Hayden, 2006; Held and McGrew, 2007: 148–150). It should be noted that no single label could adequately represent the vast range of interests represented and positions held by the participants in these groups, movements and actions. With this in mind, I describe the assemblage as a whole either as just a 'movement' or as the 'global justice movement' (within inverted commas) throughout this chapter.
2 For Bogad, these two ambitions are reciprocal: the associations the movement forges between people compromised or marginalised by what he calls 'corporate globalisation' are themselves part of its strategy of opposition to neoliberal flows of capital and power. Drawing heavily (and often explicitly) on models of social organisation developed in the global South, the movement might therefore also be read, with David Graeber, as an attempt to answer the 1996 call of the Zapatistas'

Subcomandante Marcos: 'we will make a collective network of all our particular struggles and resistances, an intercontinental network of resistance against neoliberalism, an intercontinental network of resistance for humanity' (Subcomandante Marcos, 2001: 117; cf. Graeber, 2002: 63; on the influence of the Zapatista movement on the broader 'global justice movement', see Graeber, 2002; Bogad, 2016: 40; Conant, 2010).

3 There are parallels to be drawn here between the 'cultural activism' of the 'global justice movement' and the theatrical stunts of ACT UP, of course (see Shepard and Hayduk, 2002; Shepard, 2005; Bogad, 2016: 37–38).

4 'by solemnly inscribing offences in the field of objects susceptible of scientific knowledge, they [psychiatrists, criminologists, and criminal anthropologists] provide the mechanisms of legal punishment with a justifiable hold not only on offences, but on individuals; not only on what they do, but also on what they are, will be, may be' (Foucault, 1991: 18).

5 In *On Violence*, Arendt notes that in etymological terms the word 'bureaucracy' simply implies 'the rule of the desk'. The system's purpose is thus to spirit responsibility and obligation away into the cracks of administration; it is a system characterised by smoke and mirrors in which the buck ultimately always stops with an abstract 'someone else' whose existence, when probed, dissolves into nothing: 'the latest and perhaps most formidable form of domination: bureaucracy or the rule of an intimate system of bureaus in which no man, neither one nor the best, neither the few nor the many, can be held responsible, and which could properly be called rule by Nobody' (1970: 38).

6 Foucault's 1978–1979 lecture series, entitled 'The Birth of Biopolitics', traces the development of liberal and neoliberal discourses of governmentality, and argues that neoliberalism emerges in tandem with a particular, market-focused regime of truth. The market is constituted as a site where social relations are forged and made legible, transforming politics into a secondary field which can only operate reactively to the knowledge produced through consumer exchange (Foucault, 2008).

7 From this perspective, drag is a mode of parody centred around questions of gender identity – though elsewhere, Butler is at pains to point out that it is not only this. In *Bodies That Matter*, Butler discusses Jennie Livingston's *Paris is Burning*, a documentary about the drag/transgender ball scene in 1980s/1990s New York, in which questions of gender inextricably intersect with those of race, sexuality and class in multifaceted performances of 'realness' (Livingston, 1990; Butler, 2011: 84–95).

8 Mentioning the clown and the drag artist together here does not signify any equivalence between the two beyond their respective uses of parody. I am not by any means suggesting that the drag artist is a clown, or that the two subjects share a genealogy, or operate within the same interpretive matrix.
9 *King Lear* (1608 quarto text), I.4, 145–147 (Orgel and Braunmuller, 2002: 1502).
10 For Eli Simon, clowning entails precisely these sorts of profound 'physical, emotional and psychological transformations'; it is to become something other than what one usually is (2012: 43).
11 'It doesn't matter how well you can throw a custard pie, fall over or tell a joke; if your entire being has not taken on the state of clown and isn't committed to staying with that state, then it becomes a pretence, mere acting' (Klepto, 2004: 408; cf. Klepto and Up Evil, 2005: 248).
12 'Suddenly, and with no cue, the rebel clowns travel like a tightly clustered school of fish, all making the same sound and gesture, then changing direction simultaneously and making an entirely different sound and gesture. (This is called "fishing")' (Bogad, 2011: 190; 2016: 168; cf. Interview with Private Individual).
13 As many as 160 clowns took part in 2005 (Routledge, 2012: 429). Theo Price argues that the sheer number served to dilute the group's ability to unnerve and unease, and that CIRCA subsequently 'lost its teeth' (interview with Theo Price). Private Individual similarly recalled that after Gleneagles, CIRCA 'rotted away from the inside, like a doughnut' (interview with Private Individual).
14 The Trapese Collective similarly read CIRCA as a response to the 'criminalisation of protestors and dissent' (2007: 171). The criminalisation of the G8 protests was abetted by the simultaneous 'Make Poverty History' and 'Live 8' campaigns, whose mainstream prominence was used to marginalise and delegitimise actions that fell outside their scope, aims and ambitions. Live 8 organiser Midge Ure went so far as to claim that the concerts would 'hijack' the 'anarchists' event' (attributed by Summer and Jones, 2005; cf. Gorringe and Rosie, 2008: 693).
15 'Operation HA.HA.HAA was deployed to invert the logic and expectations of the July 6th demonstrations against the G8. Instead of trying to climb the fences and disrupt the meeting, we wanted to deploy rebel clowns to keep the world's most dangerous errorists under house arrest in perpetuity. Build the fences higher, and never let them out of their five star luxury prison!'
16 There is an obvious similarity between this action and ACT UP/TAG's condom-over-the-house stunt, discussed in Chapter 5.

Conclusion: parasitic politics and world politics

I would like to begin my conclusion by returning to the same question with which I began this book: what is the relationship between humour and international politics? In my introduction, I sketched out an initial response to this problem, noting that humour already plays a constitutive role in a number of events of obvious global significance. Incidents like the *Charlie Hebdo* shootings of 2015, among others, make little sense unless one recognises the ways in which humour provokes, informs and shapes belief, desire and action. However, I also suggested that humour's relevance to international affairs goes beyond explosive and exceptional acts of violence. As an everyday practice, humour also plays an important role in the production and reproduction of social relations, across the International Relations (IR) discipline's so-called levels of analysis. How people joke and laugh offers acute insights into their (actual or desired) position within broader relational fields – including those that constitute 'the international' as a sphere of political activity.

The academic discipline of IR is ill-suited to excavating and exploring these dynamics. IR scholars have tended to think of their discipline as occupying a different plane from the fripperies of everyday (inter)action that constitute sociological or anthropological fields of study. Many have even framed the international sphere in explicitly tragic terms, in the process demanding a particular kind of analytic temperament or attitude that would appear to preclude an interest in practices like joking, irony and laughter (cf. Lisle, 2016; Wedderburn, 2018). Yet as feminists, among others, have shown, social relations *are* international relations: the patterns and textures of everyday life both reflect and shape the wider (social, political, international) fields in which people make their way. Humour, like other everyday practices, discloses important information about the matrices of inclusion and exclusion through which these fields are brought into being, maintained, secured and negotiated.

Throughout the main body of this book, I expanded and developed this argument both theoretically and empirically. In Part I, I explored humour's intimate involvement in the everyday performance of subjective identity and intersubjective relations. Humour is part of a rich and complex field of everyday practice through which subjects make claims about who they are and how they relate to (or differ from) others, and it contributes to the emotional, affective and rhythmic landscapes that give those claims purchase and weight. Drawing on ancient accounts of comedy, I suggested that humour has historically been understood in these terms – and in particular, as a way of making a claim to political subjectivity from a position of political abjection or disgrace. In Greek comedy, this function is embodied by the parasite, an ambiguous figure who oscillates across the limits of the political sphere, performatively asking questions of its terms of belonging (while also providing an opportunity for those terms to be violently re-asserted). To speak of a 'parasitic politics' is thus to speak of humour as a way of making claims to subjectivity and agency in contexts of political or even existential urgency, directing analytic attention towards the performative articulations of self and other that underpin the social, political and international fields.

My empirical chapters established and evaluated three different modes of parasitic practice, which I termed 'aesthetic parasitism', 'physical parasitism' and 'parodic parasitism' respectively. In the small but significant body of cartoons and comic strips created by detainees in French concentration camps during the Second World War, artists including Horst Rosenthal used humour to make performative claims to political subjectivity and agency within a representational sphere standing as the avatar of the material camp space. In the work of AIDS activist group AIDS Coalition to Unleash Power (ACT UP), meanwhile, humour formed part of a wider strategy in which activists physically relocated their abject (queer, HIV-positive) bodies into spaces that symbolised or worked to produce that abjection. Finally, the Clandestine Insurgent Rebel Clown Army (CIRCA) (among other activists taking part in mass protests around the turn of the millennium) used parody in order to appropriate established, powerful subjectivities and in so doing undermine their claims to truth, naturalness or necessity. Taken together, these three case studies offer a layered and multi-dimensional understanding both of the ways in which humour functions politically and of the ways it functions 'parasitically', by conveying a performative claim to political subjectivity in the face of its violent, proscriptive denial. Three conclusions emerge from these studies, and from the theoretical parasitic subject outlined in this book's first part.

First, a focus on humour provides a valuable way of tracing the symbiotic relationship between apparently mundane social practices and issues of global political concern. Everyday intersubjective interactions are a constitutive part of the systems and networks that constitute international relations, and they demand serious attention from IR scholars. At stake here is a sense of the ways in which the everyday and the international are mutually and 'transversally' co-constitutive. The everyday lives of social, political and world-political subjects, as well as those abjected from such categories, are of course shaped by global vectors of power and violence. At the same time, however, international relations are themselves produced and reproduced by these subjects, through all manner of repetitive, iterative practices that range from diplomatic receptions and coffee meetings through to the consumption of high street and/or popular-cultural commodities (cf. Solomon and Steele, 2017; Enloe, 2004).

Yet despite events like the *Charlie Hebdo* attacks and the *Jyllands-Posten* crisis, and despite humour's increasingly prominent place within practices of international diplomacy (cf. Brassett, Browning and Wedderburn, 2021), this book does not seek to establish humour as a strategically influential or causally important variable in 'international relations' as the term is usually understood. An attitude of this sort implicitly assumes what international relations are, where they are to be found and the sorts of subjects able to participate in them. The advantage of thinking about humour as a *transversal* practice, on the other hand, is instead that it reconfigures (and problematises) 'the international' as a structural or spatial category. This kind of approach offers 'an invitation to re-envision ways of engaging with entrenched boundaries, borders, and categories, as well as to analyse specific practices, especially their justifications and routines, their effects on the reproduction of particular narratives, and their contributions to the empowerment of particular groups or individuals over others' (Basaran et al., 2017: 4). A focus on humour as a transversal practice, then, demands an attentiveness to 'the international' as a problem, rather than a pregiven field.

As such, my focus on humour throughout this book should not be read as an attempt to place humour at the 'centre' of international relations. Instead, the parasite's claims to political identity and agency are valuable precisely because they ask questions of where exactly the 'centre' is and against whom it is defined. The discipline of IR has traditionally offered a strictly delimited vision of its field. Critical race theorists, postcolonial scholars, feminists and others have already done a great deal of valuable work excavating the discipline's roots in white supremacy, colonial administration and patriarchal masculinity (e.g. Vitalis, 2015; Anievas, Manchanda and Shilliam, 2015; Sylvester 2002). These literatures have shown how the discipline rests on a particular vision of 'international relations' predicated on the exclusion of certain subjects or groups of subjects from its purview. The examples of parasitic practice studied in this book engage with these dynamics of exclusion, encouraging reflection on 'international relations' as a dynamic configuration of socially constructed flows continually beset by leaks, intrusions, diversions and miscarriages, rather than as a given set of priors.

My focus on humour throughout this book should thus be understood as a way of effecting this kind of transversal problematisation by asking how people have positioned themselves in relation to global-political discourses and apparatuses predicated on their exclusion or abjection. The material and political effects of these acts of positioning has been varied: while ACT UP may have impacted the governance of HIV/AIDS in the United States in important and tangible ways, for example, Horst Rosenthal's comic strips had little consequential effect on Rosenthal's own life (and death) within the camp system of wartime Europe. Yet despite this relative powerlessness, Rosenthal's work is only 'marginal' if one has already decided in advance where the 'margins' are. It is precisely these circumscriptive decisions that everyday practices like humour probe and question. In the words of Michel de Certeau, talking about the tactical qualities of 'ways of operating':

> Strategies are able to produce, tabulate, and impose … whereas tactics can only use, manipulate and divert these spaces … [Ways of

operating] create a certain play in the machine through a stratification of different and interfering kinds of functioning.

(1984: 29–30)

The parasite's appeals to humour cannot therefore 'tabulate' a space, or 'impose' form and order. As 'play', as interference, as 'noise', they merely excite the system, and introduce a creative indeterminacy and contingency into its circuitry. In so doing, however, they demand (and perform) a reconsideration of what 'international relations' are, where they are to be found and who participates in them.

Second, humour's status as a tactical 'way of operating' – as a practice that discloses information about people's identities; their positions in wider social, relational and discursive fields; and their attempts to exert agency over these spaces – is predicated on its role in the making and unmaking of political subjectivities. Humour offers a revealing insight into the performative politics of identity, community and difference, functioning variously as a statement of subjective identity, as a means of cultivating intersubjective affinities and antagonisms or even sometimes as a shibboleth. This in turn opens a window onto the processes through which identity and agency (and abjection from these categories) are asserted, contested, negotiated or refused.

The construction and formation of subjectivity has been an important problem among critical IR scholars for several decades. Rather than inquiring as to what political subjectivity is, and how it might or might not be accurately represented, these scholars have demanded an attentiveness to the ways in which subjectivity is performatively produced. This has in turn focused attention on the practices through which subjects bring themselves into political being. I have argued throughout this book that humour is one such practice, contributing in important and often revealing ways to these processes of subject-formation. Yet my account of the parasite, rooted in the figure of the *pharmakos*, sets up an association between comedian and scapegoat that opens up terrain from which to theorise a foundational complicity between humour on the one hand and political forms of subjectivity on the other. As my reading of Aristotle's Megarian myth reveals, comedy's origins are woven into those of the Greek *polis*: each institution implies the other, insofar as both derive from the same originary moment of sacrificial violence. The origins of 'politics' as a distinct sphere of human activity are thus bound up with the origins of 'comedy' as a genre of performance.

Humour – and in particular, 'parasitic' forms of humour – thus offers a singular purchase on questions about the definition, redefinition, transformation and affirmation of what it means to be (or not to be) a 'political' subject, and about the contours and limits of the orders in which those subjectivities find meaning. It is of course true that not all appeals to humour are 'parasitic' in the way I have outlined throughout this book: as Foucault's account of grotesque power confirms, humour is often mobilised in order to reinforce rather than contest abjection (2003a).[1] Yet this only goes to confirm humour's intimacy with processes of subject formation: humour can open a window onto the construction of exclusionary political communities, as well as the subjective clefts and interstices that inevitably accompany them. In both instances, however, it is useful as a way of tracing those limits, and their everyday production and reproduction. This book's focus on humour thus makes a contribution to critical IR literature focused on the problem of subjectivity by demonstrating this problem's close association with practices like humour, comedy, joking and laughter.

Third, the parasite's appeals to humour focus analytic attention towards the political margins and towards their creation, reproduction, maintenance and contestation. It is important to note that although I have focused in this book on parasitic appeals to humour, the theoretical parasitic subject that I outlined in this book's first part offers an account of intersubjectivity that exceeds humour as a specific field of practice. Humour is not the only way to make claims to political subjectivity from a position of abjection, as exemplified by a group like ACT UP, whose appeals to humour were combined with a broader palette of emotions (most obviously grief and anger), that also fed into their claims to identity and agency. Scattering the ashes of loved ones dead from AIDS onto the White House lawn, for example, is an action that follows a similar logic to the 'physical parasitism' outlined in Chapter 4, insofar as it involved the physical recontextualisation of abject bodies (in this instance, cremated bodies) into the very spaces symbolising and working to produce their abjection. Yet despite its methodological affinity with (for example) the carnivalesque occupation of St Patrick's Cathedral, or the Treatment Action Guerrillas' condom stunt at Jesse Helms' house,[2] the humour driving these actions was (understandably) absent from the ash-scattering action.

Looking beyond this book's empirical focus on humour, its account of the parasite's claims to identity, agency and subjectivity also makes a contribution to IR's analysis of power. Power in IR is often understood in binary terms: it manifests itself in the interaction between inside and outside, between identity and difference, between self and other, and between power itself and resistance. The parasite, as a figure who traverses these binary divisions – occupying 'the third position', in Michel Serres' words (2007, *passim*) – offers a way of accounting for the dynamism and permeability of these boundaries. It is for this reason that Umut Ozguc uses Serres' conception of the parasite as a way of theorising border-spaces, and the 'noisy-subjects' who moves across and between them. Whereas borders are usually thought of as clean lines distinguishing one homogenous, sovereign space from another, Ozguc instead examines the parasitic status of subjects who do not comfortably fit into either category, figuratively introducing noise into the channels by which states seek to know and manage those crossing their borders (2020). In so doing, she demonstrates one way in which the figure of the parasite might be brought to bear on IR beyond the specific empirical focus of this book.

I would like to end the book by reflecting briefly on the politics of humour in a time of so-called 'post-truth'. The three case studies studied in this book each take as their object broadly technocratic systems of governance defined at least in part by truth claims, or by assertions of 'rationality' and 'efficiency'. For Zygmunt Bauman, for example, the camp system of wartime Europe was the awful apotheosis of an instrumental rationalism that underpinned the industrial and economic transformations constitutive of modernity – 'the rationality of evil (or was it the evil of rationality?)' (1989: 202). Some have even seen the camps' industrialisation of murder in a nightmarishly Fordist sense (what Hannah Arendt calls 'the fabrication of corpses') (quoted in Dietz, 2000; cf. Hachtmann, 2010). Similar claims also underpinned the epidemiological discourses governing HIV/AIDS in the 1980s and 1990s (which depended for their authority on their capacity to map the incidence of HIV accurately and recommend measures for its effective control), and the neoliberal techniques of global governance that CIRCA sought to parody (which rested on particular claims about the efficiency of markets as agents of social organisation).

While humour's critical and performative purchase in such contexts is demonstrated by this book's three case studies, it is less clear what humour means in contexts where authority does not depend on truth claims or on appeals to efficiency or rationality, but instead projects its own intemperance and inconsistency, its venality and opportunism, its fundamental *in*sincerity. In recent years, the capture of state apparatuses by various anti-pluralist leaders in the United States, the United Kingdom, Poland, Hungary, Brazil, Russia, the Philippines and elsewhere has been accompanied by attacks on political discourses, apparatuses and institutions and the open pursuit of personal enrichment, the cultivation of relations of patronage and/or the construction of an exclusionary vision of the nation into which is woven a commitment to the regime (cf. Werner-Müller, 2016). In contexts such as this – contexts not unlike the autocratic grotesque identified by Foucault in figures like Nero and Mussolini (2003a) – authority might be said to project a certain clownishness of its own. In such instances, humour may well lose its appeal as a way to make performative claims to identity and agency from a position of abjection. Indeed, there is a concern among some commentators that humour might even enable such political projects: what power do critical projects of problematisation and denaturalisation have on figures who themselves gleefully repudiate any sincere claim to naturalness, honesty, truth or virtue? (e.g. Smith, 2019; Grobe, 2020).

In this light, it is perhaps unsurprising that many of the most prominent global social movements of recent years have drawn upon a different emotional, tonal and methodological range from (for example) the 'global justice movement' of the late 1990s and early 2000s. The Black Lives Matter movement and the global school strikes taking place as part of youth-led demands for serious and immediate action on climate change (to take just two examples) demonstrate little interest in humour as a rhetorical technique or as a tactical methodology (which is not at all to say that their members are individually or collectively humourless). Yet both movements have made powerful and compelling claims to political agency and subjectivity from positions of political abjection. In looking towards humour, then, this thesis has ended up gesturing beyond it, towards a 'parasitic' mode of performance whose relationship to humour is obscure, ambiguous and indeterminate. It is precisely this obscurity, ambiguity and indeterminacy that constitutes the political importance not only of humour but of what I have here described as a parasitic politics, oscillating across the limits of order and, in so doing, performatively asserting the possibility (but never more than the possibility) of something else.

Notes

1 See Chapter 5.
2 See Chapter 4.

Bibliography

ACT UP Oral History Project interviews. Harvard University Library. Available at www.actuporalhistory.org/interviews/ (accessed 1 May 2020).

#004: Gregg Bordowitz (17 December 2002)
#010: Maria Maggenti (20 January 2003)
#012: Mark Harrington (8 March 2003)
#020: Michael Petrelis (21 April 2003)
#032: Ron Goldberg (25 October 2003)
#035: Larry Kramer (15 November 2003)
#040: Steve Quester (17 January 2004)
#043: Maxine Wolfe (19 February 2004)
#065: Bill Dobbs (21 November 2006)
#067: Peter Staley (9 December 2006)
#069: Heidi Dorow (17 April 2007)
#070: Marion Banzhaf (18 April 2007)
#073: David Barr (15 May 2007)
#076: Terry McGovern (25 May 2007)
#082: David Robinson (16 July 2007)
#097: Victor Mendolia (15 August 2008)
#099: Betty Williams (23 August 2008)
#102: Brian Zabcik (8 September 2008)
#109: Anna Blume (25 January 2010)
#175: Tom Keane (24 February 2015)
#186: Alan Klein (7 May 2015)

Interviews with former members of the Clandestine Insurgent Rebel Clown Army

- Private Individual, August 2016 (conducted remotely)
- Theo Price, September 2016 (conducted remotely)

Abrahamsen, R. (2003), 'African Studies and the postcolonial challenge', *African Affairs*, 102, no. 407: 189–210.

Abrams, M. H. (1991), *Doing Things with Texts: Essays in Criticism and Critical Theory* (New York and London: Norton).

ACT UP (1990), *ACT UP San Francisco Handbook* (San Francisco: ACT UP).

Acuto, M. (2014), 'Everyday International Relations: garbage, grand designs, and mundane matters', *International Political Sociology*, 8, no. 4: 345–362.

Adler-Nissen, R. and A. Tsinovoi (2019), 'International misrecognition: the politics of humour and national identity in Israel's public diplomacy', *European Journal of International Relations*, 25, no. 1: 3–29.

Adorno, T. (1997), *Prisms* (Cambridge, MA: MIT Press).

Agamben, G. (1998), *Homo Sacer: Sovereign Power and Bare Life* (Stanford: Stanford University Press).

Agamben, G. (2011), *The Kingdom and the Glory: For a Theological Genealogy of Economy and Government* (Stanford: Stanford University Press).

Agamben, G. (2015), *The Use of Bodies* (Stanford: Stanford University Press).

Aistrope, T. (2020), 'Popular culture, the body and world politics', *European Journal of International Relations*, 26, no. 1: 163–186.

Allen, M. (2006), 'I wrapped a giant condom over Jesse Helms' house'. Available at www.markallencam.com/toptenjan2006.html (accessed 14 July 2020).

Amoore, L. and A. Hall (2013), 'The clown at the gates of the camp: sovereignty, resistance and the figure of the fool', *Security Dialogue*, 44, no. 2: 93–110.

Anievas, A., N. Manchanda and R. Shilliam (2015), *Race and Racism in International Relations: Confronting the Global Colour Line* (Abingdon and New York: Routledge).

Applebaum, R. P. and W. I. Robinson, eds (2005), *Critical Globalization Studies* (New York and Abingdon: Routledge).

Appleman Williams, W. (2009), *The Tragedy of American Diplomacy* (New York: Norton).

Arad, Y. (1987), *Belzec, Sobibor, Treblinka: The Operation Reinhard Death Camps* (Bloomington: Indiana University Press).

Aradau, C. (2008), *Rethinking Trafficking in Women: Politics out of Security* (Basingstoke: Palgrave Macmillan).

Aradau, C. (2016), 'Political grammars of mobility, security and subjectivity', *Mobilities*, 11, no. 4: 564–574.

Aradau, C., M. Coward, E. Herschinger et al. (2015), 'Discourse/ materiality', in *Critical Security Methods: New Frameworks for*

Analysis, eds C. Aradau, J. Huysmans et al. (London and New York: Routledge), 57–84.
Archibugi, D. (2004), 'Cosmopolitan democracy and its critics: a review', *European Journal of International Relations*, 10, no. 3: 437–473.
Arendt, H. (1970), *On Violence* (Orlando, New York and London: Houghton Mifflin Harcourt).
Arendt, H. (2006), *Eichmann in Jerusalem: A Report on the Banality of Evil* (London: Penguin).
Aristotle (1992), *The Politics* (London: Penguin).
Aristotle (2006), *Poetics* (London: Penguin).
Arno, A. R. (1976), 'Joking, avoidance, and authority: verbal performance as an object of exchange in Fiji', *The Journal of the Polynesian Society*, 85, no. 1: 71–86.
Ashley, R. K. (1984), 'The poverty of neorealism', *International Organization*, 38, no. 2: 225–286.
Ashley, R. K. (1988), 'Untying the sovereign state: a double reading of the Anarchy Problematique', *Millennium: Journal of International Studies*, 17, no. 2: 227–262.
Ashley, R. K. (1989), 'Living on border lines: man, poststructuralism, and war', in *International/Intertextual Relations: Postmodern Readings of World Politics*, eds J. Der Derian and M. J. Shapiro (Lexington: Lexington Books), 259–322.
Ashley, R. K. and R. B. J. Walker (1990), 'Introduction: speaking the language of exile: dissident thought in International Studies, *International Studies Quarterly*, 34, no. 3: 259–268.
Assad, M. L. (1999), *Reading with Michel Serres: An Encounter with Time* (Albany: SUNY Press).
Athenaeus (1854), *The Deipnosophists* (London: Henry G. Bohn).
Barnett, M. and R. Duvall, eds (2005), *Power in Global Governance* (Cambridge: Cambridge University Press).
Bartelson, J. (1995), *A Genealogy of Sovereignty* (Cambridge: Cambridge University Press).
Basaran, T. et al., eds (2017), *International Political Sociology: Transversal Lines* (Abingdon: Routledge).
Bauman, Z. (1989), *Modernity and the Holocaust* (Ithaca: Cornell University Press).
Bein, A. (1964), 'The Jewish parasite: notes on the semantics of the Jewish problem, with special reference to Germany', *Leo Baeck Institute Yearbook*, 9, no. 1: 3–40.
Benigni, R., dir. (1997), *La Vita è Bella* (Melampo Cinematografica).
Benvenuti, A., ed. (2016), *Imprisoned: Drawings from Nazi Concentration Camps* (New York: Skyhorse Publishing).

Bergson, H. (1974), 'Laughter', in *Comedy*, ed. W. Sypher (New York: Doubleday), 59–190.
Bersani, L. (1987), 'Is the rectum a grave?', *October*, 43: 197–222.
Bigo, D. and E. McCluskey (2018), 'What is a PARIS approach to (in)securitization? Political anthropological research for international sociology, in *The Oxford Handbook of International Security*, eds A. Gheciu and W. C. Wohlforth (Oxford: Oxford University Press), 116–132.
Bigo, D. and R. B. J. Walker (2007a), 'International, political, sociology', *International Political Sociology*, 1, no. 1: 1–5.
Bigo, D. and R. B. J. Walker (2007b), 'Political sociology and the problem of the international', *Millennium: Journal of International Studies*, 35, no. 3: 725–739.
Billig, M. (2005), *Laughter and Ridicule: Towards a Social Critique of Humour* (London: SAGE).
Birnbaum, M. (2019), 'After Trump leaves NATO summit, weary diplomats delight in what they were able to accomplish on substance', *Washington Post* (5 December). Available at www.washingtonpost.com/world/europe/after-trump-leaves-nato-summit-weary-diplomats-delight-in-what-they-were-able-to-accomplish-on-substance/2019/12/05/96cefa48-0fc0-11ea-924c-b34d09bbc948_story.html (accessed 8 May 2020).
Björkdahl, A., M. Hall and T. Svensson (2019), 'Everyday international relations: editors' introduction', *Cooperation & Conflict*, 54, no. 2: 123–130.
Black, J., R. Weiss and A. Speciale (2015), 'Violent anti-austerity protests mar opening of new ECB headquarters in Germany', *Financial Post* (18 March). Available at http://business.financialpost.com/news/economy/violent-anti-austerity-protests-mar-opening-of-new-ecb-headquarters-in-germany (accessed 15 July 2020).
Blair, A. (2005), 'Chair's summary', G8 Summit, Gleneagles. Available at www.g8.utoronto.ca/summit/2005gleneagles/summary.html (accessed 15 July 2020).
Bleiker, R. (2000), *Popular Dissent, Human Agency and Global Politics* (Cambridge: Cambridge University Press).
Bleiker, R., ed. (2018), *Visual Global Politics* (London and New York: Routledge).
Bodkin, M. (1965), *Archetypal Patterns in Poetry: Psychological Studies of Imagination* (Oxford: Oxford University Press).
Bogad, L. M. (n.d.), 'CIRCA: The Clandestine Insurgent Rebel Clown Army'. Available at www.joaap.org/new3/bogad.html (accessed 15 July 2020).
Bogad, L. M. (2011), 'Clowndestine maneuvers: a study of clownfrontational tactics', in *Cultural Activism: Practices, Dilemmas, and Possibilities*, eds

B. Özden Fırat and A. Kuryel (Amsterdam and New York: Rodopi), 179–198.
Bogad, L. M. (2016), *Tactical Performance: The Theory and Practice of Serious Play* (London and New York: Routledge).
Boochani, B. (2018), *No Friend but the Mountains: Writing from Manus Prison* (Sydney: Picador Australia).
Borges, J. L. (1999), 'John Wilkins' analytical language', in *Selected Non-Fictions* (New York: Viking), 229–232.
Borradori, G. (2003), *Philosophy in a Time of Terror: Dialogues with Jurgen Habermas and Jacques Derrida* (Chicago: University of Chicago Press).
Boseley, S. (2016), 'Think the Aids epidemic is over? Far from it – it could be getting worse', *Guardian* (31 July). Available at www.theguardian.com/global-development/2016/jul/31/aids-epidemic-getting-worse-drug-resistance-cost (accessed 14 July 2020).
Boyle, M. S. (2011), 'Play with authority!: radical performance and performative irony', in *Cultural Activism: Practices, Dilemmas, and Possibilities*, eds B. Özden Fırat and A. Kuryel (Amsterdam and New York: Rodopi), 199–218.
Brassett, J. (2009), 'British irony, global justice: a pragmatic reading of Chris Brown, Banksy and Ricky Gervais', *Review of International Studies*, 35, no. 1: 219–245.
Brassett, J. (2016), 'British comedy, global resistance: Russell Brand, Charlie Brooker and Stewart Lee', *European Journal of International Relations*, 22, no. 1: 168–191.
Brassett, J. and A. Sutton (2017), 'British satire, everyday politics: Chris Morris, Armando Iannucci and Charlie Brooker, *The British Journal of Politics and International Relations*, 19, no. 2: 245–262.
Brassett, J., C. Browning and A. Wedderburn (2021), 'Humorous states: IR, new diplomacy and the rise of comedy in global politics', *Global Society*, 35, no. 1: 1–7.
Brightman, R. (1999), 'Traditions of subversion and the subversion of tradition: cultural criticism in Maidu clown performances', *American Anthropologist*, 101, no. 2: 272–287.
Brown, S. D. (2002), 'Michel Serres: Science, translation and the logic of the parasite', *Theory, Culture & Society*, 19, no. 3: 1–27.
Brown, S. D. (2004), 'Parasite logic', *Journal of Organizational Change Management*, 17, no. 4: 383–395.
Brown, S. D. (2013), 'In praise of the parasite: the dark organizational theory of Michel Serres', *Informática na Educação: Teoria e Prática*, 16, no. 1: 83–100.
Buse, P. (2015), 'Clowning and power', lecture at Central St Martins, London (26 February). Available at https://backdoorbroadcasting.net/2015/02/peter-buse-clowning-and-power/ (accessed 8 May 2020).

Butler, J. (2006), *Gender Trouble* (New York and London: Routledge).
Butler, J. (2010), 'Performative agency', *Journal of Cultural Economy*, 3, no. 2: 147–161.
Butler, J. (2011), *Bodies That Matter* (London and New York: Routledge).
Butterfield, H. (1950), 'The tragic element in modern political conflict', *Review of Politics*, 12: 147–164.
Butterworth, M. L., ed. (2017), *Sport and Militarism: Contemporary Global Perspectives* (Abingdon: Routledge).
Campbell, C. (2003), *Letting Them Die: Why HIV/AIDS Intervention Programmes Fail* (Bloomington: Indiana University Press).
Campbell, D. (1992), *Writing Security: United States Foreign Policy and the Politics of Identity* (Minneapolis: University of Minnesota Press).
Campbell, D. (1996), 'Political prosaics, transversal politics and the anarchical world', in *Challenging Boundaries: Global Flows, Territorial Identities*, eds M. J. Shapiro and H. R. Alker (Minneapolis: University of Minnesota Press), 7–32.
Campbell, D. (2003), 'Cultural governance and pictorial resistance: reflections on the imaging of war', *Review of International Studies*, 29, 57–73.
Campbell, D. (2005), 'The onto-politics of critique', *International Relations*, 19, no. 1: 127–134.
Carlomusto, J. and M. Maggenti, dirs (1988), *Doctors, Liars and Women: AIDS Activists Say No To Cosmo* (ACT UP).
Carpenter, C. (2016), 'Rethinking the political-/-science-/fiction nexus: global policy making and the campaign to stop killer robots', *Perspectives on Politics*, 14, no. 1: 53–69.
Carr, G. and H. C. Mytum, eds (2012), *Cultural Heritage and Prisoners of War: Creativity Behind Barbed Wire* (London and New York: Routledge).
Carroll, T. W. (2015), *Mobilising New York: AIDS, Antipoverty, and Feminist Activism* (Chapel Hill: University of North Carolina Press).
Christiansen, A. E. and J. J. Hanson (1996), 'Comedy as cure for tragedy: ACT UP and the rhetoric of AIDS', *Quarterly Journal of Speech*, 82: 157–170.
Cohen-Cruz, J. (2002), 'At cross purposes: the Church Ladies for Choice', in *From ACT UP to the WTO: Urban Protest and Community Building in the Era of Globalisation*, eds B. Shepard and R. Hayduk (London and New York: Verso), 233–241
Comaroff, J. (2007), 'Beyond bare life: AIDS, (bio)politics, and the neoliberal order', *Public Culture*, 19, no. 1: 197–219.
Conant, J. (2010), *A Poetics of Resistance: The Revolutionary Public Relations of the Zapatista Insurgency* (Oakland: AK Press).
Connolly, W. E. (1991), *Identity\Difference: Democratic Negotiations of Political Paradox* (Ithaca: Cornell University Press).

Connolly, W. E. (2007), 'The complexities of sovereignty', in *On Agamben: Sovereignty and Life*, eds M. Calarco and S. DeCaroli (Stanford: Stanford University Press), 23–42.

Connolly, W. E. (2009), 'Foreword: the Left and ontopolitics', in *A Leftist Ontology: Beyond Relativism and Identity Politics*, ed. Carsten Strathausen (Minneapolis: University of Minnesota Press), ix–xviii.

Constantinides Hero, A. and J. Thomas (2000), *Byzantine Monastic Foundation Documents*, 5 vols (Washington, DC: Dumbarton Oaks Research Library and Collection).

Corner, S. (2013a), 'The politics of the parasite (Part One)', *Phoenix*, 67, nos 1 and 2: 43–80.

Corner, S. (2013b), 'The politics of the parasite (Part Two)', *Phoenix*, 67, nos 3 and 4: 223–236.

Cornford, F. (2011), *The Origin of Attic Comedy* (Cambridge: Cambridge University Press).

Crimp, D. (1987a), 'AIDS: cultural analysis, cultural criticism', *October*, 43: 3–16.

Crimp, D. (1987b), 'How to have promiscuity in an epidemic', *October*, 43: 237–271.

Crimp, D. with A. Rolston (1990), *Aids Demo Graphics* (Seattle: Bay Press).

Critchley, S. (1999), 'Comedy and finitude: displacing the tragic-heroic paradigm in philosophy and psychoanalysis', *Constellations*, 6, no. 1: 108–122.

Critchley, S. (2002), *On Humour* (London and New York: Routledge).

Critchley, S. (2012), *Infinitely Demanding: Ethics of Commitment, Politics of Resistance* (London: Verso).

Croft, S. and N. Vaughan-Williams (2017), 'Fit for purpose? Fitting ontological security studies "into" the discipline of International Relations: towards a vernacular turn', *Cooperation and Conflict*, 52, no. 1: 12–30.

Cyler, K. (2002), 'Building a healing community from ACT UP to Housing Works', in *From ACT UP to the WTO: Urban Protest and Community Building in the Era of Globalisation*, eds B. Shepard and R. Hayduk (London and New York: Verso), 351–360.

Damon, C. (1997), *The Mask of the Parasite: A Pathology of Roman Patronage* (Ann Arbor: University of Michigan Press).

Dauphinee, E. (2010), 'The ethics of autoethnography', *Review of International Studies*, 36, no. 4: 799–818.

Dauphinee, E. (2013), *The Politics of Exile* (London and New York: Routledge).

Davidson, J. (1997), *Courtesans and Fishcakes: The Consuming Passions of Classical Athens* (London: HarperCollins).

Davies, M. and M. Niemann (2002), 'The everyday spaces of global politics', *New Political Science*, 24, no. 4: 557–577.

Davis, A. (1983), *Women, Race and Class* (New York: Vintage).

de Certeau, M. (1984), *The Practice of Everyday Life* (Berkeley: University of California Press).

de Goede, M. (2005), 'Carnival of money: politics of dissent in an era of globalising finance', in *The Global Resistance Reader*, ed. L. Amoore (London: Routledge), 379–392.

Der Derian, J. and M. J. Shapiro, eds (1989), *International/Intertextual Relations: Postmodern Readings of World Politics* (Lexington: Lexington Books).

Derrida, J. (1981), *Dissemination* (London: Athlone Press).

Derrida, J. (1997), *Of Grammatology* (Baltimore and London: Johns Hopkins University Press).

Derrida, J. (2005), *Rogues* (Stanford: Stanford University Press).

Dietz, M. G. (2000), 'Arendt and the Holocaust', *The Cambridge Companion to Hannah Arendt*, ed. D. Villa (Cambridge: Cambridge University Press), 86–110.

Dillon, M. (1996), *Politics of Security: Towards a Political Philosophy of Continental Thought* (London and New York: Routledge).

Dillon, M. (1999), 'The sovereign and the stranger', in *Sovereignty and Subjectivity*, eds J. Edkins, N. Persram and V. Pin-Fat (Boulder: Lynne Rienner), 117–140.

Dingli, S. (2015), 'We need to talk about silence: re-examining silence in International Relations theory', *European Journal of International Relations*, 21, no. 4: 721–742.

Dittmer, J. (2013), *Captain America and the Nationalist Superhero: Metaphors, Narratives, and Geopolitics* (Philadelphia: Temple University Press).

DIVA TV Collective, dirs (1990), *Like a Prayer: Stop the Church* (ACT UP).

Dodds, K. (2007), 'Steve Bell's eye: cartoons, geopolitics and the visualisation of the "War on Terror"', *Security Dialogue*, 38, no. 2: 157–177.

Dodds, K. and P. Kirby (2013), 'It's not a laughing matter: critical geopolitics, humour and unlaughter', *Geopolitics*, 18, no. 1: 45–59.

Douglas, M. (1968), 'The social control of cognition: some factors in joke perception', *Man*, 3, no. 3: 361–376.

Douglas, M. (1975), *Implicit Meanings: Essays in Anthropology* (London: Routledge), 90–116.

Doyal, L. (2010), 'Putting gender into health and globalisation debates: new perspectives and old challenges', *Third World Quarterly*, 23, no. 2: 233–250.

Eco, U. (1984), 'The frames of comic freedom', in *Carnival!*, ed. Thomas A. Sebeok (Berlin and New York: Moulton), 1–10.

Eco, U. (1995), *The Search for the Perfect Language* (Oxford: Blackwell).
Eco, U. (2004), *The Name of the Rose* (London: Vintage).
Edkins, J. (1999), *Post-structuralism and International Relations: Bringing the Political Back in* (Boulder: Lynne Rienner).
Edkins, J. (2013), 'Novel writing in International Relations: openings for a creative practice', *Security Dialogue*, 44, no. 4: 281–297.
Edkins, J. and V. Pin-Fat (2004), 'Introduction: life, power, resistance', in *Sovereign Lives: Power in Global Politics*, ed. J. Edkins, V. Pin-Fat and M. Shapiro (New York and London: Routledge), 1–22.
Edkins, J. and V. Pin-Fat (2005), 'Through the wire: relations of power and relations of violence', *Millennium: Journal of International Studies*, 34, no. 1: 1–24.
Edkins, J., N. Persram and V. Pin-Fat, eds (1999), *Sovereignty and Subjectivity* (Boulder: Lynne Rienner).
Eigo, J., M. Harrington, M. McCarthy et al. (1988), *FDA Action Handbook* (12 September). Available at www.actupny.org/documents/FDAhandbook6.html (accessed 14 July 2020).
el-Ojeili, C. (2005), 'Confronting globalization in the twenty-first century', in *Confronting Globalization: Humanity, Justice and the Renewal of Politics*, eds C. el-Ojeili and M. Hayden (Basingstoke: Palgrave Macmillan), 1–22.
el-Ojeili, C. and M. Hayden, eds (2006), *Critical Theories of Globalization: An Introduction* (Basingstoke: Palgrave Macmillan).
Elbe, S. (2005), 'AIDS, security, biopolitics', *International Relations*, 19, no. 4: 403–419.
Elbe, S. (2006), 'Should HIV/AIDS be securitized? The ethical dilemmas of linking HIV/AIDS and security', *International Studies Quarterly*, 50, no. 1: 119–144.
Elgot, J. (2015), 'G7 summit: 8,000 protesters gather as leaders prepare wide-ranging talks', *Guardian* (6 June). Available at www.theguardian.com/global/2015/jun/06/g7-summit-protesters-gather-garmisch-partenkirchen-germany-alpine-resort (accessed 15 July 2020).
Elias, J. and S. M. Rai (2019), 'Feminist everyday political economy: space, time, and violence', *Review of International Studies*, 45, no. 2: 201–220.
Elias, J. and A. Roberts (2016), 'Feminist global political economies of the everyday: from bananas to bingo', *Globalizations*, 13, no. 6: 787–800.
Enloe, C. (2004), *The Curious Feminist: Searching for Women in a New Age of Empire* (Berkeley: University of California Press).
Enloe, C. (2014), *Bananas, Beaches and Bases: Making Feminist Sense of International Politics* (Berkeley: University of California Press).
Enloe, C. (2016), 'Flick of the skirt: a feminist challenge to IR's coherent narrative', *International Political Sociology*, 10, no. 4: 320–331.

Epstein, S. (1996), *Impure Science: AIDS, Activism and the Politics of Knowledge* (Berkeley and Oxford: University of California Press).

Eroukhmanoff, C. (2019), 'Responding to terrorism with peace, love and solidarity: "Je suis Charlie", "Peace" and "I Heart MCR"', *Journal of International Political Theory*, 15, no. 2: 169–189.

Erskine, T. and R. N. Lebow, eds (2012), *Tragedy and International Relations* (Basingstoke: Palgrave Macmillan).

Evans, B. (2010), 'Foucault's legacy: security, war and violence in the 21st century', *Security Dialogue*, 41, no. 4: 413–433.

Fassin, D. (2008), 'The politics of death: race war, biopower and AIDS in the post-apartheid', in *Foucault on Politics, Security and War*, eds M. Dillon and A. Neal (Basingstoke: Palgrave Macmillan), 151–165.

Fiennes, S. dir. (2012), *The Pervert's Guide to Ideology* (Zeitgeist Films).

Fineberg, H. V. (1988), 'The social dimensions of AIDS', *Scientific American*, 259, no. 4: 128–134.

Fisher, M. (2009), *Capitalist Realism: Is There No Alternative?* (London: Zer0 Books).

Foucault, M. (1982), 'The subject and power', *Critical Inquiry*, 8, no. 4: 777–795.

Foucault, M. (1991), *Discipline and Punish: The Birth of the Prison* (London: Penguin).

Foucault, M. (1998), *The History of Sexuality, vol. 1: The Will to Knowledge* (London: Penguin).

Foucault, M. (2001), *Fearless Speech* (Los Angeles: Semiotext(e)).

Foucault, M. (2002), *The Order of Things: An Archaeology of the Human Sciences* (London and New York: Routledge).

Foucault, M. (2003a), *Abnormal: Lectures at the Collège de France, 1974–1975* (New York: Picador).

Foucault, M. (2003b), *Society Must Be Defended: Lectures at the Collège de France, 1975–1976* (London: Penguin).

Foucault, M. (2005), 'On method', in *The Global Resistance Reader*, ed. L. Amoore (London and New York: Routledge), 86–91.

Foucault, M. (2008), *The Birth of Biopolitics: Lectures at the Collège de France, 1978–1979* (Basingstoke: Palgrave Macmillan).

Foucault, M. (2014), *On The Government of the Living: Lectures at the Collège de France 1979–1980* (Basingstoke: Palgrave Macmillan).

France, D. dir. (2012), *How To Survive a Plague* (Public Square Films/Ninety Thousand Words).

Frazer, J. A. (1954), *The Golden Bough* (New York: Macmillan).

Freud, S. (2002), *The Joke and Its Relation to the Unconscious* (London: Penguin).

Frost, M. (2003), 'Tragedy, ethics and International Relations', *International Relations*, 17, no. 4: 477–495.

Frost, M. (2008), 'Tragedy, reconciliation and reconstruction', *European Journal of Social Theory*, 11, no. 3: 351–365.
Frye, N. (1973), *Anatomy of Criticism: Four Essays* (Princeton: Princeton University Press).
Garde, M. (2008), 'The pragmatics of rude jokes with Grandad: joking relationships in Aboriginal Australia', *Anthropological Forum*, 18, no. 3: 235–253.
Gill, S. (1995), 'Globalisation, market civilisation, and disciplinary neoliberalism', *Millennium: Journal of International Studies*, 24, no. 3: 399–423.
Girard, R. (1986), *The Scapegoat* (Baltimore: Johns Hopkins University Press).
Girard, R. (2005), *Violence and the Sacred* (London: Continuum).
Goldberg, R. (1998), 'When PWAs first sat at the high table', July. Available at www.actupny.org/documents/montreal.html (accessed 14 July 2020).
Gorringe, H. and M. Rosie (2008), 'The polis of "global" protest: policing protest at the G8 in Scotland', *Current Sociology*, 56, no. 5: 691–710.
Gould, D. (2009), *Moving Politics: Emotion and ACT UP's Fight Against AIDS* (Chicago: University of Chicago Press).
Gould, R. (1988), 'Reassuring news about AIDS: a doctor tells why *you* might not be at risk', *Cosmopolitan* (January).
Graeber, D. (2002), 'The new anarchists', *New Left Review*, 13: 61–73.
Graham-Harrison, E. (2015), 'Niger rioters torch churches and attack French firms in Charlie Hebdo protest', *Observer* (17 January). Available at www.theguardian.com/world/2015/jan/17/niger-protesters-burn-churches-charlie-hebdo-protest (accessed 28 April 2020).
Grayson, K. (2016), *The Cultural Politics of Targeted Killing: On Drones, Counter-Insurgency and Violence* (London and New York: Routledge).
Grayson, K., M. Davies and S. Philpott (2009), 'Pop goes IR? Researching the popular culture–world politics continuum', *Politics*, 29, no. 3: 155–163.
Greenberg, R. (1992), 'ACT UP explained'. Available at www.actupny.org/documents/greenbergAU.html (accessed 14 July 2020).
Griffin, P. (2015), 'Development institutions and neoliberal globalisation', in *Gender Matters in Global Politics: A Feminist Introduction to International Relations*, ed. L. J. Shepherd (London: Routledge), 210–224.
Grindon, G. (2004), 'Carnival against capital: a comparison of Bakhtin, Vaneigem and Bey', *Anarchist Studies*, 12, no. 2: 146–61.
Grobe, C. (2020), 'The artist is president: performance art and other keywords in the age of Donald Trump', *Critical Inquiry*, 46, no. 4: 764–805.
Groensteen, T. (2013), *Comics and Narration* (Jackson: University Press of Mississippi).

Grove, D. (1997), 'Fucked up models of AIDS prevention', speech at the ACT UP 10 year Anniversary Conference (22 March). Available at actupny.org/diva/CBgrove.html (accessed 14 July 2020).

H.R.5638 (99th Congress, 2 October 1986): A bill to prohibit the transfer of body fluids by Federal officers and employees or members of the armed forces of the United States who have Acquired Immune Deficiency Syndrome, and for other purposes.

H.R.345 (100th Congress, 6 January 1987): A bill to prohibit the transfer of body fluids by Federal officers and employees or members of the armed forces of the United States who have Acquired Immune Deficiency Syndrome, and for other purposes.

H.R.3058 (100th Congress, 30 July 1987): Departments of Labor, Health and Human Services, and Education and Related Agencies Appropriations Act, 1988.

H.R.3102 (101st Congress, 3 August 1989): Public Health Response to AIDS Act of 1989.

Hachtmann, R. (2010), 'Fordism and unfree labour: aspects of the work deployment of concentration camp prisoners in German industry between 1941 and 1944', *International Review of Social History*, 55, no. 3: 485–513.

Hall, I. (2014), 'The satiric vision of politics: ethics, interests and disorders', *European Journal of International Relations*, 20, no. 1: 217–236.

Hall, S. (1992), 'Cultural Studies and its theoretical legacies', in *Cultural Studies*, eds L. Grossberg, C. Nelson and P. Treichler (Routledge: New York), 277–286.

Halliwell, S. (2008), *Greek Laughter: A Study of Cultural Psychology from Homer to Early Christianity* (Cambridge: Cambridge University Press).

Hansen, L. (2006), *Security as Practice: Discourse Analysis and the Bosnian War* (Abingdon: Routledge).

Hansen, L. (2011), 'The politics of securitization and the Muhammed cartoon crisis: a post-structuralist perspective', *Security Dialogue* 42, nos 4–5: 357–369.

Hansen, L. (2017), 'Reading comics for the field of International Relations: theory, method, and the Bosnian War', *European Journal of International Relations*, 23, no. 3: 581–608.

Haraway, D. (2013), 'The biopolitics of postmodern bodies: constitutions of self in immune system discourse', in *Biopolitics: A Reader*, eds T. Campbell and A. Sitze (Durham and London: Duke University Press), 274–309.

Harman, S. (2010), *The World Bank and HIV/AIDS: Setting a Global Agenda* (New York and London: Routledge).

Harman, S. (2018), 'Making the invisible visible in International Relations: film, co-produced research and transnational feminism', *European Journal of International Relations*, 24, no. 4: 791–813.

Harrington, M. (1997), 'Some transitions in the history of AIDS treatment activism: from therapeutic utopianism to pragmatic praxis', in *Acting on AIDS: Sex, Drugs and Politics*, eds J. Oppenheimer and H. Reckitt (London: Serpent's Tail), 273–286.

Harris, C. M. (2018), *Obscene Pedagogies: Transgressive Talk and Sexual Education in Late Medieval Britain* (Ithaca: Cornell University Press).

Harvie, D., K. Milburn, B. Trott et al., eds (2005), *Shut Them Down! The G8, Gleneagles 2005 and the Movement of Movements* (Leeds: Dissent!).

Held, D. and A. McGrew, eds (2002), *Governing Globalization: Power, Authority, and Global Governance* (Cambridge: Polity).

Held, D. and A. McGrew (2007), *Globalization/Anti-Globalization: Beyond the Great Divide* (Cambridge: Polity).

Heyward, W. L. and J. W. Curran (1988), 'The epidemiology of AIDS in the U.S.', *Scientific American*, 259, no. 4: 72–81.

Hilferty, R. and R. Huff, dirs (1991), *TAG Helms* (Treatment Action Guerillas). Available at www.youtube.com/watch?v=TS-w4Pqvkuw (accessed 14 July 2020).

Hobbes, T. (2005), *Leviathan* (Cambridge: Cambridge University Press).

Hodkinson, S. and P. Chatterton (2006), 'Autonomy in the city? Reflections on the social centres movement in the UK', *City: Analysis of Urban Trends, Culture, Theory, Policy, Action*, 10, no. 3: 305–315.

Honig, B. (2013), *Antigone, Interrupted* (Cambridge: Cambridge University Press).

Hubbard, J. dir. (2012), *United in Anger: A History of ACT UP* (United in Anger, inc.).

Hurrell, A. and N. Woods (1995), 'Globalisation and inequality', *Millennium: Journal of International Studies*, 24, no. 3: 447–470.

Hutcheon, L. (1989), *The Politics of Postmodernism* (London and New York: Routledge).

Hutcheon, L. (2000), *A Theory of Parody: The Teachings of Twentieth-Century Art Forms* (Urbana and Chicago: University of Illinois Press).

Hutcheson, F. (1758), *Reflections upon Laughter, and Remarks on the Fable of the Bees* (Glasgow: Robert & Andrew Foulis).

Huysmans, J. (2008), 'The jargon of exception – on Schmitt, Agamben and the absence of political society', *International Political Sociology*, 2, no. 2: 165–183.

Huysmans, J. and J. P. Nogueira (2016), 'Ten years of IPS: fracturing IR', *International Political Sociology*, 10, no. 4: 299–319.

Ikenberry, G. J. (2009), 'Liberal Internationalism 3.0: America and the dilemmas of liberal world order', *Perspectives on Politics*, 7, no. 1: 71–87.

Inayatullah, N. and D. Blaney (2004), *International Relations and the Problem of Difference* (New York and London: Routledge).
Irigaray, L. (1985), *This Sex Which is Not One*, trans. C. Porter (Ithaca: Cornell University Press).
Jackes, M. (1969), 'Wikmunkan joking relationships', *Mankind*, 7, no. 2, 128–131.
Jahn, B. (2000), *The Cultural Construction of International Relations: The Invention of the State of Nature* (Basingstoke: Palgrave Macmillan).
Jarry, Alfred (1968), *The Ubu Plays* (New York: Grove Press).
Jordan, J. (n.d.), 'Clandestine Insurgent Rebel Clown Army', *Beautiful Trouble*. Available at http://beautifultrouble.org/case/clandestine-insurgent-rebel-clown-army/ (accessed 15 July 2020).
Kalyvas, A. (2005), 'The sovereign weaver: beyond the camp', in *Politics, Metaphysics, and Death: Essays on Giorgio Agamben's Homo Sacer*, ed. A. Norris (Durham and London: Duke University Press), 107–134.
Kaldor, M. (1999), *New and Old Wars: Organized Violence in a Global Era* (Cambridge: Polity).
Kant, I. (2007), *Critique of Judgment*, trans. J. C. Meredith (Oxford: Oxford University Press).
Klein, N. (2002), *Fences and Windows: Dispatches from the Front Lines of the Globalization Debate* (London: Picador).
Klepto, K. (2004), 'Making war with love: The Clandestine Insurgent Rebel Clown Army', *City: Analysis of Urban Trends, Culture, Theory, Policy, Action*, 8, no. 3: 403–411.
Klepto, K. and M. Up Evil (2005), 'The Clandestine Insurgent Rebel Clown Army goes to Scotland via a few other places', in *Shut Them Down! The G8, Gleneagles 2005 and the Movement of Movements*, eds D. Harvie, K. Milburn, B. Trott et al. (Leeds: Dissent!), 243–254.
Konstan, D. (1997), *Friendship in the Classical World* (Cambridge: Cambridge University Press).
Koogie, C. (2005), 'Private parts in the general mayhem', in *Shut Them Down! The G8, Gleneagles 2005 and the Movement of Movements*, eds D. Harvie, K. Milburn, B. Trott et al. (Leeds: Dissent!), 127–133.
Kotek, J. and D. Pasamonik (2014), *Mickey à Gurs: Les carnets de dessins de Horst Rosenthal* (Paris: Calmann-Lévy/le Mémorial de la Shoah).
Kristeva, J. (1982), *Powers of Horror: An Essay on Abjection* (New York: Columbia University Press).
Kuusisto, R. (2009), 'Comic plots as conflict resolution strategy', *European Journal of International Relations*, 15, no. 4: 601–626.
Laclau, E. (2007), 'Bare life or social indeterminacy?', in *On Agamben: Sovereignty and Life*, eds M. Calarco and S. DeCaroli (Stanford: Stanford University Press), 11–22.

Laertius, Diogenes (1853), *Lives of Eminent Philosophers* (London: Henry G. Bohn).

Laharie, C. (2008), *Gurs – L'art derrière les barbelés* (Biarritz: Atlantica).

Lankester, E. R. (1880), *Degeneration: A Chapter in Darwinism* (London: MacMillan & Co.).

Lawson, S. (2006), *Culture and Context in World Politics* (Basingstoke: Palgrave Macmillan).

Lebow, R. N. (2003), *The Tragic Vision of Politics: Ethics, Interests and Orders* (Cambridge: Cambridge University Press).

Lefebvre, H. (2014), *Critique of Everyday Life* (London: Verso).

Levi, P. (1959), *If This Is A Man* (New York: Orion Press).

Levi, P. (1987), *The Reawakening* (New York: Simon & Schuster).

Lewis, W. (1928), *The Wild Body: A Soldier of Humour and Other Stories* (New York: Harcourt, Brace & Co.).

Lisle, D. (2016), 'Waiting for international political sociology: a field guide to living in-between', *International Political Sociology*, 10, no. 4: 417–433.

Livingston, J., dir. (1990), *Paris is Burning* (Off-White Productions).

Lorde, A. (1995), 'Age, race, class, and sex: women redefining difference', in *Words of Fire: An Anthology of African-American Feminist Thought*, ed. B. Guy-Sheftall (New York: New Press), 284–292.

Lorenzetti, L. (2015), 'Protesters, police clash as the European Central Bank opens its new headquarters', *Fortune* (18 March). Available at http://fortune.com/2015/03/18/protesters-police-clash-ecb-headquarters/ (accessed 15 July 2020).

Lucey, C. and S. Meichtrey (2019), 'Trump leaves NATO summit after video flap', *The Wall Street Journal* (4 December). Available at www.wsj.com/articles/trump-risks-further-isolation-as-macron-relationship-sours-11575455075 (accessed 8 May 2020).

Lyons, K. and P. Wintour (2019), 'Footage appears to show world leaders joking about Trump at Nato summit', *Guardian* (4 December). Available at www.theguardian.com/us-news/2019/dec/04/footage-appears-to-show-world-leaders-joking-about-trump-at-nato-summit (accessed 8 May 2020).

Mansfield, N. (2008), 'Sovereignty as its own question: Derrida's *Rogues*', *Contemporary Political Theory*, 7, no. 4: 361–375.

Mbali, M. (2013), *South African AIDS Activism and Global Health Politics* (Basingstoke: Palgrave MacMillan).

Mbembe, A. (2001), *On the Postcolony* (Berkeley: University of California Press).

McClish, C. L. (2007), 'Social protest, freedom, and play as rebellion' (doctoral thesis submitted to the University of Massachusetts at Amherst).

McCloud, S. (1994), *Understanding Comics: The Invisible Art* (London: HarperCollins).
McGlew, J. (2002), *Citizens on Stage: Comedy and Political Culture in the Athenian Democracy* (Ann Arbor: Michigan University Press).
McInnes, C. (2006), 'HIV/AIDS and security', *International Affairs*, 82, no. 2: 315–326.
Mead, M. (2012), *Kinship in the Admiralty Islands* (London and New York: Routledge).
Mearsheimer, J. J. (2001), *The Tragedy of Great Power Politics* (New York: Norton).
Megargee, G. P. ed. (2018), *The United States Holocaust Memorial Museum Encyclopaedia of Camps and Ghettos, 1933–1945*, 7 vols (Bloomington: Indiana University Press).
Meyer, R. (2003), 'The Jesse Helms theory of art', *October*, 104: 131–148.
Michaels, E. (1990), *Unbecoming* (Virginia Beach, VA: Empress).
Morgenthau, H. J. (1947), *Scientific Man and Power Politics* (London: Latimer House Limited).
Morgenthau, H. J. (1962), *Politics in the Twentieth Century*, 3 vols (Chicago: University of Chicago Press).
Morgenthau, H. J. (1969), 'The present tragedy of America', *Worldview*, 12, no. 9: 14–15.
Morreall, J. (1983), *Taking Laughter Seriously* (Albany: SUNY Press, 1983).
Morreall, J., ed. (1987), *The Philosophy of Laughter and Humour* (Albany: SUNY Press).
Musolff, A. (2014), *Metaphor, Nation and the Holocaust: The Concept of the Body Politic* (New York and London: Routledge).
Nader, A. ed. (2007), *Traumatic Verses: On Poetry in German from the Concentration Camps, 1933–1945* (New York: Camden House).
Navarre, M. (1987), 'Fighting the victim label', *October*, 43: 143–146.
Neal, A. (2006), 'Foucault in Guantánamo: towards an archaeology of the exception', *Security Dialogue*, 37, no. 1: 31–46.
Niebuhr, R. (1938), *Beyond Tragedy: Essays on the Christian Interpretation of History* (London: Nisbet and Sons).
Niebuhr, R. (1964), *The Nature and Destiny of Man* (New York: Charles Scribner's Sons).
Notes from Nowhere, eds (2003), *We Are Everywhere: The Irresistible Rise of Global Anticapitalism* (London: Verso).
Nsouli, S. (2007), 'What is the IMF doing to help countries maximize the benefits of globalization?', speech delivered at the Crans Montana Forum (29 June). Available at www.imf.org/en/News/Articles/2015/09/28/04/53/sp062907 (accessed 15 July 2020).

Odysseos, L. (2001), 'Laughing matters: peace, democracy and the challenge of the comic narrative', *Millennium: Journal of International Studies*, 30, no. 3: 709–732.
Ollman, D., S. Price, C. Smith, dirs (2003), *The Yes Men* (Bluemark Productions).
Orgel, S. and A. Braunmuller, eds (2002), *The Complete Pelican Shakespeare* (London: Penguin).
Orwell, G. (2002), 'Shooting an elephant', in *Essays* (London: Everyman, 2002), 42–49.
Özden Fırat, B. and A. Kuryel (2011a), *Cultural Activism: Practices, Dilemmas, and Possibilities* (Amsterdam and New York: Rodopi).
Özden Fırat, B. and A. Kuryel (2011b), 'Introduction', in *Cultural Activism: Practices, Dilemmas, and Possibilities*, eds B. Özden Fırat and A. Kuryel (Amsterdam and New York: Rodopi), 9–20.
Ozguc, U. (2020), 'Borders, detention, and the disruptive power of the noisy-subject', *International Political Sociology*, 14, no. 1: 77–93.
Paik, A. N. (2013), 'Carceral quarantine at Guantánamo: legacies of US imprisonment of Haitian refugees, 1991–1994', *Radical History Review*, 115: 142–168.
Palmer, J. (1994), *Taking Humour Seriously* (London: Routledge).
Patton, C. (1985), *Sex & Germs: The Politics of AIDS* (Boston: South End Press).
Patton, C. (1990), *Inventing AIDS* (New York and London: Routledge).
Patton, C. (1994), *Last Served? Gendering the HIV Pandemic* (London: Taylor & Francis).
Patton, C. (1996), 'Queer peregrinations', in *Challenging Boundaries: Global Flows, Territorial Identities*, eds H. Alker and M. J. Shapiro (Minneapolis: University of Minnesota Press), 363–382.
Peterson, V. S., ed. (1992), *Gendered States: Feminist (Re)Visions of International Relations Theory* (Boulder: Lynne Rienner).
Pick, D. (1993), *Faces of Degeneration: A European Disorder, c. 1848–1918* (Cambridge: Cambridge University Press).
Plato (1987), *The Republic* (London: Penguin).
Plato (1997), *Philebus*, in *The Complete Works*, ed. J. M. Cooper (Indianapolis and Cambridge: Hackett), 398–456
Plato (2005), *The Symposium* (London: Penguin).
Pollock, G. (2018), *Charlotte Salomon and the Theatre of Memory* (New Haven: Yale University Press).
Powers, M. (1991), 'Legal protections of confidential medical information and the need for anti-discrimination laws', in *AIDS, Women and the Next Generation: Towards a Morally Acceptable Public Policy for HIV Testing of Pregnant Women and Newborns*, eds R. R. Faden, G. Geller

and M. Powers (New York and Oxford: Oxford University Press), 221–245.
Prozorov, S. (2014), *Agamben and Politics: A Critical Introduction* (Edinburgh: Edinburgh University Press).
Puggioni, R. (2005), 'Resisting sovereign power: camps in-between exception and dissent', in *The Politics of Protection: Sites of Insecurity and Political Agency*, eds A. Dobson, J. Huysmans and R. Prokhovnik (London and New York: Routledge), 68–83.
PWA Coalition (1987a), 'Founding statement of people with AIDS/ARC (The Denver Principles)', *October*, 43: 148–149.
PWA Coalition (1987b), 'A patient's Bill of Rights', *October*, 43: 160.
Radcliffe-Brown, A. R. (1940), 'On joking relationships', *Africa: Journal of the International African Institute*, 13, no. 3: 195–210.
Radcliffe-Brown, A. R. (1949), 'A further note on joking relationships', *Africa: Journal of the International African Institute*, 19, no. 2: 133–140.
Rancière, J. (1999), *Disagreement: Politics and Philosophy* (Minneapolis: University of Minnesota Press).
Rancière, J. (2004), *The Politics of Aesthetics* (New York and London: Bloomsbury).
Reagan, R. (1985), 'The President's news conference' (17 September). Transcript available at www.presidency.ucsb.edu/ws/index.php?pid=39125 (accessed 14 July 2020).
Redwood, H. and A. Wedderburn (2019), 'A cat-and-*Maus* game: the politics of truth and reconciliation in post-conflict comics', *Review of International Studies*, 45, no. 4: 588–606.
Rosenberg, P. (2002), 'Mickey Mouse in Gurs – humour, irony and criticism in works of art produced in the Gurs Internment Camp', *Rethinking History: The Journal of Theory and Practice*, 6, no. 3: 273–292.
Rosenthal, H. (1942a), *Mickey au Camp de Gurs*, DS-O.377, Centre de Documentation Juive Contemporaine, Paris.
Rosenthal, H. (1942b), *Petit Guide à Travers le Camp de Gurs*, BA Elsbeth Kasser / HD 122, Archiv für Zeitgeschichte, Zürich.
Rosenthal, H. (1942c), *La Journée d'un Hébergé*, DSO.92, Centre de Documentation Juive Contemporaine, Paris.
Rossdale, C. (2010), 'Anarchy is what anarchists make of it: reclaiming the concept of agency in IR and security studies', *Millennium: Journal of International Studies*, 39, no. 2: 483–501.
Rossdale, C. (2019), *Resisting Militarism: Direct Action and the Politics of Subversion* (Edinburgh: Edinburgh University Press).
Routledge, P. (2005), 'Reflections on the G8 protests: an interview with General Unrest of the Clandestine Insurgent Rebel Clown Army (CIRCA)', *ACME: An International Journal for Critical Geographies*, 3, no. 2: 112–120.

Routledge, P. (2010), 'Major Disasters and General Panics: methodologies of activism, affinity and emotion in the Clandestine Insurgent Rebel Clown Army', in *The SAGE Handbook of Qualitative Geography*, eds D. Delyser, S. Herbert, S. Aitkin et al. (London: SAGE), 388–405.
Routledge, P. (2012), 'Sensuous solidarities: emotion, politics and performance in the Clandestine Insurgent Rebel Clown Army', *Antipode*, 44, no. 2: 428–452.
Rushdie, S. (2015), 'Statement about *Charlie Hebdo*', *English PEN* (7 January). Available at www.englishpen.org/campaigns/salman-rushdie-condemns-attack-on-charlie-hebdo/ (accessed 8 May 2020).
Rusten, J. (2006), 'Who "invented" comedy? The ancient candidates for the origins of comedy and the visual evidence', *The American Journal of Philology*, 127, no. 1: 37–66.
Saalfield, C. and R. Navarro (1991), 'Shocking pink praxis: race and gender on the ACT UP frontlines', in *Inside/Out: Lesbian Theories, Gay Theories*, ed. D. Fuss (New York and London: Routledge), 341–372.
Salter, M. (2011), 'No joking!', in *Security and Everyday Life*, eds V. Bajc and W. de Lint (New York and London: Routledge), 31–48.
Saurin, J. (1996), 'Globalisation, poverty, and the promises of modernity', *Millennium: Journal of International Studies*, 25, no. 3: 657–680.
Sawyer, E. (2002), 'An ACT UP founder "acts up" for Africa's access to AIDS', in *From ACT UP to the WTO: Urban Protest and Community Building in the Era of Globalisation*, eds B. Shepard and R. Hayduk (London and New York: Verso), 88–102.
Schlembach, R. (2016), *Against Old Europe: Critical Theory and Alter-Globalization Movements* (London and New York: Routledge).
Schneider, B. E. and N. E. Stoller (1995), *Women Resisting AIDS: Feminist Strategies for Empowerment* (Philadelphia: Temple University Press).
Schopenhauer, A. (1969), *The World as Will and Representation*, 2 vols (Mineola, NY: Dover Publications).
Schroeter, J. (1972), 'The unseen center: a critique of Northrop Frye', *College English*, 33, no. 5: 543–557.
Scott, A. ed. (1997), *The Limits of Globalization* (London and New York: Routledge).
Selimovic, J. M. (2019), 'Everyday agency and transformation: place, body and story in the divided city', *Cooperation and Conflict*, 54, no. 2: 131–148.
Sellars, P. (2016), 'The AIDS activist and the banker', *Fortune* (21 July). Available at http://fortune.com/barclays-jes-staley-global-500/ (accessed 14 July 2020).
Serres, M. (1982), *Hermes: Literature, Science, Philosophy* (Baltimore: Johns Hopkins University Press).

Serres, M. (1983), 'Noise', *SubStance*, 12, no. 3: 48–60.
Serres, M. (1995), *Genesis* (Ann Arbor: University of Michigan Press).
Serres, M. (2000), *The Birth of Physics* (Manchester: Clinamen Press).
Serres, M. (2007), *The Parasite* (Minneapolis: University of Minnesota Press).
Serres, M. (2015), *Rome: The First Book of Foundations* (London: Bloomsbury).
Serres, M. with P. Hallward (2003), 'The science of relations: an interview', *Angelaki: Journal of the Theoretical Humanities*, 8, no. 2: 227–238.
Shapiro, M. J. (1988), *The Politics of Representation: Writing Practices in Biography, Photography, and Policy Analysis* (Madison: University of Wisconsin Press).
Shapiro, M. J. (1989a), 'Textualising global politics', in *International/Intertextual Relations: Postmodern Readings of World Politics*, eds J. Der Derian and M. J. Shapiro (Lexington: Lexington Books), 11–22.
Shapiro, M. J. (1989b), 'Representing world politics: the sport/war intertext', in *International/Intertextual Relations: Postmodern Readings of World Politics*, eds J. Der Derian and M. J. Shapiro (Lexington: Lexington Books), 69–89.
Shapiro, M. J. (2010), *The Time of the City: Politics, Philosophy and Genre* (London and New York: Routledge).
Shapiro, M. J. (2013), *Studies in Trans-Disciplinary Method: After the Aesthetic Turn* (London and New York: Routledge).
Shapiro, M. J. (2016), *Politics and Time* (Cambridge: Polity).
Shepard, B. (2002), 'Introduction', in *From ACT UP to the WTO: Urban Protest and Community Building in the Era of Globalisation*, eds B. Shepard and R. Hayduk (London and New York: Verso), 1–20.
Shepard, B. (2005), 'The use of joyfulness as a community organizing strategy', *Peace & Change*, 30, no. 4: 435–468.
Shepard, B. and R. Hayduk, eds (2002), *From ACT UP to the WTO: Urban Protest and Community Building in the Era of Globalisation* (London and New York: Verso).
Shilts, R. (1988), *And the Band Played On: Politics, People and the AIDS Epidemic* (New York: Penguin).
Shim, D. (2017), 'Sketching geopolitics: comics and the case of the Cheonan sinking', *International Political Sociology*, 11, no. 4: 398–417.
Shotwell, A. (2014), '"Women don't get AIDS, they just die from it": memory, classification, and the campaign to change the definition of AIDS', *Hypatia*, 29, no. 2: 509–525.
Simon, E. (2012), *The Art of Clowning* (New York: Palgrave).
Skinner, Q. (2004), 'Hobbes and the classical theory of laughter', in *Leviathan After 350 Years*, eds T. Sorell and L. Foisneau (Oxford: Clarendon Press), 139–166.

Smith, J. E. M. (2019) *Irrationality: A History of the Dark Side of Reason* (Princeton: Princeton University Press).
Solomon, T. (2014), 'Time and subjectivity in world politics', *International Studies Quarterly*, 58, no. 4: 671–681.
Solomon, T. (2015), *The Politics of Subjectivity in American Foreign Policy Discourses* (Ann Arbor: University of Michigan Press).
Solomon, T. (2019), 'Rhythm and mobilization in International Relations', *International Studies Quarterly*, 63, no. 4: 1001–1013.
Solomon, T. and B. Steele (2017), 'Micro-moves in International Relations theory, *European Journal of International Relations*, 23, no. 2: 267–291.
Somella, L. (n.d.), 'This is about people dying: the tactics of early ACT UP and lesbian avengers in New York City: interview with Maxine Wolfe'. Available at www.actupny.org/documents/earlytactics.html (accessed 14 July 2020).
Spencer, H. (1878), 'The physiology of laughter', in *Illustrations of Universal Progress: A Series of Discussions* (New York: D. Appleton & Co.), 194–209.
Staley, P. (2008), 'In memory of Jesse Helms, and the condom on his house', *POZ.com* (8 July). Available at www.poz.com/blog/in-memory-of-je (accessed 14 July 2020).
Stanley, J. (2015), 'A postcard From Paris', *New York Times* (8 January). Available at http://opinionator.blogs.nytimes.com/2015/01/08/a-postcard-from-paris/?page-wanted=all (accessed 8 May 2020).
Steele, B. (2008), *Ontological Security in International Relations: Self-Identity and the IR State* (London and New York: Routledge).
Stoller, N. (1998), *Lessons from the Damned: Queers, Whores and Junkies Respond to AIDS* (New York and London: Routledge).
Strange, S. (1996), *The Retreat of the State: The Diffusion of Power in the World Economy* (Cambridge: Cambridge University Press).
Strub, S. (2008), 'Condomizing Jesse Helms' house', *Huffington Post* (25 July). Available at www.huffingtonpost.com/sean-strub/condomizing-jesse-helms-h_b_113329.html (accessed 14 July 2020).
Subcomandante Marcos (2001), 'Second declaration of realidad for humanity and against neoliberalism', in *Our Word is our Weapon: Selected Writings* (New York: Seven Stories Press), 116–119.
Summer, K. and A. Jones (2005), 'The first embedded protest', *Guardian* (18 June). Available at www.theguardian.com/politics/2005/jun/18/live8.development (accessed 15 July 2020).
Sylvester, C. (2002), *Feminist International Relations: An Unfinished Journey* (Cambridge: Cambridge University Press).
Thalmann, W. G. (1984), *Conventions of Form and Thought in Early Greek Epic Poetry* (Baltimore and London: Johns Hopkins University Press).

Thompson, K. W. (1972), *Political Realism and the Crisis of World Politics: An American Approach to Foreign Policy* (Port Washington: Kennikat Press).
Thucydides (1843), *History of the Peloponnesian War*, trans. T. Hobbes (London: John Bohn).
Thucydides (1900), *History of the Peloponnesian War*, trans. B. Jowett (Oxford: Clarendon Press).
Thucydides (2004), *History of the Peloponnesian War*, trans. R. Crawley (Mineola, NY: Dover).
Thucydides (2009), *History of the Peloponnesian War*, trans. M. Hammond (Oxford: Oxford University Press).
Tickner, J. A. (1992), *Gender in International Relations: Feminist Perspectives on Achieving Global Security* (New York: Columbia University Press).
Townsend, J. and A. Kendall-Taylor (2019), 'NATO is struggling under trans-atlantic tensions', *Foreign Policy* (5 December). Available at https://foreignpolicy.com/2019/12/05/nato-is-struggling-under-transatlantic-tensions-trump/ (accessed 8 May 2020).
Trapese Collective, eds (2007), *Do It Yourself! A Handbook for Changing Our World* (London: Pluto).
Treatment Action Group (2002), 'Flying the coop: giant prophylactic enshrouds senator's suburban home; new era of inside/outside activism is born', *thebody.com* (1 April). Available at www.thebody.com/content/art1772.html (accessed 14 July 2020).
Treichler, P. (1987), 'AIDS, homophobia and biomedical discourse: an epidemic of signification', *October*, 43: 31–70.
Tylawsky, E. I. (2002), *Saturio's Inheritance: The Greek Ancestry of the Roman Comic Parasite* (New York: Peter Lang).
UNAIDS (2016), *Global AIDS Update 2016*. Available at www.unaids.org/sites/default/files/media_asset/global-AIDS-update-2016_en.pdf (accessed 14 July 2020).
United Nations (2000), Overview of Security Council Meeting 4087, *The Impact of AIDS on Peace and Security in Africa*, S/PV.4087 (10 January). Available at http://undocs.org/S/PV.4087 (accessed 1 May 2020).
United Nations Security Council Resolution 1308, UN S/RES/1308 (17 July 2000). Available at https://undocs.org/S/RES/1308(2000) (accessed 1 May 2020).
Vaughan-Williams, N. (2009), *Border Politics: The Limits of Sovereign Power* (Edinburgh: Edinburgh University Press).
Vitalis, R. (2015), *White World Order, Black Power Politics: The Birth of American International Relations* (Ithaca: Cornell University Press).
Waldby, C. (2004), *AIDS and the Body Politic: Biomedicine and Sexual Difference* (London and New York: Routledge).

Walker, R. B. J. (1993), *Inside/Outside: International Relations as Political Theory* (Cambridge: Cambridge University Press).
Walker, R. B. J. (2004), 'Sovereignties, exceptions, worlds', in *Sovereign Lives: Power in Global Politics*, eds J. Edkins, V. Pin-Fat and M. Shapiro (New York and London: Routledge), 239–250.
Watkin, W. (2010), *Agamben and Indifference: A Critical Overview* (London and New York: Rowman & Littlefield).
Watson, W. (2012), *The Lost Second Book of Aristotle's Poetics* (Chicago: The University of Chicago Press).
Weber, C. (1998), 'Performative states', *Millennium: Journal of International Studies*, 27, no. 1: 77–95.
Weber, C. (2010), 'Interruption Ashley', *Review of International Studies*, 36, no. 4: 975–987.
Weber, C. (2016) *Queer International Relations: Sovereignty, Sexuality and the Will to Knowledge* (Oxford: Oxford University Press).
Wedderburn, A. (2018), 'Tragedy, genealogy & theories of International Relations', *European Journal of International Relations*, 24, no. 1: 177–197.
Wedderburn, A. (2019), 'Cartooning the camp: aesthetic interruption and the limits of political possibility', *Millennium: Journal of International Studies*, 47, no. 2: 169–189.
Weldes, J. (2003), 'Popular culture, science fiction, and world politics: exploring intertextual relations', in *To Seek Out New Worlds: Science Fiction and World Politics*, ed. J. Weldes (New York: Palgrave), 1–30.
Welsford, E. (1968), *The Fool: His Social and Literary History* (London: Faber & Faber).
Wentzy, J. dir. (1992), *The Ashes Action* (ACT UP).
Wentzy, J. dir. (2002), *Fight Back, Fight AIDS: 15 Years of ACT UP* (ACT UP).
Werner-Müller, J. (2016), *What is Populism?* (Philadelphia: University of Pennsylvania Press).
White, H. (1975), *Metahistory: The Historical Imagination in Nineteenth-Century Europe* (Baltimore and London: Johns Hopkins University Press).
Wilcox, L. (2015), *Bodies of Violence: Theorizing Embodied Subjects in International Relations* (Oxford: Oxford University Press).
Wilkins, J. (1668), *An Essay Towards a Real Character and a Philosophical Language* (London: Gellibrand).
Wilkins, J. (2000), *The Boastful Chef: The Discourse of Food in Ancient Greek Comedy* (Oxford: Oxford University Press).
Willeford, W. (1969), *The Fool and his Sceptre: A Study in Clowns and Jesters and Their Audience* (London: Edward Arnold).

Williams, M. C. (2018), 'International Relations in the age of the image', *International Studies Quarterly*, 62, no. 4: 880–891.

Winsor, N. (2018), '"I paint to forget": a refugee turns to art on Nauru', *SBS News* (1 March). Available at www.sbs.com.au/news/i-paint-to-forget-a-refugee-turns-to-art-on-nauru (accessed 29 June 2020).

Wintour, P. and R. Mason (2019), 'Trump cuts short Nato summit after fellow leaders' hot-mic video', *Guardian* (4 December 2019). Available at www.theguardian.com/us-news/2019/dec/04/trump-describes-trudeau-as-two-faced-over-nato-hot-mic-video (accessed 8 May 2020).

Wiwa, O. (2003), 'Carnival of the Oppressed: resisting the oil occupation of the Niger Delta', in *We Are Everywhere: The Irresistible Rise of Global Anticapitalism*, eds Notes from Nowhere (London: Verso), 196–201.

Young, I. M. (2005), *On Female Body Experience: 'Throwing Like a Girl' and Other Essays* (Oxford: Oxford University Press).

Youngs, G. (2004), 'Feminist International Relations: a contradiction in terms? Or: why women and gender are essential to understanding the world "we" live in', *International Affairs*, 80, no. 1: 75–87.

Zalewski, M. (2007), 'Do we understand each other yet? Troubling feminist encounters with(in) International Relations', *British Journal of Politics & International Relations*, 9, no. 2: 302–312.

Zalewski, M. (2010), 'Distracted reflections on the production, narration, and refusal of feminist knowledge in International Relations', in *Feminist Methodologies for International Relations*, eds B. Ackerly, M. Stern and J. True (Cambridge: Cambridge University Press), 42–61.

Zijderveld, A. (1982), *Reality in a Looking-Glass: Rationality through an Analysis of Traditional Folly* (London: Routledge).

Žižek, S. (2008), *The Sublime Object of Ideology* (London: Verso).

Zupančič, A. (2008), *The Odd One In: On Comedy* (Cambridge, MA: Massachusetts Institute of Technology Press).

Index

abjection 4, 5, 6, 17, 28–29, 33–35, 41, 48, 51, 53, 55, 56, 69–70, 71, 177
  clowning 160
  and concentration camps 79–80, 81, 93–94
  and HIV/AIDS 117, 126–127, 128, 129, 130–131, 132, 136, 137
aesthetics 3, 5, 6, 10–11, 19–20, 73, 81, 85–86, 88–91, 92, 93, 94, 107–108, 110n.5, 110n.6, 170
  aesthetic subjectivity 19–20, 90, 102–103, 109n.2
affect 132, 146, 166, 170
Aids Coalition to Unleash Power (ACT UP) 20, 73, 74, 115, 121, 126, 127–134, 139–141, 167n.3, 170, 172, 174
  'ashes action' 139
  Church Ladies For Choice 133, 139
  Stop the Church 133–134, 149
  Treatment Action Guerrillas (TAG) 115, 134–139, 140, 141, 168n.16
  see also condom
anthropology 2, 12–13, 14
Aristotle 4, 18, 51, 52, 54–58, 74n.1, 173
Auschwitz-Birkenau 19, 73, 85, 87–88, 100, 107, 109n.1, 110n.4, 110n.6, 111n.9, 111n.11, 111n.12

Bakhtin, Mikhail 46–47, 152–153
biopolitics 74, 114, 115, 116–127, 128, 129
  and racism 116, 126–127, 141, 142n.3
Black Lives Matter 176
body 17, 34, 52, 54, 61, 68, 69, 97, 118, 132, 137, 139–140, 148–151
  embodiment 4, 15, 25–26, 32, 52–53, 55, 60–61, 67, 148, 156, 158, 166
Borges, Jorge Luis 36–37, 47, 49n.3, 61
Butler, Judith 4, 5, 6, 17, 20, 32, 33–35, 50n.4, 51, 68, 129–130, 147-8, 153–157, 167n.7

Camp des Milles 105–106
carnival 46–47, 74, 146–147, 152–153, 175
cartoons 81, 82, 88–91, 107–108, 111n.9
Chaplin, Charlie 97–98
Charlie Hebdo 1, 169, 171
Clandestine Insurgent Rebel Clown Army (CIRCA) 20–21, 74, 147–148, 153, 157–158, 159–164, 165, 166, 170, 176
  multiform 161, 164
clowning 20, 44–45, 74, 147–148, 152, 156, 157, 158–159, 164–166, 168n.8

colonialism 12, 49n.4, 54, 70–71, 142n.3, 172
comedy 4, 5, 9–14, 31, 51, 52, 54–58, 59, 60, 67, 170
   distinction from humour 7–8
comic strips *see* cartoons
condom 115, 134–139, 175
cultural activism 146, 165, 167n.3

De Certeau, Michel 18, 29, 41, 42, 46–48, 51, 62, 172–173
Derrida, Jacques 52, 54–58, 59, 64, 66, 75n.5, 76n.8
desolation 86–88
disgrace 56–58, 59
drag 154–155, 167n.7, 168n.8

Eco, Umberto 7, 42–45
Eichmann, Adolf 151
embodiment *see* body
emotions 2, 8–9, 38, 74, 86, 128, 132, 164, 166, 168n.10, 170, 174, 176
emplotment 6, 9–11
Enloe, Cynthia 2, 15, 25, 30
Epicharmus 58–59, 62, 75n.1
epidemiology 20, 74, 115, 116–127

feminism 2, 3, 14–15, 30, 50n.4, 53, 67, 68, 69, 70, 71, 82, 153–157, 169, 172
fool 148, 156, 159–160, 162, 164
Foucault, Michel 18, 36–42, 47–49, 51, 74, 76n.5, 80, 84, 117, 118, 141, 142n.3, 148, 149–153, 156, 164, 166, 167n.6, 174, 176

G8 *see* international summits
'global justice movement' *see* neoliberalism
grotesque 20–21, 74, 148, 149–153, 164–165, 174, 176
Gurs 5, 73, 91–99, 100–104, 109n.4

health 74, 114–127, 129, 132, 139, 141–142, 143n.5
Helms, Jesse 115, 120, 124, 134–139, 175

HIV/AIDS 20, 113–144, 170, 175–176
   Joint UN Program on 116
Hobbes, Thomas 37, 49n.1, 75n.2
Holocaust 5, 19–20, 73, 80–81, 151

incongruity 38–40
international summits 157–158, 159–64
   2005 meeting of the G8 161–164, 165, 166n.1, 168n.13
interruption 67, 68, 69, 70, 80, 89, 99, 162

Johnson, Boris 26–27, 45
joking 16, 31–32
   joking relationships 12–13
Jyllands-Posten 31, 171

Kramer, Larry 128, 130, 139, 141

laughter 1–3, 9, 26–27, 36–43, 44, 46–47, 49n.4, 52, 58–59, 61, 67, 93, 132, 135, 137–138, 155–156, 158, 169, 174
   injunctions against 42–43
   theories of 37–39, 49n.1
   and unlaughter 7, 31
Levi, Primo 86, 87, 88, 97, 100, 111n.12

Megarians 4, 51–52, 54, 55, 57, 58, 59, 60, 67, 75n.1, 173
Mickey au Camp De Gurs see Rosenthal, Horst
militarism 160–164, 165

narrative 9–14, 52, 75n.1, 86, 89–91, 104, 166, 171
National Institutes of Health 119, 131
Nazism 85–86, 91, 109n.2, 110n.4, 110n.7, 142n.3, 151
   the concentration camp system 85–86, 91, 110n.7, 112n.19
neoliberalism 74, 145–147, 164–165, 167n.6, 176
   the 'global justice movement' 145–146, 157–158, 166n.1, 176

Index

New York City 121, 123–124, 128, 167n.7
noise 64–65, 66, 67, 70, 76n.6, 81, 83, 173, 175
North Atlantic Treaty Organization (NATO) 26–27
Nussbaum, Felix 95–96, 111n.11

parasite 4, 5, 6, 18–19, 21, 29, 49, 51–53, 58–74, 75n.3, 80, 107–108, 109n.2, 128, 129–134, 155–157, 158, 160, 164–166, 170–171, 173, 174–177
parody 5, 147–149, 153–157, 160–161, 162–164, 165, 167n.7, 170, 176
performance 5, 7–8, 10, 16, 19, 21, 32–34, 45, 47, 51, 72–73, 97, 111n.16, 146–148, 154–155, 157, 161–164, 165, 167n.7, 170, 174, 177
performativity 3, 4, 18, 25–26, 28–29, 30, 32–35, 37, 40–41, 48–49, 51, 79–80, 94, 131, 138, 153, 155–157, 158–160, 166, 171, 173, 176
Petit Guide à Travers le Camp de Gurs see Rosenthal, Horst
pharmakos 52, 54–58, 59, 60, 61, 63, 66, 67, 70, 71, 109n.2, 158, 173
Plato 43–44, 74n.1
popular culture 46–47, 86, 107, 110n.5
post-structuralism 3, 15–16, 25–26, 34–35
post-truth 175–176

quarantine 116, 120–122
queerness 115, 124, 130–131, 139, 143n.3, 170

Reagan, Ronald 123, 134, 143n.8
resignification 20, 74, 129–131, 134, 136–138, 139–140, 152, 154, 163
resistance 1, 2, 5, 16, 18, 31, 45–46, 63, 83–84, 85, 89–90, 130–134, 147, 152–153, 167n.2, 175
Rosenthal, Horst 19–20, 73, 80, 81, 85–86, 88–90, 99, 107, 108, 108n.1, 172
La Journée d'un Hébergé 111n.15
Mickey au Camp de Gurs 91–99, 102, 111n.10
Petit Guide à Travers le Camp de Gurs 100–104, 106
Rushdie, Salman 44–45
Russo, Vito 127–128

satire 7, 9, 43–44, 45
scapegoat 52, 54, 57, 63–66, 156, 173
Schwesig, Karl 104–105
securitisation 16, 114, 116–117, 120
Serres, Michel 19, 53, 63–67, 70, 72, 76n.6, 83, 165, 175
silence 7, 14, 17, 57, 65–66, 67, 69, 71, 74, 128, 129, 134, 136, 138
sovereignty 15, 80–81, 82–86, 108
speech 3, 19, 52–53, 56–58, 60, 71, 79
Staley, Peter 131, 135–137, 140
the state 3, 14, 27–28, 30, 34–35, 54, 57, 65, 70, 82–83, 104–105, 108, 116, 145, 175–176

tragedy 6, 7–14, 169
transversality 3, 4, 6, 15–16, 19, 22n.2, 53, 71, 79, 171
Treatment Action Guerrillas *see* Aids Coalition to Unleash Power (ACT UP)
Trump, Donald 13, 22n.4, 26–28

Ubu Roi 149–151, 152, 164
United Nations (UN) 116, 117

violence 2, 55, 60, 169, 172
the grotesque 153
and sacrifice 52, 65, 174
and sovereign anti-politics 81, 85–87, 90, 102–104
visuality 86, 88–89, 107, 110n.5

Wilkins, John 36–37
World Health Organization (WHO) 116

Young, Iris Marion 33–34

Žižek, Slavoj 43–46
Zupančič, Alenka 44

EU authorised representative for GPSR:
Easy Access System Europe, Mustamäe tee 50,
10621 Tallinn, Estonia
gpsr.requests@easproject.com